THE REALITY OF SOCIAL GROUPS

ASHGATE NEW CRITICAL THINKING IN PHILOSOPHY

The *Ashgate New Critical Thinking in Philosophy* series brings high quality research monograph publishing into focus for authors, the international library market, and student, academic and research readers. Headed by an international editorial advisory board of acclaimed scholars from across the philosophical spectrum, this monograph series presents cutting-edge research from established as well as exciting new authors in the field. Spanning the breadth of philosophy and related disciplinary and interdisciplinary perspectives *Ashgate New Critical Thinking in Philosophy* takes contemporary philosophical research into new directions and debate.

Series Editorial Board:

The Reality of Social Groups

PAUL SHEEHY
Richmond upon Thames College, UK

ASHGATE

Published by
Ashgate Publishing Limited
Gower House
Croft Road
Aldershot
Hampshire GU11 3HR
England

Ashgate Publishing Company
Suite 420
101 Cherry Street
Burlington, VT 05401-4405
USA

Ashgate website: http://www.ashgate.com

British Library Cataloguing in Publication Data
Sheehy, Paul
  The reality of social groups. – (Ashgate new critical thinking in philosophy)
  1. Social groups
  I. Title
  306'.01

Library of Congress Cataloging-in-Publication Data
Sheehy, Paul, 1964-
    The reality of social groups / Paul Sheehy.
      p. cm.—(Ashgate new critical thinking in philosophy)
    Includes bibliographical references and index.
    ISBN 0-7546-5348-X (hardback : alk. paper)
  1. Social groups. I. Title. II. Series.

    HM716.S44 2006
    305.01—dc22

2005031974

ISBN-13: 978-0-7546-5348-6
ISBN-10: 0-7546-5348-X

Printed and bound in Great Britain by Antony Rowe Ltd, Chippenham, Wiltshire.

Contents

Acknowledgements

The arguments presented in this book have developed out of my work as a doctoral student on the metaphysics and moral status of social groups, for which funding from the British Academy is gratefully acknowledged, and from a series of papers published in recent years. In particular parts of the discussion in chapters 2-4 and 8 draw on the following papers:

- 'On Plural Subject Theory', *Journal of Social Philosophy* 33 (3), 2002, pp. 377–94

- 'Social Groups, Explanation and Ontological Holism', *Philosophical Papers*, 32 (2), 2003, pp. 187–216

- 'Sharing Space: The Synchronic Identity of Groups', *Philosophy of the Social Sciences* 36 (2), 2006, pp. 1–18

- 'Blaming Them: Holding Groups Morally Responsible', *Midwest Studies in Philosophy* (XXX), 2006, pp. 74–93

My employers during the writing of this book, King's College London and Richmond upon Thames College, have been extremely congenial places at which to teach and research. At some stage in its history each part of this book has been read by and discussed with colleagues and friends. I am grateful to Juliana Cardinale, Matthew Carmody, Peter Goldie, Pierre Cruse, Stephen Grant, Tom Pink, Adrian Samuel, Paul Sperring, Eilert Sundt, Alan Thomas and Mike Ward. While it would be convenient to blame their collective contribution for the shortfalls and infelicities of the following pages, I am afraid that I alone must take responsibility.

For reasons which go beyond the writing of a book it was Yasuko who made this monograph a reality. It is to her that this work is dedicated.

Introduction

Why Worry about Groups?

I   Motivation

We lead our lives in the social or human domain, the sphere of human co-existence and interaction. More particularly our lives unfold within and through our membership of groups. Much effort, ink and no little passion has been expended in assessing the nature of social groups, their relationship with their individual members and their role in description, explanation, evaluation and practical reasoning. Our language and our understanding of the world appear unable to dispense with families, tribes, gangs, peoples, cultures, teams (sporting and work based), companies, religious bodies, bureaucracies, governments, political organisations, states, economic classes, social classes, mobs and crowds.[1]

There seems nothing odd in talking of a person's character being shaped by his family when his character and goals clearly reflect certain attributes or activities of his family. An anthropologist or historian may explain an individual's behaviour or state of affairs in terms of the structure or properties of a group. A mob may be blamed for the damage it has caused, and a culture praised or condemned for the practices and values it fosters. National or racial stereotypes attach to individuals, but they are commonly predicated of a group as a whole. For example, when Frederick II wrote to European rulers in 1241 about the danger of a Mongol invasion he addressed his remarks to the different powers, picking them out in terms of national characteristics. Germany was 'fervent in arms', France 'the mother and nurse of chivalry', Spain 'warlike and bold' and England 'fertile and protected by its fleet'.[2]

---

1   Do not take this list to be exhaustive, or to represent a consensus within the social sciences that all of these groups or collectivities are universally regarded as properly qualifying as such. Mobs and crowds in particular are often excluded from the range of social groups, being categorised as mere aggregates. Also, within some parts of sociology and organisational and management science the main unit of investigation is taken it be the 'face-to-face group'. This is typically a group of no more than a dozen persons characterised by its capacity to foster communication between the individuals and for the articulation of shared goals and co-operative strategies.

2   This is recorded in Matthew Paris, *Chronica Majora Volume IV* and discussed in Clanchy (1983). The description of England was rather unusual for the time. While England was widely regarded as wealthy, the English were considered to be violent and drunken, and caricatured as possessing tails to indicate their untrustworthiness.

An elucidation of the nature of groups seems essential to an understanding of the social domain, and to the formulation of appropriate judgements and policies within it. A clarification of the sense, if any, in which groups are to be regarded as real entities is a response to the recognition that:

i.   The truth conditions of many propositions about the social world depend upon the existential or referential status of groups. In our everyday talk, and in the descriptive and explanatory discourses of the social sciences, a proper understanding of what is said – of what we mean – turns on how we are to treat the references to social groups.

ii. The justification of moral evaluations, the articulation of practical judgements and action, and the formation of policies depend upon the object of such judgements or actions being an appropriate one. In particular it must be the kind of thing capable of sustaining such judgements and of being responsive to particular policies and actions.

I shall endorse a holist or realist thesis about groups: interrelational holism. It holds groups to be material particulars which, alongside individual persons and artefacts, count as objects in the social world, figuring in our explanations and descriptions. Groups are ontologically on a par with individuals in the social world. More tentatively I argue that a group is the kind of object towards, or in respect of which, we may have obligations or duties; a group can thus possess moral status. From this claim I go on to suggest that a plausible case can be made for a group right to non-interference, and that, given a certain structure, a group can be held morally accountable to some degree.

It is not sufficient to look to the mere surface form of our ways of talking, but appearances there are a starting point. Holism is not secured by noting that a group term or name can function grammatically as a subject of predication, or because we can apparently speak meaningfully of what we think about a group or are going to do to, or with respect to it. The arguments which follow provide an analysis of groups to suggest that we should in fact take seriously the appearance of our discourse. Through such an analysis we arrive back at the surface forms via a deepened understanding of the nature of groups. In the denial that groups exist in any important sense, the individualist appears committed to something like an error theory, for she must explain why appearance is so deceptive.

II   Structure

The next chapter discusses ways in which the thesis of ontological individualism can be articulated. A plausible version of individualism is identified in which the relations between individuals is stressed. This is a lengthy chapter. Its length reflects the intuitive pull, variety and sophistication of argument deployed to articulate the claim that (in any sense that matters) groups are no more than the individuals who are their members. In Chapter 2 a recent form of holism due to Margaret Gilbert is sketched,[3] suggesting why it is inadequate as a general account of grouphood. In doing so it challenges as undermotivated and unnecessary the thesis that group formation is dependent on individuals sharing a conception of themselves as members or as being united in a common identity. The positive argument for interrelational holism is made in Chapters 3–4. In Chapter 5 a distinction is drawn between social groups and corporations. The final three chapters turn to consider the moral status of groups, group rights and the moral accountability of groups.

The ontological thesis is independent of the moral claims in that ontological realism about groups does not entail a particular conclusion about their moral or evaluative status. The methodological structure of the book is to present independently plausible arguments for the ontological realism of groups and for their candidacy to be the objects of obligations and duties, the holders of rights, and the bearers of moral responsibility. The relation between the two parts of the book is, first, one of presupposition. In discussing the moral status of groups I take it that there are groups and that groups are material objects. If ontological holism is false, then a substantive and interesting sense in which groups figure in our evaluative and practical deliberations would trivially not be available for discussion.

Second, consideration of groups in moral terms illuminates and supports the ontological thesis. The morally salient relations in which individuals stand appear to be just the kind of links between individuals that constitute them into a body. I shall propose that in our evaluations and practical judgements we must sometimes take individuals together as the object of assessment or action. In doing so we are in effect recognising that they are linked or united in a way that forms a group. Furthermore, in considering the forms of relations through which individuals constitute a group, and in virtue of which it is causally relevant, we may frequently identify just those relations through which collective or irreducibly social needs and wants arise and are articulated. For example, the needs of a people or culture may focus on the availability of material and legal resources to enable it to practise certain activities, to conduct itself in a particular language and in accordance with certain values and goals. It is just the interrelations through which these practices, values and goals are articulated, sustained and developed that a pool of individuals, changing through time, can constitute a single entity.

I observed earlier that the arguments of the moral part of the thesis are tentative. The reason for the tentativeness is that in discussing groups as sources and objects of obligations, and bearers of rights and moral accountability, a very wide, deep and complex range of issues must be confronted. Substantive, and sometimes perhaps intractable, issues lurk at every corner. Rather than attempt to engage fruitfully in debates within meta-ethics and normative theory, I aim to present a plausible basis on which certain claims about groups are true; that is, that groups possess moral status, they can have rights and they can be held responsible. In order to do this I

---

3   Gilbert (1989; 1996; 2000).

must make certain assumptions about the grounds underwriting the aptness for these kinds of moral attribution. In particular, I hold that a concern for the needs and harms of others grounds certain obligations and rights, and that a capacity to reflect upon values and deeds is essential to bear the ascription of moral responsibility. It is worth holding in mind that given realism about any kind of entity, the way in which it figures morally is a feature of our moral capacities (or sensibilities) and theory. The discussion of the moral status of groups is not a contribution to moral theory as such, but an indication of the shape of the theory if it is to recognise groups. Put another way, the discussion of the moral nature and role of groups points to the price that one may need to pay if one is to exclude them from moral consideration.

III   Ontological Status

I defend the view that our best understanding of groups is as composite material particulars formed through interrelating individuals. The idea of a material particular is of something in space and time, which can be individuated, counted and described. Such an entity can remain the very same thing while its properties change through time. Aristotelian primary substances such as men and horses are material particulars par excellence, as are Austinian medium-sized dry goods like tables and chairs. To regard groups as material particulars is to understand them as being constituted from suitably related parts and capable of standing in causal and explanatory relations in their own right. This is a form of ontological holism or realism about social groups, going beyond an acceptance that reference to groups functions as a useful shorthand, or that social concepts may be legitimately employed, or that there is a class of irreducibly social properties. Rather, groups are on an ontological and explanatory par with individuals within the social domain. Both groups and individuals count as objects within the social world, and both feature in their own right in explanations.

The argument for the material particularity of groups proceeds by four steps. First (Chapter 1), I consider the merits of ontological individualism. At a minimum individualism holds that individual persons are prior to or more fundamental than groups. This priority can be expressed in a number of ways. I examine and reject strategies of eliminativism, the identification of groups with sets, aggregates or mereological wholes, the reduction of groups to individuals, and of non-reductive individualism. The last approach explains the priority of the individual in terms of the determining relation between lower and higher levels in a supervenience relation. A more persuasive version of individualism is identified as 'interrelational individualism', which analyses groups in terms of individuals-in-relations. In doing so it holds out the prospect of capturing the sense in which individuals interact and engage together collectively without a commitment to the objecthood of groups.

The second part of the argument (Chapter 2) motivates the rejection of an influential view of holism – Margaret Gilbert's plural subject theory – on the grounds of its apparent circularity and lack of generality. In this chapter I also reject the *intentionalist thesis*. This maintains that in the formation and maintenance of a group individuals must conceive of themselves in some particular way (for example as being or forming a group, as sharing certain ends or values), or possess certain shared intentional or psychological states. All that is conceptually necessary and sufficient for the formation and maintenance of a group (or to be a member) is that individuals interact in a way that unites them as a unit, as a body with its own impact on the world – typically on them as members.

The burden of providing a positive case for ontological holism is discharged in the next two chapters. The third part of the argument (Chapter 3) considers the role of groups in explanation. It is maintained that groups are ineliminable from our best explanatory schemes.[4] There is then good reason to treat them as real objects. The individualist, though, may deny that groups *qua* objects are playing any role in explanations. Rather, individuals-in-relations instantiate certain causally salient properties or collectively produce states of affairs, without thereby engendering any ontological commitment to a new or independent object. I shall cast doubt on the ability of the individualist to successfully analyse away the reference to or presupposition of groups in such explanations.

The fourth part of the argument (Chapter 4) shows that considerations of taxonomic consistency underwrite the classification of groups as material objects. Quite in general non-simple objects are constituted from suitably related parts. In virtue of the form of the relations between those parts an object is structured with certain properties and causal powers through which it can be individuated. The compositional nature of groups – individuals-in-relations forming causally relevant entities that figure in explanations – suggests that it is consistent with our everyday and scientific practice of taxonomy to regard them as material objects. The form of holism I endorse shares with interrelational individualism the recognition of the central role to an understanding of the social world of the relations in which

---

4   The existence of groups need not be linked to their explanatory role, at least if one agrees with Ruben (1985) who claims that one could find 'that there were social entities, which played no role whatever, or no irreducible role, in the explanation of events. This would still be of great philosophical interest, for it would tell us something about the nature and structure of reality, in spite of having no interest at all from the point of view of the methodology of the social sciences' (p. 1). He is here responding to Watkins's (1957) note that presenting the issue of holism as a question about the existence of irreducibly social facts 'seems to empty it of most of its interest. If a new kind of beast is discovered what we want to know is not so much whether it falls outside existing zoological categories, but how it behaves. People who insist on the existence of social facts, but who do not say whether they are governed by sociological laws, are like people who claim to have discovered an unclassified animal but who do not tell us whether it is tame or dangerous, whether it can be domesticated or is unmanageable. If an answer to the question of social facts could throw light on the serious and interesting question of sociological laws, then the question of social facts would also be serious and interesting. But this is not so' (fn. 2, p. 169). While Ruben's point is noted, a *prima facie* reason for thinking anything real is that it features in our best forms of explanation within a certain domain of enquiry. If something has no explanatory role at all, then one may wonder why it would be individuated.

individuals stand. Consideration of explanatory role and taxonomic consistency highlights the undermotivation of the individualist denial that such recognition brings with it an ontological commitment to the material reality of groups.

In the next chapter I complete the discussion of the ontological status of groups, explaining that social groups are to be distinguished from corporations. This is the key distinction in higher-order social taxa rather than the one typically found in the social sciences between groups and aggregates. Thus I hold that a mob and a people are both groups. However, a state or business corporation is distinct from the group(s) through which its activities may be conducted. A corporation is the instantiation of a particular set of rules and procedures, and it is not existentially dependent on members in the same way as a group.

IV   Moral Status

Following the discussion of the ontological status of groups, attention turns to their moral status. Historically, this has arguably been the dominant interest with respect to groups. In particular, the question of whether there are special moral bonds between the individual and the groups to which he belongs has prompted enquiry into both the nature of such ties and of the group; for they would seem to be intimately connected. Perhaps most effort has been devoted to the bonds of obligation between state and citizen, ruler and subject. The moral bonds between the member and her group have sometimes been taken to be grounded in the 'harmony' of a certain mode of organisation.[5] For Rousseau it is in being united with one's peers in society 'which alone makes man the master of himself'.[6] For Hegel isolation from an authorised corporation leaves a man without rank or dignity, and for Bradley the individual man is what he is because of and by virtue of the community, his moral development being the acquisition of his proper station. More recently Gilbert[7] has suggested that to be a member is to have made commitments to certain ends or beliefs jointly with other individuals. Obligation inheres in the plural subject we have formed. Of course others, such as say Hobbes and Locke, regard the state and the associations of civil society in instrumental terms, constrained by the needs, nature and reason of individuals.

Perhaps now eclipsing the question of the obligations a member may have to her group(s) are questions addressing the responsibilities, duties and rights of groups themselves. The right of a people to self-determination has become enshrined in international law. The needs of communities and cultures are articulated in the public space of political debate about the proper allocation of resources and administrative structure. In the American and English courts claims have been made on the basis that governments and corporations have responsibilities and attendant duties towards,

---

5   Compare Plato's analogy of the organisation of the City and of the Soul in the *Republic*.

6   Rousseau (1968) p. 65.

7   Gilbert (1993; 1999).

inter alia, their citizens, the citizens of other nations, their employees, customers and a wider universe of 'stakeholders', ultimately encompassing anyone with an interest in the corporate impact on the environment.

Again the fact that we talk as if groups have moral status, rights and responsibilities could be merely a way of talking. Moreover, there is no reason to suppose ontological holism entails a commitment to the view that groups have moral status. After all, why should ontological realism about groups entail such status any more than realism about tables commits us to regarding tables as moral entities? I shall propose that a group may possess moral status (Chapter 6) and possess rights in virtue of the irreducibly collective needs of its members (Chapter 7). I further suggest that a group can bear moral responsibility, at least to a certain degree, if the group has a capacity for collective reflection (Chapter 8). However, groups are not moral persons in the full-blown or literal sense that individual human beings can be. They remain vital in our evaluative and practical reasoning because of their role in determining the attitudes and actions of individuals, and because in respecting individuals together or collectively our moral response is directed at the group.

V 'Spooky' Metaphysics

The holist belief that groups exist as entities figuring in our best causal and explanatory schemes has sometimes been characterised as a commitment to some form of supra-individual entity. Certainly the metaphysics of Plato's eternal realm and his analysis of the state in terms of the soul encourages such a view, as does the notion of Rousseau's General Will, an Hegelian Geist or Durkheimian *sui generis* facts.

A suspicion that appeal to holism in explanation entails rather costly metaphysical baggage may be due in part to the fact that the ontological status or nature of social wholes is rarely given any detailed attention. It has been argued that that social facts or laws cannot be reduced without remainder;[8] that the organisation of society and a grasp social concepts is indispensable to an understanding of individuals;[9] or that holism be defined as 'the view that social phenomena are to be explained by appealing primarily to the properties of social wholes, since the latter are causal factors which shape the characteristics of individual members of society'.[10] One can agree with such conclusions (or be largely persuaded by their reasonableness), but be left wondering what kind of thing a social whole or group *is*.

Whatever the explanatory pressure to include groups within our ontology, it is reasonable to expect the holist to locate groups taxonomically; to say what kind of thing a group is. If the price is deemed too high, then she does not have to pay it. However, the holist cannot also retain the benefits of holism, while eschewing the

---

8   For example Mandelbaum (1955; 1957).

9   For example ibid.; Gellner (1956).

10   James (1984) p. 79. James is here characterising holism, rather than arguing that this is the single appropriate mode of explanation.

task of making clear their ontological cost (if not actually repudiating the ontology), without indulging in what amounts to a form of 'philosophical double talk'.[11]

Of course, some are quite happy to embrace 'spooky' metaphysics, the spookiness of which may owe more to contemporary perspective or fashion than to any problem inherent in the view. David Ruben takes social substances, examples of which he suggests are France, Ealing and the Red Cross, to be spatio-temporally locatable but non-material entities.[12] As he observes, such entities are puzzling. We may have good grounds for believing them to be parasitic upon material individuals who comprise their membership, for how else could a group form, but how should we explain the membership relation? Gilbert[13] offers an analysis of groups as plural subjects, a union of individuals linked 'as a body' through a joint commitment to, for example, a belief, intention or goal. She wonders how to respond to an interlocutor who insists that there are no plural subjects *really*. Her response is to say that

> plural subjects are a *special type* of entity, no doubt about that. But as far as I can see they are not illusory or based on illusion. They depend for their existence on people's possession of a certain rather special concept, and acting successfully so that the concept be instantiated.[14]

The account I offer of groups has the advantage of identifying them as material particulars, a class of entity with which we are familiar and which is for the most part uncontroversial. Groups are not *prima facie* obvious candidates for inclusion in this class, and the burden of argument throughout is to offer a positive case for acknowledging groups as such, and not merely to rely on the shortcomings of individualism.

VI   Context

Seen through the perspective of the debate on methodological individualism, which was at its most intense in the 30 years following the Second World War, a concern for the ontological nature of groups might appear to miss the key issues. The core of the dispute between individualism and holism in the social sciences has been about the proper analysis of explanation, the role of laws and the question of the continuity of the social science with natural science. I am inclined to agree that much of the dispute in the post-war years regarding methodology was ultimately addressing questions of autonomous levels of explanations, laws and the causal efficacy of social properties. Holism was an affirmation of such an autonomy, and its ontological commitments

---

11 See Quine (1960). Of course, by preserving all the language of groups without providing an adequate account of an individualist ontology, individualists can indulge in such double talk too. The point is also made by Ruben (1985) that we ought to take seriously the apparent ontological commitments of our ways of speaking (p. 10).

12 Ruben (1985) see Chapters 1 and 2.

13 Gilbert's version of holism is discussed in Chapter 2 below.

14 Gilbert (1989) p. 434, Gilbert's emphasis.

were frequently misrepresented or presupposed as entailing supra-individual wholes hovering over a group's individual members. It may be argued, now that the nature of the dispute is clear, the ontological question can be allowed to fall away as attention focuses on issues such as whether social properties such as 'being a mayor' or 'possessing monetary value' are causally efficacious in their own right, and whether there is an irreducibly social or collective element in the explanation of certain intentional states. Indeed much recent work on collectivities has focused on the nature and role of group, collective or 'we' intentions.[15] So significant is the role of a proper understanding of intentions in an analysis of, for example, practical reasoning, judgement formation and action that one might concur with the view that:

> The issue between individualists and holists is no longer, as it once was, what kinds of entities are involved in sociality so much as what kinds of intentional contents constitute social and therefore moral relations.[16]

The nature of social properties and the proper analysis of 'we' intentions are obviously important to a complete understanding of both the metaphysical and moral dimensions of the social world. However, their importance does not undermine the motivation to consider the ontological nature of groups. Not least because our forms of explanation and description, laden with reference to groups, carry with them ontological commitments that ought to be rendered transparent. There is an epistemological and practical significance in considering what kind of thing a social group is. If we are to understand what we mean when we talk about the social world, then we ought to clarify the ontological status of social groups as they appear abundantly within our discourse. In arguing for a form of holism I also sketch the kind of theoretical commitments an individualist must endorse if she is to insist that individuals are ontologically prior to groups in anything other than a trivial sense of composition. Moreover, the question of how we should regard groups is not to be framed solely in the terms of a debate within the philosophy of social science. As I have already observed there is both a wider and more enduring demand that the ontological and moral status of groups be investigated in our concern to elucidate moral and political relations. It would be foolish to think that, for example, the role of 'community' and the constraints on the neutrality of liberalism can be explained just through a clear understanding of groups, but such an understanding may certainly cast a useful light.

---

15 See for example Bratman (1992), Clark (1984), Gilbert (1987; 1997), Searle (1995), Tuomela and Miller (1988), Tuomela (1995).

16 Swindler (1996) p. 61.

VII   A Note on Something I Shall Not Say

I shall finish this introductory section by noting that there seem to be deep parallels between the individual–group relation and the physical-mental relation. Issues and moves familiar from the philosophy of mind may therefore arise. It also seems plausible that the separate investigation of each relation could illuminate the other; perhaps revealing the dimensions of a problem because of a basic similarity in structure, or perhaps showing that the difficulties and purported solutions of one domain are not readily translatable into the other. I do not delay to consider these interesting matters, but maintain a focus upon groups and the social domain. In part the discussion in this book may show how one set of philosophical problems may be related to another, without commenting on or highlighting them as they arise.

Chapter 1

Individual and Group: Identity, Composition and Reduction

I   Introduction

The ontological thesis I shall defend is that social groups are material particulars. This ontological holism is a position motivated by the explanatory role of groups and considerations of consistency in our taxonomic practices. Opposition to the holist thesis is immediately located in the thought that a group is no more than the individual persons we call members. Before setting out the positive arguments for a holist understanding of social groups I shall survey the forms ontological individualism can take. There are a number of ways in which the sense can be expressed that a group is no more than the individual persons who are its members. The extent to which ontological individualism is plausible sets a minimum on the demands that holism must satisfy. To a degree the purpose of examining the theoretical articulation of ontological individualism is to poison rival wells. However, the primary purpose of this chapter is not to eliminate as many of the 'opposing' positions as possible. It is to clarify the shape of a coherent and *prima facie* convincing form of ontological individualism, thereby illuminating what is at stake in the debate about the ontological nature of groups. As shall become apparent in the course of the next three chapters, this is not a question of choosing one side of an individual–group dichotomy, but of whether fidelity to the significance of relations and context central to a plausible individualism is consistent with that individualism.

Ontological individualism comes in degrees. It can be formulated as the more or less flat denial that groups exist. For example, one may hold that the only material particulars in the social domain are individual persons and artefacts. In this stronger version individualism is the denial that there is in any sense a class of material entities comprising social groups. It does not rule out using the concept of a group as an heuristic device or the employment of references to groups as a useful shorthand or fiction. We do not, though, actually quantify over groups because they simply do not exist as entities in the world: the individuals, whom we might casually call 'members', just do not come together in the right way to form a material entity. Whatever being a member designates, it is not a relation between the individual and a material entity (the group) regarded as such.

A weaker, but nonetheless firmly individualist, claim is that individual persons are prior to or more fundamental than groups. This expression of individualism is weaker in that it does not entail the non-existence of groups. Rather, it maintains that even if there were groups, we would have no need or call to refer to them, because in our analyses and formation of judgements we can always go to the individual level; and indeed ought to go to the level of individuals for an ultimate or basic explanation or description. Facts, events and states of affairs at the social level are determined by the individual level, and explanations given in terms of the facts, properties, laws and generalisations pertaining to individuals. The weaker form does allow, then, that there are groups, but that in some important sense (to be determined by the individualist) everything that needs to be said or understood can be done in terms of their individual members.

One may regard with suspicion the existential claims of a class of entity as thorough-goingly otiose as groups would thus seem to be in explanatory and descriptive discourse. To say that there is no need at all to refer to groups may appear to amount to the stronger individualist claim. For the holist, though, the concern is not whether a weaker version of individualism can consistently differentiate itself from stronger forms, but the truth of its central claim that individual persons are more fundamental than groups. If this is the case, then groups would not be on an ontological par with individuals, and much of the interest and substance would be lost from any formulation of holism.

Pressed on whether the use of the notion of a group carries an ontological commitment the individualist could respond in a number of ways. For example, she may hold that groups are to be identified with sets of individuals; or with the mereological sum of individuals (or person-stages); or, perhaps, in using group terms one is really quantifying plurally over individuals. Of course, individualism must now accommodate abstract entities in the form of sets and the status of mereological sums must be clarified. However, the individualist point is that within the social domain we only need have recourse to individuals – and their artefacts, and perhaps also environmental or ecological factors with a significant impact on their lives. At bottom the individualist is saying that the only way in which we need consider persons is as individuals (standing in relations) and not as united into a distinct entity, a group. The success of an argument for ontological holism as a thesis about the material reality of groups naturally entails that ontological individualism fails in both its stronger and weaker versions.

It is worth noting that one may hold there are groups, but deny that they are material particulars. It can be held that groups are abstract entities, outside of space and time, to which we can nonetheless refer, describe and about which there are truths to be discovered. Under such a view groups would rank alongside numbers, classes, kinds and fictions. A group would be something like an Idea or Geist, in which individuals could participate and through which participation the nature of the group would to some degree be instantiated. An individualist denial that groups are material particulars is consistent with the ontological position of those who regard groups as abstract.

The problem that ensues from this combination is twofold. Those who regard a group as an abstract entity would be ill described as ontological individualists. Furthermore, the group may be held to stand with respect to its members in some kind of causal or influencing relation. It is by no means clear how such a relation should be expressed, and I am inclined to take the view that one only confronts the problem if there are pressing reasons to regard groups as abstract entities.

A quick stipulative line is to exclude from consideration the possibility that groups are abstract on the grounds that the domain of human interaction is firmly located in the material sphere. However, this looks to be merely question-begging. If our best account of groups were to maintain their abstract nature, then in as far as groups have a role in the social world they cannot simply be excluded because of their ontological nature. While there is conceptual space for the non-materiality of groups *qua* particulars, the arguments recommending such positions are less than obviously compelling. The relationship between the individual person as a member and the group seems utterly mysterious if the group is an abstract entity. To model that relationship on the part–whole or member–set relation is a possible approach, but it leaves unattended how the group or its members interact or otherwise affect or influence the other. Now grouphood may prove to be a universal or concept predicated of individuals collectively, and one may regard universals as real in perhaps a Fregean or Platonic fashion. However, this is not to say that the group as such is an abstract particular. Furthermore, the debate between individualism and holism focuses on how individuals related collectively should be regarded in this human domain. The individualist dialectical ambition is not to demonstrate that groups cannot be abstract particulars, but to show that this is all that is left to an ontological holism committed to the view that groups are particulars.[1]

In explaining that there are sound grounds for regarding groups as causally relevant material particulars, I shall show that ontological individualism fails to demonstrate that individuals are the sole non-artefactual particulars of the social world, or that individual persons are more fundamental than groups – other than in the sense that groups are composed by or constituted from individuals.

Ontological individualism can be expressed in distinct ways. I shall classify these individualist strategies as:

---

1   A further possibility is that groups may in some way be non-abstract and non-material objects. An argument for this begins from the presumption that material objects compete for space in the world and so cannot share spatio-temporal co-ordinates; groups are capable of being in the same place at the same time; therefore groups, which we can individuate in space and time, cannot be material. A related point is that if groups are non-material then individuals cannot be parts of a group, because the materiality of parts is transitive in part-whole relations (compare discussion in Ruben (1985) Chaps I and II). I address these issues in Chapter 4, finding that (a) groups are material; (b) two or more groups can be in the same place at the same time, and (c) individuals are parts of a group.

1. Eliminativism
2. Identification of groups with sets or aggregates of individuals
3. Reduction of groups to individuals
4. Non-Reductive Individualism
5. Interrelational Individualism

In section II I shall briefly comment on eliminativism, suggesting that to the extent we can make sense of it we have little reason to adopt it. The elimination of groups holds that the way of thinking that induces us to refer to groups amounts to, or arises from, a radically false theory, and that we should replace the entities it cites with those of its successor. It is not a thesis that a particular analysis of groups is wrong - for example in regarding groups as entities in their own right rather than as individuals who are analysable as such in terms of their relationships – but that we are profoundly in error to be thinking in terms of groups at all, even though in practice we may be constrained to do so by the limitations of our theoretical repertoire. Save for the employment of the notion of a group as an heuristic device, eliminativism holds that there are literally no groups.

The individualist strategy of identifying groups with sets, aggregates or mereological sums is discussed in section III. Such identification fails because it entails the identity of a group changes with every change in membership and because of the difficulties it encounters handling counterfactual claims. I assume an everyday intuition about groups. I take it that anyone prepared to admit groups into discourse regards them in general as surviving change in their membership. This does not prejudge the ontological question. It does mean that whatever the correct analysis of groups, it must under 'normal' conditions be consistent with the capacity of a group to survive a change in its membership. Or, if one's preferred analysis is not able to accommodate the intuition, then the intuition must be forsaken and this must be transparent in the way in which one talks about the social world. In sections IV–V the reduction of groups to individuals is examined. The problems in establishing systematic links between the group and individual levels dispel the apparent promise of this individualist strategy. Next, in section VI, a weaker form of individualism is considered holding that facts at the level of groups are determined or fixed by facts at the individual level. The problem faced by the individualist here is in the tension between the 'non-reductive' nature of the account, maintaining the autonomy (in some fairly robust sense) of facts about groups and the ontological priority of individuals. Having suggested why (1)–(4) above fail as adequate accounts of individualism, I sketch in section VII a plausible and robust version of ontological individualism – interrelational individualism.

I shall introduce interrelational individualism shortly, but first I should note a difference in the scope of the arguments deployed against certain of the individualist strategies. The claim against the identification of groups with sets or aggregates is 'global'. The identification of material composite objects with sets or sums of their parts fails in general. The rejection of a reductive analysis of groups is different, though, in being a 'local' claim, the argument being restricted to the social domain. Likewise, in criticising non-reductive individualism, my concern is with the relationship between the group and individual levels, and not with broader questions of how facts, events or properties at different levels of enquiry may in general be related.

Interrelational individualism is an ontological and explanatory approach apparent in the work of a number of recent philosophers.[2] Interrelational individualism is not a systematically and clearly defined body of thought, but a development of the explanatory, semantic and ontological theses of the methodological individualism exemplified by the works of Popper, Hayek and Watkins in the 1950s and 1960s. Through an analysis of our reference to groups in terms of the relations in which individuals stand to each other, and the contexts in which they must deliberate and act, interrelational individualism seems to avoid any commitment to groups or collectivities having to be counted and recognised in their own right. For groups are just individuals standing in relations with one another. As such these individuals comprise a collectivity capable (in a sense) of purposive action, but which, having no independent existence, enjoys a vicarious existential status thanks to the material reality of the individuals. Groups do not exist as entities in their own right, but analysis, description and explanation of the social world must be conducted in terms of individuals standing in relations to one another. This form of individualism recognises the collective and relational dimension in the lives of individuals and the role of relations and collective action in the formation of their psychological states, which (it holds) ultimately account for the events and states of affairs within the social world.

The holist position to be articulated and defended in the course of this book takes interrelational individualism as the most plausible and defensible version of the individualist thesis available. In explaining an alternative, holist, understanding of groups, interrelational holism, I shall argue that interrelational individualism is undermotivated in its denial of ontological holism. It is undermotivated in light of its own emphasis on relations, the explanatory role of groups considered as objects in their own right, and the way in which we regard other compositional entities such as animals and artefacts.

---

2   For example May (1987), Schatzki (1988), Carter (1990), Tuomela (1995), Gould (1996). There is no single canonical statement of this individualism, but the approaches to ontology evident in the literature are sufficiently close to merit their being grouped together.

II   The Elimination of Groups

Eliminativism is a strategy familiar from the philosophy of mind, holding that
mental talk be eliminated from any serious discourse about the nature of the world
and the way it works. There are literally no beliefs, desires, pro-attitudes, intentions
and so on. Our common-sense conception of psychological phenomena constitutes a
radically false theory, a theory so defective its principles and ontology will eventually
be replaced by a completed neuroscience.[3] The elimination of groups is not the mere
denial there are real entities that are the referents of group names, but that the very
category 'group' or 'collective' is part of a radically false theory. The question is not
whether groups should be understood in holist or individualistic terms, but of what
form the replacement theory for our 'folk social science' will take. An eliminativist
seems to be trivially an ontological individualist, but perhaps that categorisation is
just part of the theoretical framework in need of complete replacement.

    Taking elimination to be a somewhat stronger thesis than the analysis of groups
in a way that shows groups as such do not exist, but to be the demand for a complete
overhaul of our ways of conceptualising the social world, it is difficult to identify
any compelling reasons to endorse it. Ontological individualism accepts a sense in
which we may say that there are groups. That is, individuals standing in relations
who together can feature in our explanations and theory building. Individualism
may deny a mob the status of a material particular, but would not want to eliminate
the concept of a mob. Indeed, eliminativism can hardly stop at the group terms of a
theory about the social domain, but must call into question the notions of say roles
and socialised individuals. A full blooded eliminativism can not yet be expressed
in terms of a worked-out replacement theory and its new theoretical resources, and
there appears little in the issues of substance within the social world to prompt the
search for such a replacement theory.

    I am conscious that this dismissal of eliminativism may be too fast and question-
begging. It is, though, difficult to see how elimination can be progressed as a
research programme within the social sciences and philosophical consideration
thereof. Perhaps once we have attained a completed neuroscience, then folk social
science will undergo radical abandonment along with our folk psychology.

III   Identity

There may be no entirely happy way of expressing the matter simply but, crudely,
identity is a relationship between a thing and itself at and through time. A thing
stands in the relation of numerical identity to itself, and with absolutely nothing
else. A way of expressing this reflexive relation is to put it in terms of names, so that
names stand in the identity relation if they refer to the very same entity.[4] As Frege

---

    3   See for example Churchland (1981) for a statement of this view.
    4   For those unhappy with identity being expressed in terms of a relation something
stands in with itself, identity can just be thought of as a relation between names.

has made familiar, to say that 'a = a' looks merely trivial, whereas to state that 'a = b' seems informative. If it is true that 'a' is identical to 'b', then it is because 'a' and 'b' name the very same object. We should observe that 'a' and 'b' are not here names, but variables in the open sentence 'a = b'.[5] For our current purposes we can regard an object as being picked out through its being named, or possessing a name, or through a definite description. For example, the elite guard of the Ottoman ruler from the fourteenth century was the Janissary Guard. Historians can pick out that group by employing its name, which refers uniquely to a particular group. Had this elite group of soldiers never been named, an object would nonetheless have existed and it could be picked out through a description, such as 'the military unit formed by men taken as children from subject nations and raised since childhood in an elite military environment'. This is not to say that names and descriptions are synonymous, but merely that they can actually pick out the very same entity.

An object, *a*, is identical to itself. While we may always pick something out through and in terms of its being a certain kind, its *being* (this particular) is not relativised to the sortal under which it is distinguished. Opacity and ambiguities certainly arise through contextual differences and changes in tense. John may know Michael as the local priest, while Mary knows him as her lover. Bob's cat may unbeknownst to Bob roam the moors attacking sheep and tourists. Tom has seen the beast of the moor. It is a fact that they have seen the same animal, although each would learn something new in ascertaining that fact. Naturally there are many ways in which different objects are the same through being the same kind of thing or standing in the same type of relations. The conditions under which a particular entity *a* may be identified as the very same entity as *b* are suggested by Leibniz's Law. Thus for any *a* and *b*, and property(s) ϕ:

$$(LL) \ (a) \ (b) \qquad (a=b) \rightarrow (\phi a \leftrightarrow \phi b)$$

To identify some thing (be it an entity, property or event) with another is to propose that there is just one thing which can be picked out using different concepts - perhaps radically different ones. In the present context a defence of holism must examine the possibility that groups can be identified with entities acceptable to ontological individualism. The first such candidate is the set of individuals who are a group's members.

One could say that the Welsh people[6] is identical with the set of its members. The idea of membership need not here imply that there is a group *qua* entity, merely that there is some property or family of properties that lead us to identify certain individuals as Welsh. A set can be specified as a list. For example the set of prime numbers less than 10 is given by the list:[7]

---

5   Compare Kripke (1972) p. 107.

6   The group that is the Welsh people or nation, rather than the political entity or state or geographic region, Wales.

7   I do not include 1 as contemporary mathematical opinion is that 1 is not obviously prime. Thanks to Dr Mike Ward for this point.

$\{2, 3, 5, 7\}$.

Or a set can be specified as an extension of a property:

$\{x: x$ is a prime number less than $10\}$.

Taking the Welsh people as an example of a social group, the Welsh would then be identical to the set of individuals $\{i^1, i^2... i^n\}$ which represents its membership. Alternatively the Welsh could be identified as the set, S, of all i such that i is ϕ, where ϕ is a property(s) that marks out or is essential to Welshness; that is the property or family of properties that is 'Welsh-making'. On the face of it this identification is attractive to the ontological individualist because there is now no obvious commitment to any social objects other than individuals and artefacts. The Welsh could be identified as the set, S, of persons $(i^1... i^n)$ who were, are or will be Welsh – that is possess the relevant 'Welsh-making' properties. The set membership is specified diachronically otherwise the strategy of identification would fail with every change in membership.

However problems arise with counterfactual claims such as 'Maradona might have been English'[8] or 'Magwa might have been a Mohican'. Now, the difficulty arises because sets are extensional and preserve their membership across possible worlds. The identity of sets conforms to a principle of extensionality. A set *is* its members. Set A is identical to set B if and only if its constituents are the same. The set A exists at the actual world and at a possible world if its members are present in both.[9] If the English people is identified by the set S, and that set cannot survive a change in its membership, then it cannot be the case that Maradona might have been English. Maradona is not in the set S, although there is of course a set, the members of which are S and Maradona. Yet, it appears that the English people has the capacity to sustain such counterfactual claims, whereas sets do not. One member more or less makes no difference to the English, but is absolutely vital to set identity. Consider the economist who suggests that the size of the English population has a direct impact on levels of productivity. She may offer the counterfactual hypothesis that a smaller population would have been beneficial to the economic activity. In such a case the social scientist has in mind the very same group. It is just that identity of referents which is called into question by the identification of groups with sets.

Let us turn to the French. It is possible that there may never have been a French people, or it could have been the case that at some point in time the French ceased to exist as a culture or people. For example, Roland may have failed in his efforts against the Moors.

---

8   C.f Ruben (1985).
9   Ibid.

A world without the French people is possible.[10] In a Frenchless world it could also be the case that just those individuals could also exist who are actually members of the French people.[11] Moreover, if they were to exist then there would be the set of those persons. By the principle of extensionality it looks as if we are compelled to say that the French would exist as a group in such a world – set A is identical to a set B if and only if they share exactly the same members. Worlds with and without the French could have just the same individuals, some of whom in the former scenario constitute the French through time. The same set of persons exists in both cases, and so if the French People is identical with a set, the French are present in both worlds. Yet, one of the ways in which we have distinguished these worlds is in terms of the survival or existence of the French. The individualist is faced with the following set of propositions:

P1   In the actual world W the French People is identical with the set S of individuals $\{i^1..i^n\}$.

P2   There is a possible world W* in which there is no French People.

P3   In W* there is set S.[12]

By P1 and P3, P2 must be false if groups are identical to sets. The identification of a group with a set of individuals seems to require us to accept that a group can exist at a world when we have no reason to suppose that it does given the nature of that world. In W* there would, it seems, both be and not be a French People. The identification with sets gives rise to a further puzzling modal claim. It could be the case that the French People exists as a group in exactly the way it actually does so, but that it is composed of completely different individuals. Things could have been so that the French consist of individuals other than those who are actually French (and have been/will be French), while those who are actually French could have belonged to other groups. Thus we can conceive of a world in which the following claims are both true:

P4   There is a possible world W** at which the French People is identical with (a disjoint) set S^2 of individuals $\{j^1..j^n\}$.

P5   In W** there is set S.

---

10 For the purposes of this discussion we need not consider the extent of the other changes that would be necessary to make such a world possible.

11 Those who endorse the modal realism and counterpart theory of David Lewis might put this point in terms of the counterparts of the actual French individuals existing at a possible world in which there is no French people. The criticisms of the identification of groups with sets do not depend on one's position with regard to modal realism.

12 Or the set of counterparts of $\{i^1... i^n\}$.

It therefore seems that the possibility of there being two French peoples arises. There would be the French identical with S^2, speaking French and drinking absinthe, and the set S.

Now, I have yet to offer an account of the identity criteria for a group, but it seems reasonable at this stage to suppose that we can imagine a world in which some particular group does not exist, or in which its membership consists of persons different from its actual members. For there not to be a group is for individuals not to have interrelated through time in the appropriate fashion. The absence of a people for example will be detected by the lack of a group with the cultural, linguistic and historic integration characteristic of a people, which corresponds to the actual group in question. It could have been the case that a group, such as a people, developed in a way radically different from that evidenced by its actual history, so that the French could have possessed extremely different characteristics as a group than they have actually manifested. The people we individuate today as the French could have developed patterns of relations, practices and attitudes that would make them most unlike the French as we actually know that group. The language could be very different and the culture shaped by a devotion to Islam. Even though the French *as* we actually know them would not be in such a world, consideration of the historical development of the groups suggests that we should say that the same group is present in both worlds.

The non-existence of a group does not entail the non-existence of its members, unless individual existence is somehow necessarily dependent upon that of the group. This would block the possibility of individuals existing when a group does not, but it is hardly acceptable to the individualist. Indeed, it is hardly acceptable *simpliciter* unless one can offer an explanation of which group(s) could stand in such a relationship, even if one were happy that a group could do so. A more attractive move would be to question the reasonableness of the modal analyses. I have assumed the necessity of identity, so that if a set of individuals is identical to a group then that relation holds across counterfactual contexts. The necessity of identity is open to challenge,[13] and the individualist can try to argue that at least the identification of groups with sets is a contingent one. I am happy to agree that the composition of a group by a particular set of individuals is a contingent matter. As I shall explain below, this does not help the individualist because the relationship between the group and a set of individuals is never one of identity.

There is a clear sense in which a group *is* the individuals who compose it. The Mohican tribe or French People consist in the individuals that belong to them; that is, individuals who through time interrelate to form the group. Just like any non-simple object a group can be reduced to its parts.[14] It is composed of, or consists

---

13 See especially Gibbard (1975).

14 A simple object or substance is one that is not divisible or capable of being broken down or decomposed into its parts. It has no parts. Leibniz's monads are simple in this sense. Leibniz held that anything extended in space is divisible and so monads are to be carefully distinguished from the particles of physical theory. For present purposes we do not

in, appropriately related parts and one form of analysis is to decompose it. An individualist may eschew identification of groups in terms of sets, for the reasons outlined earlier or, perhaps for independent reasons, because it would entail a commitment to the existence of a kind of abstract entity, sets. Such an individualist may note that just as concrete particulars consist of suitably organised parts, so there are aggregates or sums that are also composed of parts. However, a pile of stones arguably lacks the unity of a concrete particular. It is merely an aggregation or sum, entailing no ontological commitment to entities except the pile-forming stones. That is, stones related to each other in a pile-wise or 'pilely' fashion. To introduce an entity into the world is just to reify the relations between the stones. A similar approach can be applied to groups.

There is an immediate difficulty in identifying groups with aggregates of individuals. As with sets, the identity of aggregates conforms to a principle of extensionality so that an aggregate A is identical to an aggregate B if and only if its constituents are the same. Groups must therefore inherit the fragility of aggregates, or we must accept that piles exhibit a unity through time that makes them non-identical with aggregates. A second problem is that there are reasons of explanatory and ontological and taxonomic consistency to treat interrelating individuals as constituting a material particular, as I shall explain in Chapters 3 and 4. To take groups as aggregates of individuals is merely to presuppose the issue at hand or to assume a position undermotivated in light of other of our classificatory practices.

Deferring discussion of these claims, we should at this point consider an apparently promising move available to the individualist. The identification of groups with sets has been blocked because of the fragility of set (and aggregate) identity and the modal problems arising from the attempt to identify a group diachronically with a set of individuals specified in terms of certain shared properties. Rather than identifying a group with a set or mereological sum of individual persons, one could adopt an approach outlined by David Copp in seeing groups as mereological[15] sums of stages of persons linked by a unity relation.[16]

---

need to investigate the nature of simple objects, but merely hold the intuitive thought that such an object is fundamentally basic in a compositional sense. The metaphysical possibility of the decompositional reduction of something to its parts is not to be confused with the epistemological question of whether we can (ever) come to know about those parts or the practical question of whether we have the means to effect such a decomposition.

15 Mereology is the mathematical theory of parts. Formal mereologies are axiomatic systems, taking as primitive the part-whole relation and defining a proper part as a part not identical to the whole.

16 Copp (1984). In this paper Copp opposes what he calls 'ontological individualism', which he characterises as the view that there are no collectives or that our ontology need not countenance collectives (p. 251). His purpose is to sketch a theory of collectives or groups that accounts for the 'intuitively obvious fact that collectives do exist, and in some sense collectives are just collections of individual persons' (p. 252). That sense is elucidated as an identity relationship between mereological sums of person-stages and groups. I regard Copp as setting out a weak ontological individualist thesis.

The mereological sum of a set of entities is that entity which overlaps with every part of every entity in the set, and with nothing else. For objects a and b, there is an entity c of which a and b are parts. Something is discrete from c if and only if it is discrete from both a and b. We have seen that the identification of a group with the mereological sum of persons is incompatible with the survival of a group's identity through change in its membership – a change in the identity of the individuals who compose the group. However, it is open to the ontological individualist to regard a group as a complex of its stages, whereby a stage of a group is the 'mereological sum of stages of its persons, or a person-stage sum; more accurately the stage of an aggregate at a time is the mereological sum of the stages at that time of the persons who are its members at that time'.[17]

The switch from persons to person-stage sums does not rescue the account from the same kind of problems faced by the earlier purported identification of groups with sets or sums. In particular any proposal that a group is identical with a mereological sum must face a consequence of the principle of collectivism. Any entities, no matter how scattered or diverse in kind, can have a mereological sum. Defining a group in terms of a unity relation between person stages does not rule out the identification of the group in question with just the sum of those parts, no matter how or whether they are related.

A strategy of identifying groups with sets or aggregates or wholes fails because it does not permit a group to survive change in its membership. Our counterfactual analyses of groups also go wrong in a deeply counter-intuitive fashion if they are identical with sets or mereological sums. Ontological individualism must therefore take a different form if it is to account for or persuasively revise our intuitive understanding of groups. In the next section I shall make some clarificatory remarks about composition and then move on to address individualism in its reductive and non-reductive forms.

IV   Composition

Unless a particular is indivisible, and hence simple, it is composed of other things. That is to say it consists in or is comprised of its parts. Ontological reduction is the thesis that all non-simple material entities can be reduced to their parts. In its

---

17 Copp (1984) p. 253. Copp divides groups into aggregates and organisations, and regards them both as mereological sums of temporally unified person-stage sums linked by a unity relation (compare p. 257). A stage is a slice or temporal part of a continuant entity. Copp cites Lewis (1976), who in discussing the stages of a person observes that they are just like persons and can do many of the same things, but their existence is momentary. The notion of temporal parts has been criticised by for example Thompson (1983), but the criticisms here of Copp's proposal will not depend upon the rejection of the notion of temporal parts. Of course, if one feels there are well-motivated reasons for being suspicious about them, then Copp's proposal will be singularly unattractive. For a fuller discussion of Copp's account see the Appendix to this chapter.

strongest and historically most common form it also holds that ultimately every thing can be reduced to the same level of 'basic' matter. This is a concomitant of substance monism, the belief that all material entities are made up of the same basic 'stuff'. Material particulars are entities whose constituents are organised in a certain form through time. Some may have an ephemeral existence, just long enough perhaps to be picked out. Those we encounter for the most part are continuant, in that they exhibit a continuity of form through time. We recognise an entity as a certain kind through the way in which its parts are arranged and the fashion in which it characteristically behaves. Our individuative principles do not appeal merely to an enumeration of an entity's components, but to how its parts are organised in terms of form and behaviour. Dogs and tables, for example, survive changes in their composition. Or, if one holds they do not, then one must surely pay the high price of revising our ordinary notions, and for what gain? Everything is yet to be said on why groups are material particulars, but that they (typically) consist in a changing membership does not tell against the very suggestion.

One could deny that there are really objects composed of or consisting in their parts. Atomism pares down the ontological inventory to indivisible entities – whatever they may turn out to be.[18] Our reference to composite individuals, masses and wholes is ultimately via plural quantification over basic indivisible particulars. Thus an object, x, of certain kind, K, consists of X, where X are simple entities arranged k-wise. Our references to basic everyday particulars such as tables and dogs is a useful fiction. There are not really dogs or tables, but simple elements arranged in, for example, a 'dog-forming' fashion. Such continuant entities are eliminated from our ontology, but the facts about the world are not. Rather, the facts about the spatio-temporal regions occupied by an arrangement of simples are expressible via the fiction that there is this entity, Rover the dog sitting there. The unity through time vital in our individuation of entities does not inhere in the nature of a dog or a table, but in the continuity of the 'k-wise' arrangement of simple entities through time.

Atomism could prove to be the view that there are only groups, or that there are groups and individuals if and only if groups and/or individuals are ontologically simple. Since I believe the most plausible view of groups (and indeed of the medium-sized dry goods of the everyday world) is as composite continuant material particulars, this is not an analysis I could consistently adopt. I regard the parsimonious ontology of simples as coherent, but it is not one that a materialist individualist can espouse without also abandoning the claim that individuals are the sole objects of the social world. Arguably, a weak form of ontological individualism with its insistence on the priority of the individual is consistent with atomism in as far as the individualism is confined to questions arising within the social domain. Such a position hardly recommends itself, however, since atomism ultimately entails a commitment to the denial that there are individuals as such. The individualist may bite this bullet, in which case talk of individuals is just as much a useful fiction as talk of groups.

---

18 The main candidates are probably the fundamental entities cited in particle physics, selves, or souls.

Of course, then the individualist motivation to favour individualism in the social domain on the would presumably be the view that the deployment of group fictions is explanatorily otiose: and that claim is not settled by a commitment to or truth of atomism.[19]

V   Reduction

The identification of a group with the set or aggregate of its component members is not a promising strategy for the ontological individualist. In large part difficulties arise because the purported identification demands that one abandon the intuitively compelling notion that groups can survive changes in membership. In itself this is not yet an argument against a radical revision in our understanding of groups. Rather it is simply to make clear part of the price that must be paid if one is to insist that groups as such do not exist because they are identical to sets or aggregates of individuals. The balance is payable in the elucidation of the ontological commitment to sets or aggregates and their relationship to everyday and social scientific descriptive and explanatory discourse.

However, ontological individualism need never embark on a strategy of identity. Ontological individualism of a non-eliminativist stripe can accept a sense in which realism about groups is true. It sees groups as composed of individuals and as being individuated through the predication of properties and facts about them. Individuals, though, remain ontologically and explanatorily prior to or more fundamental than groups. Rather than identifying groups with some more acceptable kind of entity, groups as social objects are reduced to individuals in a way that goes beyond compositional analysis. That is, the properties of a group, the social generalisations or laws that are predicated of it and in virtue of which it is individuated, are reduced to properties and generalisations predicable of its individual members. Reduction is an approach whereby one domain of things is shown to be absorbable into or dispensable in favour of another domain.[20]

---

19 If there are not really groups or individuals the explanatory worth of a fiction is a matter that can only be settled by an appeal to prevailing convention. Perhaps, more tellingly, there is reason to reject an ontology of simples as a response to the problematic existence of groups (and individuals) because as such a response it runs together a thesis about basic substance(s) with one about taxonomic practice. The latter is a function of the relationship between the world and our theoretical and interest-laden perspective, and it is within this practice that the debate about the status of groups and individuals arises. An ontology of simples can be regarded as a thesis about the basic compositional units, and the associated development of a semantics to express the facts of the world in a way that is referentially pure, where purity restricts the quantificational domain to those indivisible entities. For a defence of atomism and the analysis of, *inter alia*, composite objects in trem sof plural quantification see for example Hossack (2000).

20 Compare Kim (1989; 1992); this is what Ruben (1985) seems to mean by 'reductive identification' (pp. 5–8).

Crudely, then, the truths about groups are held to be expressible, without loss, as truths about individuals. The reductionist about groups accepts that there are groups, but that the science or body of generalisations in which facts about groups are explained can be reduced – typically the reduction of the social sciences to psychology (plus certain aspects of other relevant bodies of knowledge such as biology and ecology). Through this procedure one domain is said to be reduced to the other. Examples of reductionist programmes include the reduction of numbers to sets, chemical properties (such as solubility) to the properties of molecules and atoms, mental properties to physical properties, and the laws of 'special' sciences to those of physics. Similarly, it has been proposed that social groups, properties and the laws of the social sciences can be analysed in reductive terms. Indeed Pettit has noted that the standard tradition of recent individualism takes the regularities of social science to be reducible to intentional regularities, with the social-structural properties involved in social regularities being defined in terms of intentional psychology.[21] The appeal of reduction is held to be its ontological economy and conceptual unity in promoting explanations and descriptions couched in unifactorial terms. It may appear, moreover, to touch deep epistemological and ontological truths in revealing to us the gap between our ways of talking and the structure of the world.

Reductionism is associated with a global thesis that every domain can be reduced ultimately to that of physics, a view associated with the belief that science can constitute a single unified project that has come to be known as the 'unity of science'. Such unity has been presented as a 'working hypothesis' supposing there to be an hierarchical organisation of objects in which the objects at each level are formed through the complex arrangement of objects at the next lower level. We can thus envisage an increasing complexity of organisation as we move from elementary particles through atoms, molecules, living cells, multi-cellular organisms to social groups.[22] Each level is subject to a programme(s) of investigation governed by the principles and practices of a particular domain of science aiming to uncover the principles and laws governing the behaviour of the objects at that level. A proper whole within the terms of discourse at a level N is reducible into proper parts in a universe of discourse at a lower level N–1. This reduction also consists in the derivation of the laws governing the behaviour of entities at each higher level from those governing objects at the next lower level. Such reduction calls for the knowledge of bridge principles or laws identifying kinds of objects at the higher or

---

21 Compare Pettit (1996) p. 145.

22 Oppenheim and Putnam (1958) is the *locus classicus* of this notion of 'micro' reduction. Advances in physics and molecular biology appeared to them to confirm the robustness of a reductive research program aiming to explain macro-phenomena in terms of their micro-structure (for example the reduction of thermodynamics to statistical mechanics, optics to electromagnetics). Associated with micro-reduction is the idea of theoretical reduction (compare Kemeny and Oppenheim (1956)). Roughly, this posits a hierarchy of theories. A theory about one level of objects is derivable from another theory about simpler entities and identities between entities of the reduced (higher level) theory and structures of entities of the reducing theory.

reduced level with arrangements or organisations of objects at the lower or reducing level. Through the transitivity of the reductive relations a unity of science is taken to hold, with the laws of the 'special sciences' being ultimately derivable form those of fundamental physics and the bridge principles.

Now, at bottom this is an empirical hypothesis and reduction is an empirical achievement resulting from the identification of suitable bridge principles.[23] There has been no programme establishing universal and systematic connections between types of entities, properties and laws at different levels, all of which are ultimately connected through the transitivity imparted by bridging principles between adjacent levels.[24] This does not in itself deny the possibility of type–type reductions, but to point at the very least to the absence of any practical advance demonstrating that the types of one level are systematically connected to those of another. Sometimes we may find systematic links between kinds at different levels, but the practical endorsement of the global reductionist claim here is hostage to counterexample. Furthermore the model of a unified scientific project has been criticised as being thoroughly unsupported by consideration of and reflection upon our practices and standards of taxonomy and of the laws and generalisations employed in different scientific domains. Models of the world distinctly at odds with the hierarchy, determination and predictability (in principle) of reduction include an ontologically promiscuous realism of countless (cross classifying) ways of ordering nature and a patchwork of laws governing local domains.[25]

I have sketched in the barest outline the thesis of global reduction because if it were to prove our best model of the world, then there would be a sense in which individuals are more fundamental than groups. Equally, though there would be yet more ontologically and explanatorily fundamental levels relevant to our understanding of the social domain. Nonetheless, the dispute between ontological holism and individualism is perhaps best construed as a local one, which seeks to cast light on the descriptive, explanatory and evaluative forms at a particular level of discourse. As such, then, the question is whether there is a persuasive case for a local reduction of social groups to individuals. Naturally, if we feel warranted in recognising the irreducibility of groups, so doubts will grow about the global reductionist programme. My endorsement of realism about groups is consistent with a model of the world in terms of cross-cutting classifications and domains governed by their own local principles. However, I shall not merely presuppose these views,

---

23 Compare Mellor (1982) pp. 51–2. We should note that the possibility of reduction is not hostage to the state of our scientific practices or the epistemological limitations of creatures like us. It could be a property of the world that one domain is reducible to another. Whether its reduction becomes part of our body of knowledge depends upon our capacities and our adopting a suitable perspective or theoretical interest to discover the reduction. I assume here that our knowledge and the construction of theories depends at least in part on a world independent of our theory construction, conventions and attitudes.

24 For arguments against unity as a working hypothesis see for example Fodor (1974); Dupré (1993).

25 By Dupré (1993) and Cartwright (for example1994) respectively.

but argue from the localised dispute within the social domain that our best model of that domain is one in which groups (the facts and generalisations about them) are irreducible to individuals.

Now, first we must remember that it is not the compositional claim at issue here. Groups are just individuals in a compositional sense; just as individuals are composed of their arms, legs, torsos, organs and so on; and these are composed of flesh, muscle, sinews, blood and bones; and these are composed of ... and so on. The reduction of groups to individuals is the reductive analysis of the properties, facts, events, generalisations or (social scientific) laws through which groups are individuated as entities in their own right and in which groups figure. It is sufficient for (a weak) individualism to show that the properties of, facts about or generalisations or laws applying to groups, and which feature in the formulation of counterfactual conditionals, can be reduced to properties, facts or laws applying to individuals. Note that this neither requires nor entails a semantic reduction of group terms or predicates to individual ones. The success of reduction could be said to turn on whether it can show that groups lack causal and explanatory potency in their own right. The idea that for something to be real *it* must possess causal powers is clearly captured by Alexander:

> ... to suppose something to exist in nature which has nothing to do, no purpose to serve, a species of noblesse, which depends on the work of its inferiors, but is kept for show, might as well, as undoubtedly would in time, be abolished.[26]

Reduction must therefore explain the (apparent) causal and explanatory role of groups in terms of the properties of and generalisations pertaining to individuals as such.[27] A reduction of groups to individuals (or more precisely group properties, facts about groups, generalisations or laws within a theory about them) would take the form of an explanation of facts about the group in terms of the dispositions, beliefs, actions, resources, interrelations and situations of individuals. This reductive strategy is at the core of Methodological Individualism. Thus, a characteristic statement of the approach holds that,

> (E)very complex social situation, institution or event is a result of a particular configuration of individuals, their dispositions, situations, beliefs and physical resources and environment. There may be unfinished or half-way explanations of large-scale social phenomena (say, inflation) in terms of other large-scale phenomena (say, full employment); but we shall not have arrived at rock-bottom explanations of such large scale phenomena until we have deduced an account of them from statements about the dispositions, beliefs, resources and interrelations of individuals.[28]

---

26 Alexander (1920, vol. II) quoted in Kim (1992) p. 134.

27 For generalisation one can read 'ceteris paribus, special science or higher level law'. Unlike the laws of physics those of say biology, engineering and sociology are not exceptionless. Whether the laws of physics should be regarded as exceptionless or truly basic is itself subject to much debate (compare Cartwright, 1994; Dupré, 1993).

28 Watkins (1957) repr. O'Neill (1973) p. 168.

Methodological Individualism has been criticised as lacking precision in its formulation,[29] and there is indeed no single account of it. This is unsurprising given that different writers have developed their own theses, which typically share an emphasis on the explanatory priority of the individual, her psychological properties and an hostility to macro or social level laws (*sui generis* sociological laws). For the present, though, it is sufficient to see Methodological Individualism as a suitable framework in which a reductive analysis of groups could be pursued.[30]

The individualistic analysis need not be framed in terms of the actual individual members, but in terms of 'ideal types' or 'anonymous individuals' who characterise the membership of that group. One would construct an ideal type by 'discerning the form of typical, socially significant dispositions and then by demonstrating how, in various typical situations, these lead to certain principles of social behaviour'.[31] The notion of an ideal type, introduced by Weber and employed by Watkins, is used to explain social phenomena in general. An ideal or hypothetical type is an abstraction from the personal preferences, different kinds of individual knowledge persons possess in a particular context, and typical relations between individuals and between individuals and resources.[32] The abstraction is conceived by Watkins to be to an ideal actor, probably without an empirical counterpart, in terms of whose attitudes, beliefs, dispositions, relations, and contextual setting a particular social phenomenon or fact can be examined. Thus a range of social facts or phenomena could be analysed such as the process of capital accumulation within a market economy, or the tendency of a particular group to display certain properties such as the mercantile spirit of French Huguenots. Within this framework groups can be conceived as entities individuated through their instantiation of patterns of social behaviour and of particular properties. A reductionist programme would aim to correlate a kind of group, say trade unions or peoples, with a kind of individual, in terms of whose dispositions, attitudes, actions and relations with others the facts and states of affairs associated with the group can be explained.

It may be objected that in the formation of a group the kind of individual is less important than the kind of relations between individuals (whatever their 'kinds'). To bring out the point that groups are to be analysed in terms of individuals standing

---

29 For example Ruben (1985); Carter (1990).

30 Watkins (1955; 1957) provides classic statements of the principle of methodological individualism. The principle never pretended that a semantic reduction of social predicates to individual ones were possible, but that explanations could be given of social events or facts in terms of individual beliefs, actions and dispositions. As shall become clear my criticism of methodological individualism is that it presupposes that groups do not exist in their own right, rather than offer within its own terms a persuasive case against their existence. In a sense it mirrors one bad holist argument to the effect that reference to groups by an individual entails they therefore do exist. Methodological individualism tends to take the obliquity of expressions in 'that' clauses as suggesting there is no reason to think they might exist. Compare Currie (1984) p. 347.

31 Watkins (1955) repr. O'Neill (1973) p. 165.

32 Watkins (1952) repr. O'Neill (1973) p. 144.

in relations a reductionist programme employing ideal types would then need to be framed in terms of the correspondences between certain kinds of interrelations between individuals and kinds of groups. If there were to be some such systematic correspondences, then, at least for those kinds of groups, it seems that a reductive analysis may be available. However, how likely is it that there is a single kind of relational structure between individuals forming a kind of group? Intuitively simple and clearly individualisable kinds of group such as a family or a tribe can be formed through a diverse range of forms of relations between individuals. Of course they would share certain features, but it is not open to the individualist to define the nature of the relations by reference to or in terms citing the group. For example, the individualist may not define the family as those who mutually recognise themselves as members. Perhaps, though, the individualist can find a non-circular way of expressing the kind of interrelations corresponding to the group type.

In the case of the family the obvious set of relations may be biological. Yet, the question remains of why a particular set of relations counts as determining the 'limits' of the group. In other words how do we establish the principles that link a set of interrelations with a kind of group? It may be that there is an inevitable degree of vagueness in the reduction of a group, but that a core of relations can be identified – and that this is sufficient to establish the priority of the individual. However, as I shall explain in Chapters 3 and 4 the nature of the individuals and their relations is influenced by the groups to which they belong in a way that undermines the claim of the individual to ontological priority. For now, though, I turn to a different problem for reductionism. The same kind of group can be realised through multiply various forms of interrelations, which are not amenable to abstraction to a single ideal kind or family of relations.

If reductionism is to proceed by systematically linking kinds of group with kinds of individuals or kinds of relations, which when individuals stand in those relations constitute such a group, the kinds of the higher level must be co-extensive with those of the lower level. In attacking the global reductionist programme Fodor defines the natural kind predicates of a science as those whose terms are the bound variables in its proper laws, and notes that if (global) reductionism is true, 'then *every* natural kind is, or is co-extensive with, a physical natural kind'.[33] The reasons he suggests for thinking it 'intolerable' that every natural kind term of a special science must correspond to a physical natural kind term apply directly to the case for rejecting the identification of social or group terms with individualistic ones. Adjusting Fodor's original for the 'local' social scientific case we could say that the reasons it

---

33 Fodor (1974) p. 102. Fodor remarks on the implausibility of reducing Gresham's Law to physics. Gresham's Law makes a generalisation about monetary exchanges in certain conditions. Those exchanges can take an indefinitely large number of distinct forms – the exchange of beads, pieces of paper designated as dollar bills, pieces of paper issued as cheques and so on. It looks unlikely that a disjunction of physical predicates covering all such events expresses a physical natural kind with which monetary exchange could correspond.

is unlikely that every social or group kind corresponds to an individual kind or kind of interrelations between individuals are that:

(a) interesting generalisations (such as counterfactual supporting ones) can often be made about groups, their properties, relations and associated events whose individualistic descriptions have nothing in common;

(b) it is often the case that whether the individual events, properties or relations subsumed by such generalisations have anything in common is irrelevant to the truth of the generalisations, their interest or significance from the point of view of the science or perspective in question.

The social sciences attempt to establish (to some degree of approximation to practical and predictive usefulness) counterfactual supporting generalisations about groups such as the ruling class, the poor, tribes, families, gangs, work units, cultures and religious communities. Understanding a group may involve an analysis of the individual beliefs and values. However, generalisations about a (kind of) group can not always be reduced to generalisations about individuals, their relations, beliefs and practices. Consider the family, a primary social group typically defined in terms of parents and their biological off-spring. A group individualisable as a family can vary greatly across cultures and times in the forms of interrelations amongst its members. Those forms of interrelations define the barriers of entry to the group.

A contrast in the relations, practices and norms that constitute a family can be found between the traditional Chinese notion of the family, *jia*, and the Japanese concept of family (or household), *ie*. In Chinese society membership of a family is strictly biologically based, but 'proper' or 'full' membership extends widely to distant cousins. There is no obvious distinction between 'family' and 'relatives'.[34] Around a core of parents and children there are overlapping circles of cousins and distant cousins tracing their lineage to a shared ancestor. These extended families may look more like clans or small tribes from an Anglophone perspective of predominantly small nuclear families. Indeed, it is common in southern China for families to share common property, such as land in a certain area or a hall in a village, and for there to be family records in order that membership claims can be demonstrated and tested. Membership of the family is the source of feelings of loyalty and the focus of the primary duties and obligations of individuals. Wealth and assets have also tended to be distributed through the equal division of estates amongst male heirs, thereby tending to preserve individuals' positions within a network of relations.

The Chinese family structure contrasts with traditional notions of the family in Japan. The core of the family is the parent-child relationship. However, relations within the family are defined in terms of their role and functionality, particularly with

---

34 For the discussion that follows see Fukayama (1995) pp. 90–91; pp. 171–83; also Lebra (1989). The anthropological and sociological studies suggest that the model of extended biological families is predominant in S.E. China.

respect to the maintenance of family interests and honour. There is little distinctive in this end, but the occupation of roles within the family and the capacity to stand in those family-making relations is not constrained by biological background. The extent of the family is more restricted than in China, and the concept of a family is more closely aligned to that of a household. That is, of a unit whose purpose is to sustain itself and to develop and preserve its reputation and assets for future generations. The role of head of the family usually passes from father to son. However, it is perfectly acceptable for a son to be adopted. The most common way for a family without a male heir, or at any rate a competent one, to sustain the relations and roles vital for the family structure is to marry a daughter to a man who would take her name, and thereby be absorbed into the family. Inheritance would pass through him and the filial piety characteristic of social relations come to focus upon him when he becomes family head. Unlike the Chinese practice of equal division of the estate, the Japanese family has tended to transmit wealth and assets through primogeniture. Effects of this practice would be to enhance the role of the head of the *ie*, to encourage smaller family units than in China, not least because younger sons would tend to move on. The traditional Japanese *ie* lacked the potential self-sufficiency of an extended clan-like family and this would have an impact on the shape and dynamics for the nature of relations across the culture. Furthermore the Japanese *ie*, is one of several groups which compete as the primary claim on an individual's loyalty and duties, and as the source of his goals and ambitions. Companies, political parties, shrines, temples, sports and craft associations, and gangs are all voluntary in a way that families cannot be. Nonetheless the hierarchical structure and patterns of obligations and duties owed by followers and leaders mirror those of the family, and they are no less keenly felt.

Now the point here is that beginning from a simple biological notion of family and the understanding that families play a role in the structure and function of a society, we can individuate families across different contexts. However, there is no single pattern of interrelations, practices or norms that correspond to the type of group, 'family'. Nor, does the family inhabit a single or clear cut role within the life and functioning of a society by which it might be singled out.

It may be objected that 'family' does not mean the same across different cultures, and that a reduction is possible of the *jia* and *ie* to their respective sets of relations. Theories of meaning and mental content which take the meaning of a word, and the content of our thoughts, to be fixed at least in part by the essential properties of the object to which we refer, or by communal practices,[35] encourage the view that what counts as a family is determined by cultural context. From the perspective of social science, or our everyday way of going on, we have little reason to think that differences in the structure or character of families means that the concept or meaning of family is relativised to a culture. For a start, social science proceeds by noting the way in which kinds of groups, institutions and practices are variously realised. Families are similar enough across cultures to be recognised by 'outsiders'

---

35 See for example Putnam (1973) and Burge (1979).

as corresponding to what they would count as a family. Furthermore the (family) resemblance amongst families can arise at the level of function and role within the structure of a culture. It is the role or function of the family within the structure of a culture that individuates it, rather than just its possession of some particular internal set of relations. A similar consideration applies to an institution such as money. Means of exchange through the symbolic transformation of value can take many different forms, which tend to share certain key features in terms of their role within a culture. Equally, the possession of money may play very different roles across cultures. In some cultures monetary wealth may be the prime determinant of social status, while in others it plays no such role.

A similar lack of correspondence between group type and types of interrelations are apparent when we consider the diversity of religious groups and institutions. We may doubt that a social kind 'religious group' can be identified with any kind or ideal type of individual or pattern of relations. This is because the beliefs, interrelations and dispositions of the individuals who together constitute a religious group could vary considerably. For example, the kind of individual ideal type constituting a single kind of group could vary considerably. One set of individuals may be characterised by monotheistic beliefs, focusing on a principle of resurrection and by a disposition to defer to the authority of those individuals playing certain roles within the doctrine of the religion. This would contrast with individuals committed to polytheism, blood sacrifice and disposed to follow the dictates of the priest of their favourite deity. Of course they share the property of being members of a religious group, and as such their behaviour under certain conditions may be predictable. For example, members of religious groups may tend to respond to external threats in a way that gives the fullest expression to the central tenets of the religious doctrine.

However, this kind of response can vary in form and, moreover, it seems to be an explanation couched in terms presupposing the explanatory salience or autonomy of the group. Individualism faces a difficulty in establishing the priority of individual dispositions and beliefs so that the explanatory currency of the social sciences is coined in individuals alone. For the moment though the issue is the practical one arising from the fact that if reductionism were committed to an identity of kinds it must regard a potentially indefinite disjunction of kinds of individual beliefs, practices and dispositions as fitting the right-hand side of statements such as:

x is a religious group $\leftrightarrow$ *I1* v*I2* v... v *In*

where *I1* and so forth represent each kind of combination of individual dispositions, practices, beliefs and relations that constitute religious groups.

We can formulate generalisations such as 'the increasing formality of religious groups correlates with an increased bureaucratic sophistication of secular governance'. For example, the conversion of pagan kingdoms to Christianity in Saxon England may have been directly linked to the rapid growth of kingly power, centralisation and the revival (in part) of a sophisticated Romano-British taxation system.[36] The association of the secular authority with spiritual authority and the organisational infrastructure of the church enhanced the capacity of the secular ruling groups, because the nature of those groups underwent certain important changes through the conversion. On the basis of these kinds of generalisations social science can engage in counterfactual analysis. Historians and sociologists may find, for example, that generally it is true that whenever religious groups are characterised by a formalised set of practices secular government grows in its bureaucratic sophistication. However, short of a complete enumeration of the ideal or constructed kinds that form religious groups we will not analyse the claims reductively, where reduction entails generalising from one disjunction of individual facts type-correlated with group ones to another disjunction of individual facts type-related to another group fact. This model of type reduction in social science would look like this where S1 and S2 are facts about groups, and *I1* etc. facts about the beliefs, dispositions and actions of individuals:

$$S1 \qquad\qquad \rightarrow \qquad\qquad S2$$
$$\downarrow \qquad\qquad\qquad\qquad\qquad\qquad \downarrow$$
$$(I1\text{v } I2\text{v } ... \text{ v}In) \qquad \rightarrow \qquad (I^*1\text{v } I^*2\text{v } ... \text{ v}I^*n)$$

The problem here is not with whether there need be a strict nomological link between the social and the individual kinds. Rather, and leaving that issue to one side, the criticism is that the reduction of a social or group level generalisation does not *explain* what is happening at the social level. The reduction just tells us that any one of a whole set of individual facts could give rise to or 'realise' the fact about the group via the generalisation between one set of individual kinds and another. To gather such individual facts together as a kind does not furnish any explanatory gain. In particular it does not secure an explanation of why the generalisation is a valid one at the group level. Now, to the extent this casts a shadow over the reduction of kinds of groups, or kinds of facts about groups, to kinds of individual dispositions, beliefs and actions and facts about them, it is not yet an argument that can secure ontological holism. Individualism can hold that groups are eliminable from our best explanations just because they do not function in any causally salient fashion, and so there are no generalisations about the social world in which reference to groups is anything other than metaphorical. For the moment though I shall consider an alternative individualist response, which is to accept the failure of type–type identity and to embrace what we may call 'non-reductive individualism'.

---

36 For a discussion of this period see for example Campbell (1986).

VI   Non-Reductive Individualism

Let us grant that groups are individuated by their properties, and particularly their causal powers and role. Reductionism may encounter difficulties in establishing identities between group and individual kinds, but the individualist may feel she can explain the priority of the individual through appealing to a weaker relationship between the group and individual levels. It would be sufficient to demonstrate that the social is dependent upon the individual – that social phenomena or facts supervene upon individual ones. Such an ontological individualism is realist about social phenomena and social properties. It can accept that facts arise and certain properties are instantiated or become predicable in virtue of individuals standing in certain relations or engaging in certain patterns of activity together. There is a class of facts and states of affairs that are social through only being capable of being brought about by individuals standing in certain relations or acting collectively. A social property may be predicated of a thing such as a piece of paper functioning as money, a pattern of activity such as the raising of hands to vote or the deliberations and procedures involved in a trial and of individuals, such as George being the mayor or tribal elder. A property is social when it arises because there is an interlocking set of beliefs and expectations that constrain the reasons individuals have for action in a particular context.[37]

Supervenience is the thesis that one domain of phenomena (D1) depends entirely on another (D2) even though there are no systematic links between them, and in particular even though there is no causal relationship between D2 and D1. The state of D1 is given by the state of D2, and there can be no change in D1 without some change in D2 (although the converse relation does not hold). Thus a group could not alter in any respect without a change at the individual level. The English could not become more tolerant without a change at the level of individuals. In addition to being a proposal about how one class or level of properties or facts determine another, supervenience is typically formulated as being a non-reductive relationship. That is, the supervenient properties or facts are not taken to be necessarily reducible to the base ones.[38]

The concept of supervenience as deployed in contemporary philosophy has its origins in accounts of the relationship between moral and non-moral properties. Although the term was never used by Moore, the idea of a non-reductive relation of dependency is reflected in the anti-naturalistic thesis that 'good' stands for a non-natural property.[39] The term 'supervenience' was introduced into the contemporary

---

37 A group can also have properties that are not social. The nature of the group need not depend upon social properties either. However, the normal case is that groups are formed through and sustain the instantiation of social properties.

38 It may be the case that where x is reducible to y, then x supervenes on y. However, supervenience does not depend on there being any reduction – at least in its standard formulations.

39 Moore (1922).

philosophical lexicon by Hare,[40] according to whom all evaluative predicates supervene on the 'descriptive' characteristics of something. No two things (for example persons, acts, states of affairs) can differ in evaluative terms without also differing in their non-evaluative properties. The basic idea of supervenience has lent itself readily to generalisation. In particular it has featured in the formulation of a non-reductive physicalism in the philosophy of mind.[41] In the philosophy of the social sciences it has been suggested that the notion of supervenience allows us to defuse the tension between individualism and holism in general, and to expose as misleading the dichotomy between these different approaches. Social phenomena are here held to supervene on individual phenomena. The supervenience thesis appears to offer the prospect of serving

> as the metaphysical 'hard core' of a research programme for the social sciences. Such a programme would recognise the holistic nature of social concepts and their resistance to characterisation in terms of individualistic equivalents (nomic or definitional). But it would affirm the claim that the domain of individual facts is more fundamental than the domain of social facts.[42]

As the hardcore of such a programme it seems supervenience conjoins the compositional truth about groups with their explanatory dependence on individuals and their properties. Group or social level discourse can be maintained, but all of the social facts are determined by the individual ones. An understanding of and discourse in the social world thus employs the conceptual dualism of holistic and individualistic properties, events and generalisations and predicates, while holding individuals to be in some way ontologically fundamental. A group can be regarded as possessing properties in its own right, and as there being facts about it. In virtue of these properties and facts the group can be individuated. At the same time the individuals who compose the group are possessed of properties, and there are facts about them. Supervenience holds that facts about individuals determine in some non-causal way facts about the group, and that in virtue of that determination the former be taken as fundamental.[43] If the social does supervene on the individual in this way then holism that does not go beyond supervenience collapses into this kind of non-reductive individualism. In the remaining part of this section I shall suggest that non-reductive individualism is not a stable position.

---

40 Hare (1952).

41 For example Davidson's (1970; 1980) anomalous monism; also see Hellman and Thompson (1975) for an influential statement of physicalism without reduction.

42 Currie (1984) p. 355.

43 It is important to note here that a group and individual can share properties. A group and a man may be brave or just or large. Both a group and a man may be a ruler. Social properties as defined are not only predicated of groups. The supervenience claim is that whatever the properties or facts by which we individuate groups, they are dependent on the properties and facts about individuals.

The supervenience of the social on the individual needs to be given a more precise formulation. Supervenience is expressed as a relation between one class of facts or properties and another. For example, a class of properties or facts, S, supervenes on a class of properties of facts, I, if any two objects which are indiscernible with respect to their I properties are also indiscernible with respect to their S properties. For example, mental properties (S) are held by many to supervene on physical ones (I), so that two individuals with indiscernible physical properties have indiscernible mental properties. This notion can be formalised as a 'weak supervenience' claim:

(WS)   For any possible world w and for any objects x and y, if x has in w the same I properties that y has in w, then in w x has the same S properties as y.

Under this formulation of supervenience it appears we must talk about the social or holist properties of a group and its individual properties. To treat a social group as an object with individual properties seems rather problematic. In the case of the supervenience of the mental on the physical, or the moral on the descriptive, the idea is that one thing, typically an individual person, possesses distinct sets of properties. The individual properties of a group might include its size and its other spatio-temporal relations, and its character as expressed though its actions and attitudes. If a group has these properties itself then in treating the group as an individual we have moved beyond ontological individualism. It is certainly controversial to suppose that a group can have mental properties. The thought underlying the supervenience claim is not that some of a group's properties supervene on other of its properties, as would be the case if the character of a group supervened on its size and relationship to the environment. The claim that facts about the group supervene on individual facts is that the group is dependent on the nature of its individual members.

One can certainly talk about the properties of the individual members, and the supervenience claim might therefore be better understood in terms of the properties of a group's individual members. Any two groups which are indiscernible with respect to their members (and their properties) are indiscernible in terms of their own I properties *qua* groups (or we could have expressed the matter in terms of facts). It is thus the properties of the individuals who are the members of the group that determine the properties of the group. Allowing for the moment that those individual properties do not actually presuppose the existence of the group, there remain nonetheless problems in adopting this approach.

First, non-identical groups can have co-extensive memberships.[44] The groups differ in their properties, but they consist in just the same individuals whose (non group-dependent) properties are held constant 'across' groups. One may wish to say that some psychological properties of the individuals subvene one group and

---

44 Co-extensive memberships of distinct groups is discussed in Chapter 3. For the moment the point rests on the intuition that, say, the male voice choir and the rugby team are distinct entities even if they happen to have identical memberships.

some the other. Allowing this to be the case, we must then determine how the relevant subvenient properties are to be individuated. The clearest way to do so is to individuate them by reference to the group itself. Either the group features directly in the content of the state, or the possession of certain psychological states by individuals determine certain group facts. In either case, one must appeal to the group to pick out the subvenient states, which is hardly satisfactory for the individualist.

Furthermore, the modal force of WS appears too weak to yield the counterfactual dependency required of the determination relation at the core of supervenience. If S properties or facts are determined by I ones, then the counterfactual 'If it were the case that I, then it would be the case that S held' ought to be true. WS only implies, however, that objects with the same I properties within a world have the same S properties in that world. A group, x, can have the social property, F, at w. Naming the conjunction of the individual properties of its members in w, G, we can see that WS only implies the truth in w of the universal conditional 'For all x, if $G(x)$ then $F(x)$'. This is compatible with x lacking F at the nearest possible world, w*, even though G is true of its members.

A stronger formulation of supervenience allows the relation to hold across possible worlds. Of groups and their members one could say that:

(SS)   For any possible worlds w^1 and w^2 and for any groups, x and y, if x has in w^1 the same I properties that y has in w^2, then x has in w^1 the same S properties as y has in w^2.

This certainly captures at first glance the idea that it is the individual properties of or facts about the members that determine the properties or facts about the group. However, the asymmetry in the dependency relation is not really captured. As Kim has noted, if S strongly supervenes on I, this neither implies nor precludes that I also strongly supervenes on S.[45] For example, the intolerance of a group may strongly supervene on the individual characteristics of its members. The tolerance of the group strongly co-varies with the prevalence of certain individual characteristics of its members such as the possession of certain beliefs, attitudes and dispositions; perhaps there is even co-variance with manners of dress. SS just tells us that the social and individual properties or facts co-vary, not that the latter are dependent upon the former.

Moreover, even where there is in fact no social change without individual change, SS does not show that the appropriate form of dependence relation is in place. Both could be dependent upon a third factor.[46] Indeed the (in)tolerance of the group and the individual properties of its members could both be dependent in some way on, for example, environmental factors or on a non-material social substance or Geist. There are certainly reasons to reject any such non-material social entity, but strong

---

45 Kim (1990); Beckermann et al. (1992: Introduction). For example the surface area and volume of a sphere appear to stand in just this kind of relationship.

46 Again, compare Kim (1990).

supervenience cannot in itself be one since it is compatible with such a dualism of 'social substances'. It may be true that in any possible world the tolerance of the French (for example) would increase if and only if the individual properties of its members were to develop in a certain way. However, this does not yet express the kind of explanatory determination that prioritises the individual, which promises to show that it is *in virtue of* matters at the individual level that things are arranged thus and so at the group level.

The supervenience thesis has thus far been expressed as the relation between properties of or facts about objects. I have proceeded notwithstanding the awkwardness in expressing this relationship in terms of groups. I have skated over the question of whether it is acceptable to talk about the 'individual(istic)' properties of a group in the sense that these are the properties of its parts. In part this is because WS and SS look unpromising candidates to express the determination of social or group level facts and properties by individual ones. More importantly, the sense in which the nature of groups along with all other social facts are determined by individual ones is perhaps best captured by the notion of global supervenience. Here supervenience does not depend upon an axis of indiscernibility between particular objects, but between worlds. It is the totality of individual facts that determine the totality of social facts, so that the latter is properly said to supervene on the former.[47]

(GS)   Any two worlds, w^1 and w^2, which are indiscernible with respect to their I properties and facts are also indiscernible with respect to their S properties and facts.

This idea can be made more precise by 'comparing' worlds synchronically. Thus the supervenience of the social on the individual can be put in terms of the indiscernibility of the individual histories of worlds up to some time, t. Therefore any two worlds that have the same individual history up to t have the same social states at t.[48] I believe that it is true that worlds with indiscernible individual histories have the same social states, or at least share the probability of being thus indiscernible. GS is, however, compatible with there being a world that differs from the actual world in some infinitesimal respect with regard to individual history, but which is radically different in terms of its social state. For example a people, f and f*, in two possible worlds w^1 and w^2, may be exactly alike in terms of their memberships and their individual histories, yet differ radically in their cultural and linguistic practices and characteristics. The difference is accommodated within the framework of GS because a difference anywhere in the individual histories of w^1 and w^2 is consistent with a radical difference between the groups. Imagine a world in which a particular person (oneself perhaps) is not born, and then consider the impact this would have on a group with which that person in fact has no connection. While GS captures

47   Currie (1984) argues for the global supervenience of the social on the individual in these terms.

48   Compare Currie (1984) p. 350.

the idea that there can be no social change without individual change, it permits the social to be determined by trifling changes in what must be regarded as a maximally extended subvenient base. In so doing we move away from the thought that the nature of a group is determined by facts about *its* members.

A reply to this line of criticism is that there is simply no need to limit the set of facts supervened upon to those about the members of the group itself. It is after all possible that changes that are distant from the group could nonetheless have a significant impact on it. The study of non-linear systems has suggested that patterns of change and development can be complex and difficult to predict, and apparently unconnected elements do prove to be importantly linked through causal chains. A world in which a single fifteenth century Suomi Reindeer herder died on one day rather another could have developed in such a way that there is today no longer a French people. This is not an incoherent position, but absent an account of the possible nature of the determining relation and it looks to support no more than the claim that there is no social change without some change at the individual level. This does not seem, however, to be in line with the non-reductive individualist claim that the social is determined by the individual, since it again expresses a relation of co-variation rather than determination.

The non-reductive individualist is committed to the facts about and properties of individuals being fundamental in the social domain. Our descriptions and explanations admit both individualist and holist concepts. When we talk of groups or other social phenomena we are referring to facts, properties or states of affairs that have arisen in virtue of the actions, beliefs, attitudes and dispositions of individuals. Reference to groups is to a certain arrangement of individuals. The social facts are neither identical to types of individual facts nor can they be reduced to individual facts or properties in our explanatory and descriptive discourse. However, non-reductive individualism faces pressure on two fronts. First it requires more than the co-variation of individual and group facts. It must demonstrate that the individual facts determine the group ones in order to secure the 'fundamental' position of the former. The formulations of the supervenience relation considered do not seem to express such a determining relationship. Perhaps there are better ways of expressing the supervenience relation, but the second problem suggests that this would not save non-reductive individualism from being an internally unstable position.

The second reason to suspect the internal instability of non-reductive individualism and thus to doubt that it shows the individual level to be more fundamental is briefly as follows. We individuate groups through their causal role, by the effects they have in the world. I take this to be uncontroversial here as it is held by non-reductive individualism:

> Institutions are individuated, I suggest, by the effects they have on individuals. A bank affects its owners, directors, employees and clients in various ways. It has an effect of a more distant kind on individuals less closely related to it...It would be plainly absurd to

insist that while institutions *a* and *b* were indistinguishable with respect to their effects on the totality of individuals, they were yet *distinct* institutions.[49]

Although social groups are singled out through their causal impact, non-reductive individualism holds the domain of individual facts to be more fundamental than social facts. This finds expression in the direction of determination in the supervenience relation. The social facts are set by the individual ones. The fact that a group has a certain impact supervenes on (the totality of) individual facts. Now, because the relationship is non-reductive it looks like social groups are causally autonomous in some fairly robust sense. A group has an effect as such – in its own right and in virtue of its properties or dispositions. We also know from the supervenience relation that any change at the group level is accompanied by a change at the individual level. Moreover, any change at the social level is determined by the individual level. If the social level is to be genuinely causally relevant[50] *it* must exert a causal influence (in some sense) over the individual level, since the only way to cause something at the social level is to cause its subvenient base to be present.

Imagine that a group becomes increasingly hostile to non-members. Perhaps a society confronted with economic problems is becoming a less tolerant and more xenophobic one. The group, through its changing character, has an impact on its members and those who find themselves confronted by it. Tourists and migrants find it more difficult to gain entry or to sustain a living in the midst of such a society. Its own members find a shift in norms and values that promote some practices while eroding others. The change in the group may cause other groups to adjust their attitudes and practices. Let us say, for example, that the increasing nationalism of a particular people causes growing hostility to them by other groups, where that nationalism and hostility is not merely in the breasts of individuals but expressed through the practices and structures of the groups. Now, according to the supervenience thesis, the hostile response of other groups is determined by individual facts and properties. If the Serb People, for example, become more nationalistic and cause other groups to react with hostility, then the Serbs must have brought that about by causing the appropriate subvenient changes at the individual level.

Yet if this is the case, the one-way dependence of the social on the individual has broken down. Indeed if groups have an impact on individuals it is hard to see how they cannot be genuinely causally relevant and difficult therefore to accept that social facts are determined asymmetrically by individual facts. Non-reductive individualism faces a tension between its realism about group facts and properties and the implications of the determination relation. It is an unstable position because

---

49 Currie (1984) p. 357.

50 I return to the issue of what is for a group to be causally relevant in Chapter 3. Briefly, a group is causally relevant when the group is the cause in its own right of an effect, *e*, (say, individuals acting in a certain way) or when the group brings it about (without itself causally intervening) that *e* occurs. In the first case we can say the group is causally efficacious. In the second we can regard the group as 'programming' that individuals act in a certain way (compare Jackson and Pettit (1990); Pettit (1996).

its proponent seems compelled to give up something she very much needs to retain. One could give up the determination of the social by the individual, but this is to give up the sense in which the thesis is at all individualistic. Alternatively, the determination of the social by the individual via the supervenience relation can be maintained, and the claim dropped that groups are causally relevant in their own right. Now, though, the properties we ascribe to groups in descriptions and explanation appear to be epiphenomenal. This secures the priority of the individual, but at the expense of the idea that groups possess some kind of a causal and explanatory punch, which was a motivation in the articulation of the position. It is possible to allow that the group and individuals are both causally relevant, so that events in the social domain can be over-determined. Leaving aside all discussion of overdetermination, such a view fails to protect the priority of the individual. If supervenience is meant to show that the individual level is fundamental in the social domain, then we should perhaps re-appraise supervenience as a weak form of reductionism. From a 'God's-eye' perspective complete knowledge of how things are arranged at the individual level would allow one to infer the complete description of things at the social level.[51]

Ontological individualism's best option is to deny that groups as such have causal or explanatory relevance. This is not to eliminate groups from our discourse, but to regard them as analysable in terms of individuals-in-relations, a position developed from Methodological Individualism.

VII   Interrelational Individualism

Interrelational individualism is an ontological and explanatory thesis emphasising the need to understand groups as individuals standing in relations. In focusing on the relatedness of individuals it avoids a crude individualism in which the only relevant explanatory factor is the psychological states of particular individuals. In restricting its ontology to individual persons it denies that there is a class of entity, namely groups, individualisable through causal impact and explanatory need. Discourse about the social domain need only employ group terms as a shorthand for the relations in which individuals stand, and their collective modes of action. This form of individualism does not take the collective and concerted action of a team of rowers or of a mob as it storms the barricades to be constitutive of an entity. Rather, it is just a pattern of activity and relations between individuals. Interrelational individualism advances a core set of claims:

---

51 Compare Dupré (1993) p. 97.

    i. individuals are the only social particulars;

    ii. individuals exist in relations with one another;

    iii. social wholes possess only an intentional existence (such as as psychological
          constructs, concepts or posits).

This form of individualism can be formulated in either the weaker or the stronger sense. It purports to allow a sense in which there are groups, albeit a sense in which everything said about groups can be reduced in the explanatory context to statement about individuals and their relations. More strongly it can take the form of a version of fictionalism, denying that there is any sense in which we might talk of groups to be reduced. Instead there are only persons and the relations in which they stand. However, the idea or concept of a group plays a significant role in explaining the actions of and relations between individuals. For example Raimo Tuomela holds that groups possess only an intentional existence (for example as psychological constructs, concepts or posits).[52] His 'individualistic interrelationalism' rejects the need to posit social wholes in the explanation of phenomena such as group intentions or actions. The fact that we do refer to such things as 'groups', 'nations' and the like can be explained in terms of the relations between and attitudes of individuals. The (actual) existence of social wholes is rejected, while there is an acknowledgement of the:

> intentional existence of social wholes viz., that concepts of social wholes can and do
> exist in peoples' thoughts, they have no real existence, viz., existence outside the realm
> of thoughts.[53]

Larry May takes himself to be an ontological fictionalist about groups in explaining that:

> relations among individuals do have a reality, a distinct ontological status which is different
> from the individuals who are so related. However the reality of these relations is not
> sufficient to ensure that the groups, which are composed of individuals *in relationships*,
> have reality independently of the individuals who compose these groups.[54]

Groups play a role in explaining the actions of individuals because the existence of common interests relate individuals, giving rise to a (Sartrian inspired) 'solidarity' amongst them. Those individuals perceive themselves to be linked through a common interest, and as such to be members of a group. The group, though, is a fiction 'applied to those collections of persons which are interrelated in such ways as to be able to engage in joint action or have common interests'.[55]

---

52 Tuomela (1995).
53 Tuomela (1995) p. 367.
54 May (1987) p. 23.
55 Ibid. p. 29.

For her part Carol Gould understands groups to be

> constituted entities, that is, they come into being by virtue of actual relations among their constituent individual members, but are not reducible to the individuals distributively, taken apart from these relations. We may observe that constituted entities are not less real for being constituted; but they do not exist independently as Platonic universals. Rather, they exist only in and through the individuals related to each other in the group and cease to exist when these relations no longer hold.[56]

Put thus, it is possible to read Gould in an holist light. However, I read the constitutive nature of a group to be such that it is real only in so far as its members are, and the reality of the group is not a function of what the group as such does or the properties predicated of it. For Gould a group is individuals standing together in a pattern of relations, and no more. When we talk of the group we are talking about individuals collectively. However, their being joined together in some way does not place a collectivity on an ontological par with individuals.

> The ontological priority of the individuals is retained, however, in virtue of their agency, as a capacity to change these relations and to choose new ones (either by themselves or together with others).[57]

Without ascent to Plato's heaven we have a firm grasp of something that is constituted from its parts, but that is over and above those parts, and which figures as such in our explanatory schema. Although Gould refers to groups in realist terms she holds it to be an error to understand the group as independent of or abstractible from its constitution by individuals. However, the constitution of the group by individuals, linked through certain relations, does not foreclose on the possibility that the group be conceived as an entity in its own right.

Gould is less a fictionalist than a constructivist about groups. In general constructivism about social facts holds that facts about groups, social properties, institutions, processes and events are determined by the beliefs, agreements or conventions established between individuals. John Searle[58] has argued that social facts are possible because as creatures with the capacity to think and act in the first person plural – we can think and act together by each possessing a 'we' thought – we impart functionality on the world. A piece of paper counts as money or a collection of men as a team, because we can agree to bestow status and function onto things in the world. 'X counts as Y in C', where X is an item or collection to which a function Y is attributed in some particular context, C. Our formation of groups, and their individuation, is then to be understood as a way of agreeing to go on together. It

---

56 Gould (1996) p. 75.

57 Gould (1996) p. 74.

58 Searle (1995). I should add at this point that constructivism need not be committed to an individualist ontology. The point at the moment is simply that an emphasis on the relations between individuals does lend itself to individualist conclusions. In discussing Gilbert (1989) a holist constructivist position will be examined.

is a form of interrelating in accordance with certain norms or canons of behaviour appropriate for the context. Because the social fact (the group) is generated by the actions, discourse and agreement of the individuals there is presumed to be no commitment to any entities beyond those individuals.

Theodore Schatzki explains that in regarding social reality to be made up of actions, factors determining the intelligibility of such actions, entities found in contexts or settings and interrelations, he is committed ontologically to:

> a form of individualism. The essence of individualism lies in the exclusion of formations and structures that are something independent of or in addition to individual lives or people; and on my account there is nothing more to social reality than the elements and interrelations between individual lives.[59]

For Schatzki social facts are just facts about on-going interrelated lives, in which individuals employ and are influenced by social concepts. Thus an individual may have the concept that 'P is a bank clerk', or that 'in certain contexts individuals behave collectively in characteristic ways'. It appears groups do not figure in his ontology because the empirical reality of the social world is exhausted by the interrelations of individuals in contexts which render those relations and their actions meaningful. Individual lives 'hang together' through practices which integrate and demarcate individuals within certain spheres, and which orchestrate lives through providing and articulating commonalities in goals and mutual dependencies. Thus to belong to a voluntary association is to share in a range of practices and goals that are determined by and shape what it is to belong to such a collective, and which provide individuals with roles and a location or position relative to others in the relevant context. Related to the practices through which our lives interrelate are the settings and physical environments in which they take place, and which again can be shaped by and in part shape those practices.[60]

Alan Carter has set out a position he labels 'interrelationism' as a sensible middle ground between the overly simplifying individualistic psychologism of methodological individualism and the holist (or in his terms, collectivist) commitment to an explanatory and causally independent whole affecting its parts. Methodological individualism is best understood in terms of an approach to the analysis of the social domain. As such, it is in practice expressed through a range of ontological and explanatory theses, holding that both a head count and any explanation in the social world would be conducted in terms of individuals' beliefs, attitudes, dispositions and relations. For Carter interrelationism marks a clear departure from methodological individualism through its emphasis on the relations between interacting lives. Its distinctiveness as a middle-position, rather than a development of and within individualism, hangs partly on Carter's view that the claims of methodological

---

59 Schatzki (1988) p. 247–8. Earlier (p. 242) he notes his general intuition of social reality as 'the concrete, empirical reality of actual social life'. That is those objects, actions, properties and relations which constitute human co-existence.

60 Schatzki (1996) develops the notion of commonalities.

individualism to take seriously the interrelations and context of individuals should be discounted. In locating explanations in the psychology of individuals, thinkers such as Popper, Hayek and Watkins must at vital points in explanation eschew discussion of the causes of these supposed ultimate explanations (that is the beliefs, desires intentions and so on of individuals). Carter presses the point that it is insufficient to merely say that one takes into account the interrelations and contexts of individuals, but the explanatory schema must actually do so. Thus,

> (I)t is all very well saying that relationships are significant, but when they come to be ignored at crucial points, then the position which so frequently ignores them can justifiably be criticised on that count.[61]

In my view it is unclear that individualists such as Watkins were ever committed to a bare reduction to individual psychological states that could not accommodate relations. Whether the illustrations he gives of his methodological recommendations and analyses succeed in making the point is a different matter. More to the present point, though, is Carter's contention that his interrelationism marks a middle ground. He characterises the ontological claims of individualism and holism contrastively as the views that there are only individuals or that there are only groups. 'Individuals-in-relations' stakes out a middle ground, carrying no mysterious holist commitment to a new kind of entity, but able to escape the individualist neglect of relations. Although Carter seeks to define the individualist and holist positions in as contrasting ways as possible in order to clarify what is at issue (what he calls exercising a 'principle of uncharity'), the holist position clearly need not be that there are only groups, but that groups and individuals both figure in the social domain. If, as I shall argue, groups are objects composed of individuals standing in certain patterns of relations, it is hardly open to Carter to claim a middle position. His interrelationism will be consistent with the claim that groups are material objects, or he must defend individualism by explaining how individuals-in-relations (always) remain *qua* individuals prior to or more fundamental than groups.

(It is worth noting that those characterised above as interrelational individualists range from regarding relations as real[62] to believing 'that there are no (holistic or other) social properties', understanding social predicates as linguistic entities.[63] The characteristic feature of this version of individualism is that everything one wants to say about groups is expressible in terms of individuals interrelating and sharing certain common practices and goals).

I shall not attempt here a detailed consideration of the works mentioned, which each offer subtle accounts of the social with their own emphases. They are representative of an approach which continues the dialogue between individualism and holism in social ontology, by introducing a greater attention on the relations between individuals. It is a plausible form of individualism, retaining our group

---

61 Carter (1990) pp. 26–7.

62 For example May (1987), Gould (1996).

63 For example Tuomela (1995) p. 368.

language, but ultimately analysing away its apparent commitment to groups as entities or objects by offering an explanation of the relational and collective dimension of our lives in terms that need only cite individuals and their relations. It is my contention, however, that interrelational individualism does not provide an adequate account of the ontological status of groups. It does not provide an adequate framework for explanations in the social domain, and, given its stress on relations between individuals, it is ultimately undermotivated in its denial of the ontological reality of groups in light of our other taxonomic practices.

I shall make these criticisms of ontological individualism through the defence of interrelational holism. Both these forms of individualism and holism begin from the recognition of the core importance of focusing upon individuals and their relations in an understanding of the social domain. They diverge in what is taken to be an adequate form of explanatory framework and the ontological commitments of our most compelling explanations and our taxonomic practices and standards. In Chapter 3 I consider why we have good explanatory reasons to regard groups as material particulars: in particular because the appeal to analyses of group phenomena in terms of individuals-in-relations – interrelational individualism – fails to yield adequate explanations.

Before presenting the positive arguments for interrelational holism I turn in the next chapter to consider a version of holism developed by Margaret Gilbert. She analyses social phenomena in terms of the joining together of individuals in a way that renders them jointly committed to certain goals, intentions, beliefs and so on. Her work is probably the most fully worked-out and influential contemporary constructivist approach to the social world. It is constructivist in the substantial sense that grouphood is dependent on individuals intentionally coming together in certain socially salient ways and intentionalist in its dependence on individuals conceiving themselves as members or as being united. I explain that Gilbert's plural subject theory faces a problem of circularity if it is taken to be an account of grouphood in general, and that such a general account is not to be premised on what I have called the intentionalist thesis.

APPENDIX

Copp's Mereological Analysis of Groups

In Section III I rather summarily point out that the attempt to identify groups with mereological sums of person stages suffers the same defects as the identification of groups with sets of persons. In this appendix I sketch Copp's proposal and explain more fully why it does not underwrite the endorsement of ontological individualism.

A kind of group (say an audience or gang or tribe), K, would consist in stages or 'time slices' linked by the appropriate form of unity relation for that type of group. Thus:

a stage of an aggregate kind, K, is a temporally unified mereological sum of stages of persons with property K', where K' varies with the kind K. That is, different kinds of aggregate will incorporate stages of persons with distinctive properties: being a discussant in the case of a discussion group; paying attention to a performance in the case of an audience and so on.[64]

An individual can be designated as a member of a group at a particular time if and only if a stage of hers is a part of the unified person-stage sum that is the group's stage at that time. The stages of the group must be related in such a way that they can be ordered through time and so that later stages are descendants of prior ones. The group will have a history related in terms of the continuity between each successive stage. Copp observes that the degree of historical continuity and the precise nature of the unity relation may vary for different kinds of group, but is likely to emphasise continuity in the salient properties characterising that kind of group. Copp talks of a nation as a group whose members by and large identify with a common tradition and history, and who desire the formation or maintenance of a state for that group. Stages of a nation are linked by 'an appropriate degree and kind of historical continuity',[65] such continuity typically inhering in the gradual change in the composition of the nation's membership and the maintenance and traceable development of the practices and attitudes that mark out an individual as a member.

Underlying this ontological thesis is a view of a group as consisting in individuals sharing certain patterns of activities, practices, attitudes and beliefs through time. On its face this analysis of groups is amenable to ontological individualism because there is no commitment to a group existing as an entity in its own right. It is just a mereological sum, individuated at and through time by the typical practices and attitudes of individuals standing in certain relations. The view is also compatible with the ascription of action and valuational predicates to groups in at least the minimal sense that a mereological sum is held by Copp to be a material entity, and as such satisfies a necessary condition for the performance of an action. Copp sets a constraint on a theory of the nature of groups that it be a desideratum of any such theory that it accommodate the claim that groups can and do perform actions.[66] At a minimum, a theory ought not entail that groups belong to a kind of entity incapable of acting. Since, according to Copp, 'it is logically impossible for a set, or for any other similarly abstract entity to pay taxes, declare wars, or violate human rights ... an account (of groups) is inadequate unless it shows collectives are not sets or any other kind of abstract entity'.[67] It would seem that an audience applauds or a mob attacks a building through the actions and attitudes of individuals. To say that the group has done something, and to evaluate those actions, is to note that its members have acted. Because of the relationship of those individuals to the mereological sum that is the group there is a vicarious or indirect sense in which the group has

64 Copp (1984) pp. 253–4.
65 Ibid., p. 255.
66 Ibid., p. 250.
67 Ibid.

acted. The mereological sum(s) at a certain time(s) does not act as such, but rather individuals act collectively, perhaps typically towards some common goal they share for the group.

Furthermore, according to Copp, when a group is understood ontologically as a mereological sum we can retain the sense in which its identity can survive change *and* the sense in which it is no more than the sum of individuals. While the same group cannot be identical with a succession of sets or mereological sums of persons, a group can be identical with the mereological sum of united person stages. The identity of a group through time is analysed in terms of its stages and their being appropriately linked. Each stage is just the mereological sum of the person-stages of those individuals who are engaged in the relevant practices, possess the salient properties and share the appropriate beliefs. The membership of this set of persons can change over time, but the group is never identical to a set of persons. Rather each momentary and successive group stage is identical with a mereological sum of person stages, itself possessing a momentary existence. The group is a succession of stages. Following Lewis[68] on personal identity (as Copp does) the group's stages are not more 'basic' or smaller bits of it, but temporal slices of the group. The group and its stages are not to be counted twice over, but are part-identical: the stages are parts of the group.

This account of the ontology of groups purports to explain the referents of group terms or names as mereological sums of a particular kind. According to Copp we are thus warranted in speaking of groups, while eschewing an ontological commitment that takes us beyond individual persons. Moreover, in its account of groups there is the recognition that the understanding and individuation of groups takes place through an analysis of the being and doing together of individuals, and the relations in which they stand, the shared goals and beliefs they possess and the capacity of practices and attitudes to develop and be maintained through time by a changing constituency of members. However, as with the attempt to identify groups with sets or aggregates of persons, an identification with mereological sums of person-stages fails.

First it may be objected that a mereological sum is a kind of mathematical or logical entity. However, the account could be adjusted so that groups are abstract objects. After all their parts are not persons, but sums of the temporal slices of persons. Membership is mediated by the parthood of one's person stage to the group as a whole. Such an approach is hardly appealing given the intuitive constraints on a theory of groups. In any case while a mereological sum may be a mathematical entity, there seem to be numerous examples of material entities that are most adequately thought of as mereological sums.[69] A pile of bricks is the mereological sum of a certain set of bricks; a deck of cards, suit of clothes and groups[70] are likewise mereological sums

---

68 Lewis (1976).

69 I put things in this way since we could think of anything as a mereological sum. Equally we can take any things and from their mereological sum we have an object.

70 Compare Copp (1984) p. 252; p. 267.

of entities whose materiality is transitive to the whole. In as far as a mereological sum is material groups are material. However, an analysis of groups as mereological sums of person stages just repeats the confusion of composition with identity.

At any time any object, o, is a mereological sum, namely the sum of the parts organised 'o-wise' at that time. Here we can distinguish between kinds of objects such as natural or artefactual continuants – say cats and tables – and those gerrymandered objects that are merely mereological sums – say the entity whose parts are Basil (the cat) and the desk at which I am working. The distinction arises in the potential arbitrariness or conventionalism inherent in the appropriate 'o-wiseness'. A contingent fact about, for example a people or gang, is that a group will be composed of a certain mereological sum of person-stages through the course of its existence. To *identify* the group with such a mereological sum will give rise to modal problems familiar from the previous discussion of sets. The identity of a mereological sum of person stages is as sensitive to change as a mereological sum or set of persons. A difference in the membership of a group entails a difference in the parts of the group's stages, and hence in the parts of the group.

This line of criticism may be too hasty, however. Let us remember that a group is the mereological sum of its stages, each stage being itself a temporally unified sum of person-stages. While the classical axiomatisation of mereology makes the part–whole relation transitive, so that the parts of the stages are parts of the group, it has been suggested that this is too strong a condition.[71] A person-stage ought not to be seen as a 'significant' part of group in the same way that a door knob is not a significant part of a house[72] or my arm part of my nation. The significant parts of a group are then the stages of united person-stages, and change in their parts does not matter in questions of whether *this group under these changed counterfactual circumstances would count as the same group.*

However, the problem possesses a certain tenacity. Allowing that sums of person-stages are the significant parts of groups, is it not possible that the same group could have had different stages? In some cultures it has traditionally been the norm for families to maintain their structure and ultimately line – both male and female – through adoption.[73] We can identify the same family, F, through several centuries. The mereological approach informs us that it is actually the sum of a succession of stages of person-stage sums. Let us name this mereological sum M. Now, it is possible that at some point in its history the then youngest generation of that family could have died; perhaps as a result of the combination of war and disease. The adoption of non-biologically related individuals restores numbers and refills roles within the

---

71 Discussed by for example Simons (1987) and Cruse (1979). A similar point is made briefly by Copp (1984).

72 Cruse (1979) notes that a handle is part of a door, which is part of the house, but it may seem that the handle is not part of the house. Cruse is concerned with linguistic evidence for the failure of transitivity. I am simply taking the example to suggest that there is an intuitive case for the notion of a significant part to be distinguished from the technical notion of a proper part.

73 Compare discussion in Section V above.

family structure. More to the present point the very same family seems capable of consisting of stages that are different from the actual ones. We can name the possible mereological sum of stages M*. There are then two worlds in which the same family would be held to be identical with a succession of distinct sums of stages, namely M and M*. While this is a compositional possibility it cannot be the case that the same family is identical with different mereological sums if things true of the family are to be true of the mereological sum(s) with which it is identified. Although any part of a group's stage may not count as a 'significant' part of the group, it is the case that a person-stage is part of the group stage. If there is enough change in the person stages there is a change in the identity of the group stage,[74] and thus of the mereological sum of stages. The mereological approach tells us that F is identical with M, which is not identical with M*. Therefore, F cannot be identical with M*. However, it does violence to any plausible (holist or individualistic) view of groups to say that F could not have been M*, because surely what is meant when we assert such a modal claim is that F could have been composed of M*. The identity conditions for the group as such are not merely given by its composition.

One should remember that the mereological analysis under consideration specifies that a group is the mereological sum of temporally unified person-stages linked by a unity relation. Now the unity relation is just the pattern of salient practices, attitudes, goals and so on that make a collection of individuals individualisable as a group. Depending on the nature of the group there may be greater or lesser need for long term continuity of membership (it is worth noting that there is nothing in the unity relation itself that pre-judges the ontological status of groups). As long as stages are linked by the unity relation the group can be said to exist. An audience dissipates as it leaves a theatre, the individuals no longer collectively engaging in, *inter alia*, the watching of a performance and applauding. A people may come to cease to exist as individuals gradually fail to engage in certain linguistic and cultural practices. The role of the unity relation is to set a limit on the stages of person-stage sums that are to be considered as being identical with a group, for the (trivial) reason that a group can cease to exist. Only stages standing in the appropriate relation make up the whole. If a group is meant to be identical rather than just composed of a mereological sum, the introduction of the unity relation appears to be something of a cheat in order to side-step problems from the principle of collectivism.

Collectivism holds that entities, no matter how scattered (or diverse in kind), can have a mereological sum, implying that the assembly or disassembly of an object does not affect its existence as a mereological sum. The unity of being an audience

---

74 Cruse's (1979) suggestion that some things are significant parts of some other thing, while other kinds of constituents are not significant, could lead to similar problems we encounter with proper parts. Say a 'piece' of wood, is a significant part of the door handle, although not a significant part of the house. If enough pieces are removed there will be a different door (or no door if they are not replaced). If there is a new door then, if a house is identical with the mereological sum of its significant parts, there is a 'new' house. The difference may be that with significant parts it can be a vague matter whether the house has changed.

or a mob does not constrain or impose some kind of limit on the existence of the mereological sum of the individuals' person-stages. The very same person-stages form a mereological sum whether or not they are linked through a unity relation. The point here is that the unity relation is shorthand for the practices and continuities through which groups are singled out. By employing the unity relation we are able in principle to identify (roughly) the temporal boundaries of a group and to thereby identify the person-stages in which the group has consisted. However, there is no principled basis by which a unity relation can regulate what is to count as a mereological sum of person-sum stages *simpliciter*. The existence of such a sum is independent of there being any kind of unity relation.

Chapter 2

On Plural Subject Theory

I   Introduction

Margaret Gilbert's plural subject theory of our vernacular social concepts tells us that groups are real entities.[1] Gilbert is a realist in the sense that groups cannot be reduced or analysed out of our best explanations and descriptions of the social world, and plural subject theory tells us that groups are characterised by two essential features. First, groups are formed by individuals who share a commitment to certain ends, intentions, attitudes or actions and that commitment is common knowledge amongst them: the theory can be said to be *intentionalist*. Second, the individuals make the commitment as a *unit* or *body* or *whole*. I shall suggest *contra* Gilbert that there is no obvious reason for thinking the first condition necessary, arguing that plural subject theory does not adequately discharge the burden of explaining why intentionalism ought to be regarded as necessary. I then go on to explain that the second (supposed) essential feature of a group actually generates a dilemma for the plural subject theorist. Either the theory is circular because of a *de facto* presupposition of the notion of a group, or, in escaping circularity, it is unable to provide a general account of the nature of groups.

Since Gilbert sets out to elucidate paradigmatic everyday social phenomena and concepts, it is presumably an object of plural subject theory to provide an account of grouphood. That is, in as far as plural subject theory looks at the ontological nature of groups, it is not about a kind or sub-class of social group, but pursues the general or global question of what kind of thing is a group. Indeed, Gilbert asks '(W)hat precisely is a social group?',[2] and in setting out how individual persons come to stand in group-forming relations Gilbert develops a conceptual framework to examine, *inter alia*, conventions, agreements, promising, political obligation and collective emotions. If, as I shall explain, plural subject theory does not have the degree of generality to answer Gilbert's own question, then it may be more aptly regarded as a theory about a certain kind of group within a more general account.

---

1   See Gilbert (1987; 1989; 1996; 2000) *On Social Facts* is the major statement of her views, which have been developed in a series of papers (collected with introductions in her 1996 and 2000). Gilbert's work amounts to a consistent defence and elucidation of the position set out at length in *On Social Facts*, and it is the core concept of a plural subject which is the object of critical scrutiny in the present chapter.

2   Gilbert (1989) p. 1.

In the next section I outline how plural subject theory regards the sharing of certain propositional contents as necessary in the formation and maintenance of a social group, and how the theory takes obligations to inhere in the group-constituting joint commitment of individuals. Then I explain that there is no principled reason for realism to be committed to intentionalism (section III). The rejection of the intentional thesis is not a local criticism of plural subject theory, but of the sociological and philosophical tradition within which it is located. Furthermore, the claim that individuals must conceive of themselves as united as a unit or body or whole raises serious problems for Gilbert's account (section IV). Finally, I note that notwithstanding the difficulties entailed by the nature of its intentionalism, plural subject theory is plausibly read as being committed to the material particularity of groups (section V). The ontological commitment of plural subject theory offers support to an understanding of groups as material objects, even if plural subjecthood does not itself furnish a global account of the ontological status of groups.

II   Plural Subject Theory

Gilbert's project begins from an understanding of persons as social individuals. We are 'beings both independent and interdependent', leading our lives in terms of a personal and collective standpoint.[3] The main aim of plural subject theory is an interpretation and elucidation of the collective standpoint: the perspective from which we possess shared goals, beliefs, values and so on.[4]

The core of Gilbert's account of everyday social phenomena is her analysis of groups as plural subjects. For Gilbert a social group is a plural subject and any plural subject is a social group: 'in order to constitute a social group people must constitute a plural subject *of some kind*. And *any* plural subject is a social group',[5] which includes families, tribes, corporations, religious bodies, literary associations, peoples and states. A plural subject is formed when agents jointly commit as a body to do A or be X (or express a preparedness to so commit on the basis that joint commitment requires the corresponding commitments from the relevant others). Plural subject theory is explicitly intentionalist:

---

3   Gilbert (1996) p. 1.

4   Now, it is worth noting that plural subject theory is broad and ambitious in its scope. It is not seeking to answer questions that arise for particular sociological schools or perspectives, but looking to provide the conceptual framework in which our experience of the social world can best be understood. It is probably true to say that plural subject theory will be more appealing to some sociological perspectives rather than others. For example given Gilbert's emphasis on the role of shared intentional contents an approach such as symbolic interactionism may see much relevance in plural subject theory. On the other hand, a Marxist sociology may be relatively uninterested in a theoretical framework which stresses how groups are formed rather than how they interact in light of the distinct interests assigned to them.

5   Gilbert (1990) p. 188.

First, plural subject concepts apply only when certain individual people are in specific psychological states, that is only when they are jointly committed with certain others in some way. Second, one cannot employ a particular plural subject concept [i.e. speak of a plural subject of a belief, intention etc.] without employing the concept of the relevant psychological attribute ... such as belief, having such-and-such goal, and endorsing such-and-such principle.[6]

This commitment must be made under conditions of common knowledge. Very roughly, it must be out in the open between the agents that each has committed to do A as a body, that each knows that each has expressed preparedness to be jointly committed to do A, and knows that each knows and so on.[7] Each agent is thus committing with each of the others that they together, as a body or unit, do A. The plural subject is not formed of a sum of individual commitments to do A, say to go for a walk or bomb the embassy, but symmetrical and reciprocal commitments on the part of each individual to act together as a body. The commitment of each individual is to act jointly with the others – a joint commitment to act as a body. Taking a two-person group as the vehicle for more general analysis Gilbert has observed that:

Quite generally, if Anne and Ben are jointly committed, they are jointly committed to doing something as a body, or if you like, as a single unit or 'person'. Doing something as a body, in the relevant sense, is not a matter of 'all doing it' but rather a matter of 'all acting in a such a way to constitute a body that does it'. Doing is here construed very broadly. People may be jointly committed to accepting (and pursuing) a certain goal as a body. They may be jointly committed to believing that such-and-such as body. And so on.[8]

Such a Gilbertian group can be the subject of beliefs, desires, it can hold intentions and act. All these collective phenomena are susceptible to an analysis in terms of agents jointly committing to, say, hold certain pro-attitudes or to produce certain acts as a body.

For Gilbert then,

Human beings X, Y, Z constitute a collectivity (social group) if and only if each correctly thinks of himself and the others, taken together, as us* or we*.[9]

For a group to hold a belief it must hold a belief *qua* plural subject, and this is cashed out in the following terms:

(i) A group G believes that p if and only if the members of G jointly accept that p. (ii) Members of a group G jointly accept that p if and only if it is common knowledge in G

---

6   Gilbert (1996) p. 9. My insertion.

7   Gilbert has devoted considerable attention to elucidating, criticising and developing the notion of common knowledge introduced by David Lewis (1969).

8   Gilbert (1999) p. 147.

9   Gilbert (1989) p. 147. Gilbert employs the star to indicate the technical use of the terms.

that the individual members of *G* have openly expressed a conditional commitment to accept that *p* with the other members of *G*.[10].

To jointly accept a certain proposition, to constitute a plural subject of a belief:

> two or more people must be jointly prepared to accept the relevant proposition jointly. Or, as I prefer: they must be jointly committed to accept the proposition *as a body (as a unit, as one).*[11]

To hold an intention as a group its members must be jointly committed to some end. As Gilbert puts matters:

> Persons P1 and P2 have a shared intention to do A if and only if they are jointly committed to intending as a body to do A.[12]

It is possible according to Gilbert to be coerced into a joint commitment, to commit oneself with another(s) to do something as a unit.[13] It does not, however, seem possible to have anything other than an intentional participation in a plural subject. This is not to say that individuals must intend to form a plural subject at the outset of their interactions. Gilbert observes that 'joint commitments are not necessarily brought into being with any clear conscious intent to do so'.[14] For example, Peter and Paul may just fall into a joint commitment as their impromptu decision to have dinner after the faculty meeting becomes a regular fixture. After a couple of occasions each may surmise that 'in effect each is ready to be jointly committed with the other to accept as a body the plan of having dinner together after work'.[15] Although an original or motivating intention was not present, each comes to think of himself as related to the other in a saliently group-forming fashion.

Becoming party to a plural subject has agreement-like features. While recognising that there is a problematic vagueness in identifying when and what might constitute an agreement, Gilbert maintains that,

> (T)he exchange of conditional commitments of the will that I have argued is central to plural subject phenomena is of course not conceived of as involving understandings of the form 'I promise if you promise'. Nor is it of the form 'I promise to do A if you do B'. Like an agreement it is a device whereby a set of persons can simultaneously and interdependently become bound to act in certain ways.[16]

---

10 Gilbert (1987) pp. 198–9.

11 Gilbert (1996) p. 8.

12 Gilbert (1997) p. 22.

13 See Gilbert (1993) especially pp. 301–3. In the case of coerced agreements there may often be a moral duty not to honour its terms.

14 Gilbert (2000) p. 6.

15 Ibid.

16 Gilbert (1989) p. 382.

Although the formation of a plural subject need not arise from nor amount to a full-blown clear cut agreement it is certainly to be understood as agreement-like in the meshing of obligations and expectations. A group has a structure as if arrived at through an agreement, although the group may actually be formed by a process, which is more subtle and involve nothing obviously characterisable as an out-and-out agreement. Gilbert illustrates the kind of circumstances in which this might arise by showing how people can join together in regular trips to have coffee, or to go for walks. In entering into a joint commitment to do or be something as a body or whole, individuals are expressing a conditional commitment or a contingent preparedness to act *with* the relevant others as such a body.

Gilbert argues that a joint commitment is not simply a matter of there being corresponding and entwining personal commitments. A joint commitment does not have separable parts composed of the constituent persons. Once the expressions of commitment are in place the agents are subject to a single commitment – no single agent is the author of that commitment. Rather together, as a body, the commitment is formed. The commitment to do A as a body provides each agent with a reason for action. Moreover, the reason is not personal in the sense that the commitment can not be rescinded by the individual's change of mind, for she is not its sole author, as in the case of a personal intention. Rather, 'in being subject to a commitment such that she is not the sole author of the commitment ... she does not have the authority to unilaterally rescind it'.[17] Agents are seen as having an obligation to conform to the joint commitment in virtue of the commitment being the creation of the group. Each person has a commitment-based reason over which he can not claim sole authorship. Obligations and entitlements between agents thereby inhere in the joint commitment so that:

> If Anne and Ben are jointly committed to doing something as a body, each owes the other appropriate actions by virtue of their commitment ... I shall say that a joint commitment *obligates* the parties, one to the other.[18]

Gilbert has expressed one way of understanding the formation of the social group as the pooling of individual wills to be directed at a collective goal, under conditions of common knowledge, remarking that there appear to be similarities between Rousseau's *volonté générale* and her notion of plural subjecthood.[19] Agents are bound together, wills transformed or mapped onto the collective plane through agreement or agreement-like structures.

---

17 Gilbert (1997) p. 21.

18 Gilbert (1999) p. 151.

19 'At a late stage in writing this book I realised that I had come close to Rousseau's conception of what makes a collection of human beings into a genuine people as opposed to a mere aggregate' (1989, p. 438). ' ... I do not claim, nor need to claim, that I am certain what Rousseau had in mind. However, it and several other passages in the book [*The Social Contract*] clearly bear some resemblance to what I want to say about plural subjects' (1990 p. 190).

III   Intentionalism

The emphasis which Gilbert places on individuals sharing a conception or understanding of themselves as linked through a common belief, attitude or goal, has been widely endorsed by social scientists and philosophers as essential in the formation of a group. In this respect Gilbert is firmly in the mainstream of the sociological and philosophical tradition approach to groups. Briefly stated, the *intentionalist thesis* holds that individuals can constitute a social group only when each believes or understands himself to be linked in some salient way with the others, or when each conceives of himself as a member of the group. The relevant ways in which individuals can be linked range from entering into clear and open agreements and undertakings with others to the recognition that oneself and others share certain goals, values or attitudes, and that it is in virtue of this commonality that one stands with them in a group.[20] In this section I defend the claim that intentionalism be rejected. The formation of a group does not depend upon the understanding (broadly construed) individuals have of themselves as members or as sharing a common identity.

At a minimum it is often claimed that members of a group must see themselves as such. For example, Giddens defines social groups as:

> Collections of individuals who interact in systematic ways with one another. Groups may vary from very small associations to large-scale organizations or societies. Whatever their size, it is a defining feature of a group that its members have an awareness of a common identity.[21]

A similar stress on the shared conception of membership is found in Cooley's notion of primary groups, like families or factory work teams, which are:

> characterised by intimate face-to-face association and co-operation. They are primary in several senses, but chiefly in that they are fundamental in forming the social nature of and ideals of the individual. The result of the intimate association, psychologically, is a certain fusion of individualities in a common whole, so that one's very self, for many purposes at least, is the common life and purpose of the group. Perhaps the simplest way of describing

---

20 It is not a criticism of the intentionalist thesis to note that engaging in identical forms of practices or sharing the same goals or values is not sufficient to unite individuals. Consider the science fiction staple of an alien world indistinguishable (internally so to speak) from our actual one in its inhabitants' practices and so on. There is no reason for the intentionalist to say that a group on the actual world forms with its counterpart a single group. That is because the relevant others are indexed or bound to a particular world. A problem does lurk for the intentionalist in specifying whether group membership is limited to those who actually share certain attitudes. If it does, then cases in which individuals are unthinkingly parts of a group or unaware of their membership are ruled out. Perhaps the intentionalist position can be nuanced by requiring that one must possess *or potentially upon reflection* recognise that one has certain salient attitudes.

21 Giddens (1997) p. 585.

this wholeness is by saying that it is perhaps a 'we', it involves the sort of sympathy and mutual identification for which 'we' is a natural expression. One lives in the feeling of the whole, and finds the chief aims of his will in that feeling.[22]

Here, then, we see the group as such being assigned a significant role in explaining certain features of individuals, while its very existence – the wholeness or unity in which it consists – depends upon members standing in relations of sympathy and recognition. The concept of a primary group has become a basic staple of sociology, and its influence is reflected in the definition of a psychological group provided by an introductory text for university and MBA students on organisational behaviour.

> The idea of a group is well known to most people who work, live and play in groups...It is important to maintain a distinction between mere aggregates of individuals and what are called psychological groups. The latter are so called because they not only exist through the (often visible) interactions of members, but also in the (not observable) perceptions of their members. The term group is thus reserved for people who consider themselves to be part of an identifiable unit, who relate to each other in a meaningful fashion and who share dispositions through their shared sense of collective identity.[23]

Gilbert's own work is self-consciously inspired by Georg Simmel for whom the awareness of being part of a body with others is central to the notion of a collectivity. Identifying the process of forming a group ('sociation') as ranging 'all the way from the momentary getting together for a walk to founding a family ... from the temporary aggregation of hotel guests to the intimate bond of a medieval guild',[24] Simmel goes on to address the question of how a society is possible by urging that it is a unity of a particular kind. Namely, 'the consciousness of constituting with the others a unity is actually all there is to this unity'.[25] Plural subject theory clearly sets out its endorsement of intentionalism:

> the view that according to our everyday collectivity concepts, individual human beings must see themselves in a particular way to constitute a collectivity. In other words, intentions (broadly construed) are logically prior to collectivities.[26]

In being a member of a group each person conceives of herself as linked in some relevant fashion with the others. It is maintained that individuals must share certain goals, commitments or psychological states in order to constitute a group. Briefly

---

22 Cooley (1964/1909) p. 311. Also cited in Worsley (1977) p. 343.

23 Buchanan and Huczynski (1985) p. 131.

24 Simmel (1971) p. 24. Also cited in Gilbert (1990) p. 178.

25 Gilbert (1990) p. 75 See Gilbert 1989, Chap. IV for an extended discussion of the Simmelian influence on plural subject theory.

26 Gilbert (1989) p. 12. The way in which individuals must see themselves is as being committed together to a belief, goal, intention and so on, and for such a commitment to be common knowledge. Gilbert's 'pro-intentionalist stance finds its positive basis (in the argument) that people must perceive themselves as members of a plural subject' (ibid., p. 13).

stated, then, individuals can constitute a social group only when each believes or understands himself to be linked in some salient way with the others, or when each conceives of himself as a member of the group. Now, the claim here is not just that our (or their) sharing salient beliefs or attitudes is sufficient for us (or them) to constitute a group, but that it is necessary that we (or they) do so.

Intentionalism may resonate with much of our ordinary experience of groups. After all, being a member of a group may frequently involve one's knowing participation in the practices that amount to the on-going constitution of the group; and joining, engaging with others, and endorsing and departing from the practices and goals of a group, are things we do intentionally. Moreover, when we are engaging with others as parts of a group it is surely plausible to think that one does so because one has a conception of oneself as linked with them; as a member of the group. The intentionalist thesis thus draws together a claim about what is necessary for individuals to form and maintain a group (the possession certain shared psychological states that are common knowledge) with a commonplace feature of our experience of being in groups (the awareness that oneself and others are together members). In effect plural subject theory identifies a common feature of group membership with a necessary condition for the existence of a group.

A motivation for the intentional thesis may be the belief that as language and concept deploying creatures we more or less self-consciously construct the social world, and that its nature is (at least potentially) transparent to us.[27] Of course, it is through our modes of communication and the possession and development of shared concepts that much our lives in the social world unfold, and through which groups are formed and develop. Many groups, perhaps those of most interest to the social sciences, are 'self-identifying' in the way suggested by the intentionalist thesis, for their members conceive of themselves as such. Yet, as I shall argue in the remaining part of this section, the burden of the argument continues to rest with Gilbert (and intentionalists in general) to show that the intentionalist feature of groups is a necessary one.

We should note that plural subject theory is not to be read as claiming that intentionalism is necessary because it is obviously or trivially true. Even if Gilbert (and the other thinkers cited) thinks this is the case her analysis does not rest upon, for example, the isolation of an *a priori* reason to suggest that individuals who do not share salient intentional contents are unable to interrelate in a group-constituting fashion. Rather, plural subject theory *assumes* intentionalism and then appeals to its explanatory power in analysing paradigmatic social phenomena. This is insufficient to allow Gilbert to make her case convincingly because, first, methodologically Gilbert seems to conflate the individuation of groups *as such* with the formulation

---

27 I shall not attempt to trace the development of the thesis. At (one of) its root(s) in modern social science may be the claim due to Vico that the nature and workings of society, the subject matter of the social sciences, ought to be transparent to social agents.

of an account of how groups are formed; and, second, she ignores possible counter-examples to the intentionalist thesis.

It is at least an open possibility that a group could be established and maintained by individuals who do not share the kind of beliefs, attitudes or goals upon which intentionalism insists. The individuals would nonetheless form a body through standing in certain patterns of relations, and that body would be individualisable in virtue of its causal powers and explanatory role. The methodological confusion in plural subject theory is that an explanation of the process by which a group is formed and maintained is not identical to the criterion(ia) in virtue of which a group is individuated *qua* group in explanation or description.[28] Quite in general the individuation of entities depends upon their causal and explanatory role. For example, let us agree that a basic fact about the ecology of the oceans is that they support medium – large scale animals (i.e. measurable without the aid of specialist magnifying equipment) which spend their entire lives in the sea, and many of which depend upon other such animals for food. A much finer grained taxonomy of sea-living animals is possible once we discover more about the variety of kinds that inhabit the oceans – not least by gaining knowledge of the differences in physiological forms. In the first instance, though, we can pick out a class of sea-living animals by reference to the impact they have on their environment and each other. Of course, we must be operating within a theoretical or conceptual framework which affords us the notion of an animal or organism. This is, though, a very high order or general level taxonomic category. The question of whether a whale is a fish or a mammal follows that of whether it is an animal.

Likewise, in the social sciences the term 'group' can be thought of as a high order term. In providing a description and explanation of the social world one of our first tasks is to pick out the explanatorily salient entities. We individuate groups in the explanation of both particular events, such as the storming of the Bastille or the Watts riots in Los Angeles, and in analysing certain kinds of events, such as wars or revolutions. We may cite the role of groups in studying processes and structures like the maintenance and transmission of cultural norms, the development of capitalism, the institution of slavery within certain cultures, the long term accumulation of capital within an economy, and the correlation between states of affairs such as poverty rates and levels of criminality. Nor is an interest in groups confined to macro-level phenomena, for we may explain the development, character and actions of an individual through the groups of which he is a member and with which he has had contact.

The *prima facie* role of a group in explanation depends upon the properties and powers that are attributed to it. That does not appear to require intentionalism, which is a claim about a necessary feature in the formation and maintenance of a group. Groups as such figure in explanations because a relevant property or power is only

---

28 This is not to say that the structure of a group does not explain (at least in part) why it possesses certain properties by which it is picked out, but it is the possession of those properties which is immediately relevant to the group's individuation.

appropriately predicable to the group *qua* entity. If we ask why the barricades fell or why the soldier was afraid, perfectly good answers might cite the way in which rampaging individuals interacted in a certain environment to form a charging mob or the way in which when individuals stand in certain group forming relations the group has the property of inspiring fear in others. The question of whether the group was formed and maintained *intentionally* is a further and distinct one. Moreover, it is one that does not seem to need answering in order to individuate the group in question.

To hold that this leaves Gilbert with the explanatory onus may appear to be overstating the case. After all, plural subject theory shows how groups as diverse as couples meeting for coffee, nations and crowds can be analysed as plural subjects. The burden is surely with the critic to illustrate how groups can be formed and maintained non-intentionally. The plural subject theorist can agree that the *prima facie* case for individuating groups does not depend on the intentionalist thesis, but that an analysis of the concept of a group reveals an interesting and profound fact about them: intentionalism is a necessary property of any group.

Intentionalism is then a claim about what has to be true of individuals for it to be true that they constitute a group. In holding that individuals must share certain psychological states, intentionalism requires that group-making individuals have a certain mental content in the process of its formation and on-going maintenance. There is, though, scope for a distinction to be made between the psychological facts about individuals and the explanatory concepts used in elucidating social facts. The beliefs individuals have about their own actions and relations may not report the true or full nature of those actions and relations, in that they do not reveal to the individual the fact that he along with relevant others constitutes a group.

Let us imagine four egoists each of whom has escaped independently from a prison. By chance they arrive at the same river bank where a large oared boat is moored.[29] The boat is the only means of escape from the pursuing guards and dogs. The boat's size is such that it is evident to each of them that no individual rower would be able to propel it. Now, whether they leap into the boat and just start rowing, or begin rowing after exchanging significant looks or after each has affirmed his commitment to share in the rowing, none of the escapees considers himself to be part of a collectivity or group, even though each recognises the necessary contribution of

---

29 The story could be equally told using four walkers who independently arrive at the river, and each of whom has a singular desire to cross it. The point is that, unlike, say, the passengers on a plane, which is hijacked, the prisoners or the walkers have no shared history as elements in an aggregate prior to a change in circumstances, which may encourage a group-forming pattern of relations. The story of the rowing escapees is indebted to Hume's example of two men rowing a boat in his analysis of conventions (Hume, 1978, p. 490). It is unclear what (if any) was Hume's view of the ontological status of social groups, although there is reason to suppose that Hume was no realist about groups. Nonetheless, interrelational holism parallels Hume's account of the development of society and of the Artificial Virtues. Neither account relies upon a prior notion of agreement or convention, and both recognise the central role of interaction as the motor for conceptual development.

the others.[30] They all share the belief that 'I am escaping' and, in the circumstances its entailment, 'we are escaping'. There is no basis, though, to suppose that they have as a goal their ('our') escape, but only each's ('my') successful flight.[31]

It seems to me that they do constitute a group, even though each may sincerely deny that he is linked or united or constitutes a group with the others. It is not the individuals' beliefs about themselves and their peers that are essential to their 'grouphood', but the relations in which they stand. It may often be the case that our relations with others are bound up with our shared beliefs, including those beliefs about the beliefs of others with respect to oneself. However, a group is formed through the ways in which individuals interrelate and interact, and group-constituting patterns of relations are not necessarily those in which the kinds of beliefs essential to the intentionalist thesis will feature.

The object of each prisoner's belief, 'I am escaping', is the escape in which he is participating. The truth, warrant or assertibilty of the proposition 'I am escaping' depends upon the actions and the contribution to the prevailing state of affairs (with respect to the rowing boat) that the escapees collectively produce. The escape in which they are engaged is analysable in terms of the action tokens of each individual, and in this case the most obviously relevant actions would be the rowing. However, the rowing of each is affected or constrained by the collective rowing, and the production of the overall state of the boat. The actions and attitudes of each is partly shaped by the impact of the states of affairs produced by each-plus-the-others, and each escapee responds to and stands in a relation to the events and actions of them (that is including himself) all together. Thus prisoner A, who may be even more anxious to escape than the others, may not be able to significantly increase the speed of the boat because of its overall velocity. The actions of each must have regard to the actions of them all as manifested in the state of the boat; thus the rate at which each can row may be constrained by the danger of 'catching a crab' at the current speed of the boat, which is the product of their collective action.

The fugitive prisoners come to form a group in the rowing of the boat and, as far as the story goes, the group is maintained by their on-going rowing of it. Motivated by the purely selfish desire for flight, the processes and interrelatedness of the rowing unites the individuals into a unit, independently of their beliefs and attitudes about the others. The extension of 'we' is the group as a collectivity or whole, while it

---

30 The escapees' actions are social in Weber's sense, according to whom an action is social when 'by virtue of the subjective meaning attached to it by the acting individual(s) it takes account of the behaviour of others and is thereby oriented in its course' (Weber, 1978/1922, p. 88).

31 If captured and questioned what he thought he was doing, each escapee could answer: 'we were escaping', taking the extension to be an aggregate of individuals. An interrogator may take 'we' to refer to either an aggregate of individuals considered severally or to a body or group of individuals considered jointly or united. The belief expressed depends significantly on the sense in which 'we' is understood. Even if each prisoner has the belief 'we were escaping', the object of the belief varies depending on the referent of 'we'. Compare Perry's (1975) discussion of the 'essential indexical'.

also remains the case that each prisoner is indifferent to the fate of the others, and is possessed only of singular goals. Nonetheless, the rowing of the boat is effected by a body, formed through the interrelations of the prisoners, which constrains and influences the rowing of each individual.

Consider also a commodities market consisting of selfishly motivated individuals who do not regard themselves as being members of a group – the market.[32] The performance of the market is the outcome of the complex array of interactions between the traders. The totality of these interactions both constitute the market at any time, and are in part made possible or constrained by the state of the market. Furthermore the market has an influence on the wider economy, determining to a greater or lesser degree price behaviour and levels of activity elsewhere – but particularly in those sectors utilising the commodities traded on the market, or influenced by the pricing of financial assets traded. It is possible to develop a model of interlocking sets of practices or domains that are mutually dependent, and the understanding of which can only be attained within the context of a practice's relations to the whole pattern of interrelating domains. It may be that the London Metal Exchange and the Chicago Mercantile Exchange are best understood as individual entities constituted by the complex interactions of those who trade in them, and individuated within the social world by tracing their impact upon, for example, individuals, companies and governments. Like the escaping prisoners there is no need for traders to think of themselves as members of a group, or as united with fellow traders. Indeed, it may be more likely that they conceive of themselves *qua* traders in specifically atomistic and adversarial terms. Furthermore, it is the case that some trading methodologies take the market to be an entity in its own right, to be assessed and predicted in virtue of its properties and its (historic) relations to other markets. Far from conceiving themselves to be part of a group, such traders take themselves to be engaging directly with another entity in the world, the market itself.[33]

Now, if there is a non-intentionalist mode of group-constitution, then it may still be true that a social group is only capable of formation by creatures with a certain cognitive capacity. However, the forms of interrelations from which a group

---

32 It may be objected that in fact traders frequently must be members of a market in order to gain access to it, and that therefore no trader in, say a Chicago futures pit is likely to fail to think of him or herself as a member. However, the formal and institutional requirements regulating certain markets should not be confused with the ontological status of the market itself. The corporate and institutional framework of a market is distinct from the group, which may be constituted by the often adversarial and selfishly motivated actions of the individual traders.

33 One approach to trading commodities and financial instruments is to make purchase and selling decisions on the basis of one's interpretation of charts recording the performance of the market, and perhaps its relationship with certain others. The charts record the 'life' of the market, from which some traders claim to be able to extrapolate predictively valuable generalisations. The point is that the strategy is premised on taking the market to be an entity in its own right, and decision making screens out any source of information other than facts about the market's past performance.

is established and sustained need not be restricted to those characterised by shared beliefs, attitudes and so on. Or at any rate intentionalism in general and plural subject theory in particular must discharge the burden of explaining why the sharing of beliefs and so on is necessary for individuals to constitute a group in the face of the kind of considerations adumbrated above. In the absence of such an explanation intentionalism is not a principle realism has either the need or warrant to endorse. It should perhaps be emphasised here that many significant kinds of group are as a matter of fact constituted by individuals who share goal, values and conceive of themselves as united as members. It also seems possible that a group (such as a nation perhaps) may be formed by a complex and diverse set of relations between individuals so that there could be a mix of those who do conceive of themselves as members and those who do not. The key point is that intentionalism does not mark out a necessary condition on the formation and maintenance of social groups. Furthermore, and independent of the general intentionalist thesis that individuals must share some kind of shared attitude or belief, plural subject theory faces a problem of circularity arising from what it identifies as a necessary part of either the content or understanding of the joint commitments of group members.

IV   Bodies

Gilbert quite deliberately explains the formation of a plural subject as the coming together of individuals as a *body* or *unit* or *whole*.[34] A group consists in the joint commitment (under conditions of common knowledge) by agents to ϕ as a body. Thus, according to plural subject theory, Paul and Peter can form a group through their commitment as a unit to dine together after the faculty meeting, as can a much larger number of individuals (say, a people) who share a commitment to value as a body certain ends or practices. The requirement that individuals join together as a *body* or *unit* or *whole* gives rise to a significant problem for plural subject theory. Either it is circular in its tacit dependence on a prior notion of group, or it evades circularity at the cost of abandoning its claim to provide a general account of grouphood. Beginning from an obvious, but plainly circular reading of body/ unit/whole as simply being synonyms for 'group', I consider alternative ways of interpreting this aspect of plural subject theory, concluding that it is unable to offer a well-motivated non-circular and general account of groups.

   An obvious way of reading Gilbert is to regard 'coming together as a body or unit or whole', or 'sharing in an intention or belief together,' just to mean that individuals are coming together and committing to do certain things or hold certain beliefs or attitudes as a group. For how else is a realist to regard a social group but as a body or unit or whole? The notion of acting or being a body or unit just is the notion of being a group: we constitute a group in virtue of our joint commitment, because joint

---

34 A plural subject is maintained by individuals who continue to share certain attitudes and so forth as a body or whole. The plural subject forming attitudes or goals or intentions may change over time.

commitment is essentially the coming together of agents as a body or unit – that is, as a group.

The formation and maintenance of a plural subject presupposes that its constituents possess a concept of body or unit, such that they can intentionally commit to act as such. While a class of group may indeed be formed in just this way, the presupposition means that plural subject theory is a poor candidate as an analysis of the concept of a social group. It is hardly informative to hold that a social group consists of those who have come together to act as or be a body or unit or whole when this is just to say that they are committed to certain ends etc. as a group. On the face of it, then, the plural subject account of a group looks to be a circular one. Moreover, it is not clear that the circularity is benign, arising from the inevitable interdefinability of closely linked concepts. To avoid the charge of circularity and to maintain the generality of its scope plural subject theory must be able to distinguish the sense in which it requires individuals to join together as a body, unit or whole and the sense in which a plural subject *is* a social group.

Arguably it could be maintained that the idea of jointly committing as a body is innocent of presupposing the notion of a social group. For example, we could say that agents are employing a conception of being a body or of being unified that is quite naturally associated with our own bodies, other organisms and artefacts. In conceptualising our commitment to, say, endorse as a unit the belief that *p*, we are committing to be united or linked with others in a way already familiar from our experience of non-social unities. Under this view there remains the task for plural subject theory of explaining why this way of thinking about our relations with others arises. In order to provide a general account of social groups an elucidation is owed of why individuals come to think of themselves as being united or forming a body. Perhaps we could think of individuals making a joint commitment to come together *as if* they were a body or a unit. They would not be presupposing that they are a particular kind of body – a social group – merely that they are prepared to act or be a particular way under a general conception of being united as a whole. This approach would suppose that the concept of a group is to be understood as a restriction on, or application of, a more general conception of a body or unit. If one is to employ this account to explain the nature and formation of groups in general, then one is already committed to the view that groups are not amongst the things in the world through or in virtue of which we develop a concept of an object or unit.

I shall not here attempt to furnish an argument that groups are material objects alongside artefacts and organisms. However, *if* groups are objects in the world, then this fact would certainly have a *prima facie* claim to explain why they figure in certain explanations and why we conceive of membership in terms of being part of a body, unit or whole. One of the ways in which we establish groups would thus be through the self-conscious application of the concept of a group, a concept developed through our encounters with and reflection upon the objects in our world and relations with them. Under this view groups would be prior to our conceptualisation of them and the application of our understanding of them in our interrelations. The point of immediate concern is that the application of a general notion of a body preserves plural subject theory as an account of grouphood only by presupposing that groups are not amongst the bodies or wholes through which we develop the very conception of a body or whole.

An interpretation of plural subject theory as employing a general concept of a unit, whole or body leaves the theory assuming as a fact about groups a claim that an account of their ontological status ought to be investigating. Plural subject theory would need to exclude groups from the class of objects, our experience of which explains the development of a general concept of a unit. If it did not do this, then plural subject theory would not be a general account of grouphood as it would already have (tacitly) acknowledged the existence of groups. Yet, there is no clear principled basis for presupposing that groups ought to be excluded from that class of objects. The exclusion (and indeed inclusion) of groups from this class would be an interesting fact about groups and a substantive claim for a realist to make. To maintain the generality of the account, plural subject theory seems forced to assume rather than explain why groups are not amongst the 'basic' objects of the world.

Now, it may held be that a basic conception of a unit or body is innate to us, and it is in virtue of this conceptual capacity that we are able to individuate objects in experience. Plural subject theory could be read in terms of individuals deploying this innate concept in certain of their social interactions. However, even if there is such a built-in conceptual capacity, the question remains of whether groups as such (as objects) could be formed without that concept being employed in the interrelations of individuals. Moreover, if we are endowed with an innate concept of unit through which we pick out objects in the world, it could remain the case that groups would be individualisable prior to their conceptual taxonomisation if a group can be formed non-intentionally. An appeal to an innate concept of a body might remove the immediate threat of circularity (at the cost of accepting a certain view on the conceptual content of experience), but it does nothing to demonstrate the necessity of individuals conceiving of themselves as a body in order to constitute a group.

An alternative understanding of Gilbert's position is that we should not take a description of agents jointly committing as a body to entail that they have a concept of a body as part of the content of their commitment (or their mental content in committing). According to this interpretation we should see agents as coming together in agreement-like relations, and in doing so they are coming together as a body. This is a judgement that can be made, so to speak, externally of the group in virtue of the way in which the individuals are bound together through the joint commitment. *The notion of a body or unit would not figure in the content of their beliefs or intentions.* While this would preserve plural subject theory from presupposing the notion of a group, there is an instability in the interpretation of plural subjecthood as being a unity through the agreement-like relations of its members. The instability emerges from the need of plural subject theory to analyse agreements in terms of the relations constitutive of a plural subject, which ultimately presuppose the concept of a body. Let me explain.

Agreements bind their parties. To enter into an agreement is to engage in a practice with a constitutively normative element. Gilbert explains that in jointly committing to something individuals acquire obligations with respect to each other. These 'obligations of joint commitment' are internal to or constitutive of jointly committing. Gilbert argues that in being bound together by our joint commitment, 'it is appropriate to speak of joint commitments producing not just reasons for action but obligations. The word "obligation" comes, after all, from the Latin *ligare*, to bind'.[35] The joint commitment of plural subject formation therefore provides a way of understanding our central notions of agreement and of obligation. As Gilbert, following Brandt,[36] notes there is a range of senses in which we deploy notions of agreement, obligation and duty. Nonetheless, Gilbert has proposed a 'joint commitment account of everyday agreements',[37] maintaining that '(I)f we are to understand agreements and promises, and the hold they have upon us, we must understand the nature and structure of joint commitment'.[38]

The bindingness of the obligations of joint commitment is not then to be explained in terms of the general features of agreement, for these features are to be explained by a consideration of joint commitment. Instead we must conceive of the persons forming a plural subject being linked in virtue of their joint commitment in a way that entails obligations owed by each to all, and the right of each that no other can unilaterally rescind the joint commitment. As co-authors of a joint commitment we are permitted only to rescind it together.

Under this interpretation a body is formed through individuals being bound together by obligations inherent in their joint commitment to hold some belief, intention or attitude. However, the fact that obligations inhere in the joint commitments of plural subject formation does not furnish plural subject theory with an account of agreement-like relations, which can make the formation of a plural subject independent of a prior notion of body. The normative cement of an agreement (and presumably of agreement-like relations) is explained as a result of the binding together and co-authorship of entering into a joint commitment. Individuals are normatively bound together just in the process of jointly committing as a body. The very understanding of agreement and obligation depends on this account upon Gilbert's conception of a plural subject. A group cannot then be analysed as individuals standing in agreement-like relations without presupposing that they have a prior conception of a body or whole. The problem of a circular dependence on a notion of a body to explain the constitution of a plural subject thus re-appears. Obligation may well be a plural subject phenomenon. However, if it is, an elucidation of obligation ultimately rests on a prior conception of a group rather than being part of the explanation of the nature of grouphood.

The presupposition of a notion of a body in the understanding of joint commitment, and the reliance of Gilbert's explanation of agreements on her conception of joint commitment, undermine Gilbert's account as a general or global analysis of the

---

35 Gilbert (1993) p. 295.
36 Brandt (1965).
37 Gilbert (1999) p. 243.
38 Gilbert (1996) p. 11.

ontological status of social groups. Unable to attain the degree of generality required to answer the question of what kind of thing a social group is, Gilbert's intentionalist account is perhaps then to be better interpreted as marking out a particular kind of group in terms of the characteristic features of and nature of the relations between its members.

V   The Ontological Commitment of Plural Subject Theory

Whatever the explanatory pressure to include groups within our ontology, it is reasonable to expect the realist to locate groups taxonomically; to say what kind of thing they are. If the price is deemed too high, then she does not have to pay it. Gilbert denies that her formulation of a plural subject presupposes a commitment to a 'body', which carries any ontological weight:

> In some places I have written that a joint commitment is the commitment of 'two or more individuals considered as a unit or whole'. I do not mean to introduce the idea of a new kind of entity, a 'unit' or 'whole'. I could as well have written 'a joint commitment is the commitment of two or more individuals considered together' which would not carry any such suggestion (1997, p. 18).[39]

Well, it seems to me that in the context of her argumentation *individuals considered together* makes no advance on individuals being considered as a unit, whole or body. As is clear from the bindingness of a joint commitment, being considered together is not to be associated with others in just any fashion. It is to be linked or united with others in a very particular way. Individuals are party to a commitment to think or act in a way that is not just coincident, but in which their actions and attitudes mesh together as inseparable elements of a single subject. To be considered together as parties to a joint commitment is, by Gilbert's own lights, to be united or linked. Gilbert's alternative formulation is just another way of saying that they are to be conceived as a unit.

The suggestion that we consider individuals together may be motivated by the challenge that holism must in the end be committed to the introduction of new ('weird') kinds of entities, and so is ontologically extravagant. I doubt that 'unit' or 'whole' distinguishes any unique kind of entity. They are nouns which can stand in the predicate place in descriptions of (*inter alia*) material objects. Indeed to have a certain unity and wholeness is a hallmark of such things. The question of present interest is whether Gilbert is committed to regarding plural subjects as material entities. I believe that plural subject theory is committed in this way.

In considering what it means to accept or require something as a body Gilbert maintains that:

> The phrase to 'accept as a body' is just one of the possible phrases with which the relevant idea might best be indicated. One might also write 'accept as a unit', for instance, or

---

39 Gilbert (1997) p. 18.

'accept as a single person'. The relevant joint commitment is a commitment, if you like, to constitute as far as is possible a single entity with a certain psychological property (in this case accepting or requiring something).[40]

It is important to note that these are ways of talking about plural subjects, ways of describing plural subjects without ontological extravagance. It is clear that Gilbert does not think that plural subjects *are* persons, nor does she simply wish to leave it that plural subjects are bodies or units. Instead, Gilbert sees plural subjects as a *'special type* of entity ... But as far as I can see they are not illusory or based on illusion'.[41] For the most part Gilbert does not discuss the ontological status of the unity of agents as conceived in terms of a plural subject. In large measure this may be due to the fact that much of her work has focused on the light the notion of plural subject casts on topics such as political obligation, social convention and collective beliefs and emotions. Towards the end of *On Social Facts* Gilbert does address the question of the reality of social groups.[42] Taking plural subject theory to be in agreement with Simmel's view that societies are real unities and Durkheim's claim that societies are *sui generis* syntheses of human beings,[43] she asks how a conception of an individual as a complex system differs from that of a plural subject:

We might say that for there to be a singular agent is for there to be a system which contains as a crucial element a conception of the system. This conception of the system powers the system in the sense that leads it to acts of will and physical motions. Now, how is this complex system, the singular agent, different in kind from the plural subject? Someone may say that it alone is 'self-contained'. It is in the trivial way of having all its essential components packaged up in a single human body. But how can that fact contribute to a difference in the reality of one thing as opposed to another. Surely a plural subject, as characterised in this book, is the same kind of system as a singular agent. Its physical components are two or more human bodies. The movements of the system occur in response to the conception of the system which is contained contemporaneously in its physical parts, and which is based on the perception of what is taking place in each .... The existence of the complex plural subject system does not entail the existence as a lower order component of two singular agent systems [*sic*]. In any case, it is hard to find a good reason for denying the reality of either type of system.[44]

Naturally Gilbert's observations are riddled with intentionalism. A metric of similarity between a person and a plural subject is that both act under a conception or understanding of what it is to be a certain kind of agent. If we are to read Gilbert as regarding agents as real in the sense of being material objects (being composed of physical parts), then to the extent that groups are the same kind of system constituted

---

40 Gilbert (1999a) pp. 84–5 I shall not consider here whether a plural subject is apt to be regarded as possessing psychological states.

41 Gilbert (1989) p. 434.

42 Gilbert (1989) pp. 432–4.

43 Ibid., p. 431.

44 Ibid., p. 433.

from physical parts ('two or more human bodies') they too are real *qua* material entities.

Plural subject theory does not provide an explanation of the nature of groups – it fails as an analysis of the concept of a social group – but it does not presuppose the truth of holism. Instead it seeks to offer a comprehensive theory of our core social concepts, and this results in Gilbert's Simmelian inspired holism. In this respect, and notwithstanding its problems, Gilbert's account offers support to a more general or global account of holism that recognises the material reality of groups. In the next chapter I turn to the task of explaining why we ought to be motivated to regard groups as real, material objects.

Chapter 3

Social Groups, Explanation and Ontological Holism

I   Introduction

A good reason to be a realist about groups is that reference to groups is ineliminable or indispensable from our descriptions and explanations of the social world. In this chapter I shall show that the explanatory role of groups offers *prima facie* support for the plausibility of ontological holism. I take it that we *do* refer to groups in our everyday and formal social scientific discourse and that we do so in a way that suggests that we take such reference at face value. The claim that there is a *prima facie* case is a weak one in that it is merely a starting point for investigation. After all, a culture that believes spirits intervene in the lives of the living will refer frequently to spirits. Of course this does not underwrite the existence of spirits, but the systematic and coherent use of spirit concepts and reference to spirits does demand that the fact be explained that spirits do not exist.

In the social sciences and our ordinary discourse groups figure in, *inter alia*, explanations of events, of why and how states of affairs arise, and the persistence of trends. The mob was responsible for the rioting and damage; widespread anti-Semitism in central and eastern Europe has been explained in terms of the values and character of the majority cultural groups, the economic stresses faced by certain groups and the education systems encouraged by others. The characteristics of individuals are explained in terms of their membership of particular groups. Sometimes we are asked to pardon someone's attitude because he is from a certain group, not merely a racist (or whatever). The possibility of an individual of a certain character rising to prominence is partly explained by the nature and attitudes of groups within his milieu. A striking example here is to be found in theories of the rise of Hitler in which he is seen as 'the representative individual' whose elevation satisfied the needs of certain groups.

Of course, as with cultures committed to the existence of spirits, it is insufficient to merely point to our referential use of group terms. Not least because individualism is frequently adopted methodologically by social scientists.[1] The ontological holist must

---

1   Compare Stern (1984): 'Unlike many social scientists I take it for granted that what is at work on the données of the social world is an *individual* a single man with the relative and realistically determined freedom that is reflected in his choices and decisions' (p. 23).

provide an account of why we are justified in taking at face value the appearance of groups in certain explanations. In explaining why we are entitled (at least sometimes) to treat our references to groups in a realist fashion I assume, first, that reference to groups in social scientific and everyday discourse appears to be ineliminable. Second, I judge ineliminability from our best theoretical model to be the hallmark of realism. Therefore the apparently ineliminable role of groups in our discourse provides a *prima facie* reason for taking them to be objects capable of standing in causal and explanatory relations with other things in the world. On the face of things, then, we have reason to regard groups as material particulars. An opponent of holism who grants the link between ineliminability and realism is committed to explaining how groups can be systematically analysed out of explanation, thereby denying them the ineliminable role required for holism.

The first assumption about the appearance of talk concerning the social world has an intuitive force. Groups do figure abundantly in our descriptions, explanation and judgements with respect to the social world. The idea that we are committed to the existence of the entities cited in our best theories and explanations has been formulated in various ways, and much discussed in the philosophy of science. Arguments are advanced for scientific realism on the basis of considerations of truth, objectivity and the relationship between the success of science and the literal truth of its propositions. Quine has also recommended scientific realism on the grounds that we have no basis but to be committed to the existence of those things our best theories take to exist. He has advanced the view that we add to an ontology of medium sized bodies the unobservable posits of natural science, such as electrons and protons, and also the mathematical items appearing in our best scientific theory. Roughly the Quinean argument that our ontology embrace entities such as protons rests on three premises:

1. Our best (most successful, the one(s) we actually use) scientific theory tells us that there are atoms, molecules and so on.
2. 'There is' is univocal. It means just the same across contexts. Any theoretical claim that there are *x*'s commits that theory to the existence of such entities. 'To be is to be the value of a bound variable'.[2]
3. Scientific method is justified within its own terms, within the scope of its own practice, and is not subject to criticism or justification from an 'extra-scientific tribunal'.

In a sense, *if* this is our best theory there is nothing more to be said with respect to the entities in the world. In the social world, then, ontological holism is supported if we can show that our best explanations (or, perhaps, more strictly the best set of explanations) in that domain rely on the role of groups. This approach to motivating the case for ontological holism brings with it the burden of explaining how we should understand the nature of explanation.

---

2   See Quine (1948, repr. 1980). I am not suggesting Quine would be a realist about groups.

Quite in general a plurality of explanations may be available for any single event or state of affairs *depending upon its description*. The actions constitutive of a wedding ceremony can be explained in terms of basic physics, physiology or sociology. The appropriate explanation is one that is responsive to the question asked, one that addresses the theoretical perspective or needs of the enquiry. An explanation aims to provide an understanding of why or how something has occurred or exists. It shows why or how something has a certain form, or behaves in a particular way. In explaining something we try to do as well as we can, but must face constraints in the form of the information available to us, cognitive limits on what we can discover and understand, and the limits imposed by the abilities and attitude of an explanation's intended audience.[3]

A critical feature of explanation in general is that it must be pitched at the appropriate level of enquiry and directed at the relevant frame of interest or need. That is, an explanation must address an enquiry within the terms set out by a particular investigation. Of course, if the enquiry has been framed in terms that are in some sense self-defeating, impossible to address or otherwise clearly impaired in relation to the intent evident in the formulation of an enquiry in the first place, then this must be reflected in the explanation. Nor does the need to frame the explanation in appropriate terms rule out reductive explanations, because reduction may be informative in the right way given the domain of interest and particular set of circumstances. The best account of why a particular chemical reaction occurs may in fact be given via the laws of physics. The point here is that description matters in an explanation.

If we had to explain the regulation of traffic flow by traffic lights, we would not do so by saying that cars move because the lights sharing the same colour as grass become illuminated. It is a true, but contingent (and irrelevant) fact that green is the colour of both. The drivers move (their vehicles) because there is a convention governing action on the road. There is then the further explanation of how such a convention can arise, and be sustained. The significance of description is not that it will automatically give groups a place in certain explanations. Rather, it means that the redescription of a group in terms of individuals-in-relations must furnish an understanding of at least the same order as the explanation featuring the group. In short explanations must be pitched at the right level, so that they are at least informative, and explanations aim to be at least approximately true. For groups to figure in such explanations it must be demonstrated that the explanation cannot be structured in terms of individuals-in-relations.

---

3   Our most robust explanations are those in the form of laws, or at any rate generalisations, which for the most part support counterfactual conditionals and which do in fact prove predictively successful. It has become commonplace to observe that the social sciences lack the law-like character of the natural sciences. This does not rule out the possibility that the appropriate kinds of regularities are present, nor should the contrast be taken at face value in light of challenges to the status of laws within the natural sciences made by, for example, Cartwright (1983; 1994).

It might be objected that the strategy of defending ontological holism by defeating a range of criticisms directed at its motivating intuitions covertly relies upon further assumptions: that the ontological individualist accepts reference to groups does provide holism with an initial plausibility and that ineliminability does underpin realism about a class of entity. Although I offer no argument to this effect it seems that the rejection of either of these assumptions is an unpromising strategy for the individualist. After all, the point the individualist seeks to establish is that even if there is some sense in which we may refer to groups, it is individuals and their relations which enjoy ontological and explanatory priority. The core issue between ontological individualism and holism is ultimately the modality of the ineliminable role of groups in our forms of discourse. Individualism maintains that, notwithstanding the appearances and presuppositions of ordinary and social scientific talk, there are compelling reasons to conclude that groups *cannot* play the role holism requires.

Before proceeding it is important to note that holism has been defined as the 'view that social phenomena are to be explained by appealing primarily to the properties of social wholes, since the latter are the causal factors which shape the characteristics of individual members of society'.[4] Formally, this notion of holism does not entail the existence of groups. One can imagine a world in which there are systems of laws, economic trends and cultural norms, but which is without social groups. Holism as an overarching explanatory thesis is committed more to the explanatory priority of

> any way of acting, whether fixed or not, capable of exerting over the individual an external constraint; or: which is general over the whole of a given society whilst having an existence of its own, independent of its individual manifestations.[5]

Ontological holism is not committed to the scope of this conception of holist explanation in its subordination of the role of the individual. Ontological holism admits both individuals and groups, and other social wholes, into explanations on an equal footing. Unlike explanatory holism it is not wedded to counterfactuals of the form: if person, P, or persons $\{p...p^n\}$ had not been there/had been different in some relevant aspect/had done x instead of y etc., then event, E, or state of affairs, S, would still have arisen.[6]

---

4 James (1984) p. 79.

5 Durkheim (1982) p. 59

6 Compare James (1984) Chap. VI and discussion of Miller (1978). One might also note that, interestingly, ontological holism is in a sense compatible with Watkins' conception of methodological individualism, which only denies 'that an individual is ever frustrated, manipulated or destroyed or borne along by irreducible sociological or historical *laws*' (Watkins, 1957, repr. O'Neill (1973) p. 176). This seems to allow groups to exist and to stand in causal relations, provided the ultimate explanation of the causal interchange is not cashed out at a sociological level. We are realists about mountains, but there are no laws about mountains. The shadow cast by the mountain and its features can be explained by laws of physics, geology and geophysics. Yet we are not embarrassed to refer to the mountain, nor do we refrain from developing a body

I shall proceed by saying a little more about the motivating intuitions for ontological holism by appeal to the influence and significance of groups (§II). Next three arguments are considered and rejected, each of which purports to show that groups cannot play the indispensable explanatory role that motivates ontological holism (§III). I conclude by suggesting that, although more work needs to be undertaken to complete a holist account, there is a strong motivation to take seriously our reference to groups.

II   The Influence and Significance of Groups

To begin, let us consider briefly the ease with which groups do in fact figure in explanations within the social sciences and everyday discourse. Groups are taken to have a role in explanation in virtue of their possession of certain properties and causal powers. We pick out groups in the explanation of both particular events, such as the storming of the Bastille or the Watts riots in Los Angeles, and in analysing certain kinds of events, such as riots or revolutions. Likewise, we cite the role of groups in studying processes and structures, institutions and states of affairs.[7] Nor is an interest in groups confined to macro-level phenomena, for we may explain the development, character and actions of an individual through the groups of which he is a member and with which he has had contact. Sometimes, we may explain some aspect of a group in terms of the impact of an individual. The impact and force of a charismatic leader may be best explained by the effect he has on a certain culture or people conceived as a unit, rather than upon many individuals severally.

A mob is perhaps the most ephemeral of social groups.[8] More significantly, its impact is relatively easily identified. Mobs typically charge, burn and destroy.

---

of generalisations about mountains and their features, which we do not reduce to or analyse in terms of 'scientific' laws.

7   I have employed the notions of event, process, structure and state of affairs in a loose, non-technical way. It is not my aim to taxonomise the modes or areas of social scientific investigation. Ruben (1985) talks of a variety of social entities: 'substances' like France and the Red Cross; 'social types' like dictatorship, capitalism and bureaucracy; 'events' like the assassination of Allende; 'processes' like the Decline of The Roman Empire, and 'states' like class antagonism and the sexual division of labour (pp. 8–9). James (1984) begins by remarking on the diversity of things that stand in need of explanation in the social world – the range of 'diets, laws, courtesies, kinship systems and rulers ... is bound to strike us, and the things we should like to understand about it are correspondingly diverse, ranging from a fascination with the foibles of the Russian czars to a desire to empathise with the perception of the Other among the Boogys' (p. 1).

8   Some 'mobs' though seem to have been more enduring, and to have had fairly stable identity conditions. The mobs of eighteenth century London and Paris seem to have been well established groups. Mob tends to be used in a pejorative fashion. In the context of the present discussion I would also include short-lived gatherings of individuals into disciplined marches or demonstrations, such as those which protested against the (then) proposed invasion of Iraq

Whether it is the Bastille of 1789, the barricades of 1848, the police lines during the London 'poll tax' marches of the early 1990s, or the marble and granite banking halls of financial centres targeted by anti-capitalist protesters of the late twentieth century, we most often talk of mobs when we are explaining the events comprising an occurrence of civil disorder. Reference to a mob does not explain why individuals have taken to the streets, but, more directly, what has occurred on them. It is the collective movement of the individuals forming the mob that exerts a causal impact on the world. It is their charging the barricade together that forces it to give way, and puts the guard to flight. There is an immediate perceptual unity to a mob, like that of a flock of birds, pack of wolves or shoal of fish. It is the movement of the whole that we trace, and it is in response to that movement and its pace that others respond.

The holist may have to complete the account by explaining how the unity of a mob arises, but in the first instance she can point to the fact that the movement of a mob is a property or action of the entity constituted by the individuals together. I have suggested that a mob appears to have an immediate unity of form that accounts for the effects it exerts. Sensitive to the distinction between constitution and identity, the ontological holist has *prima facie* grounds for drawing support from our reference to mobs. Why were the barricades breached? Why was Trafalgar Square inaccessible? The answer to these questions is that a mob was active, charging about, moving through the city bringing about a set of effects attributable to its size, pace and actions. The mob, like all social groups, is dependent upon its parts, and the particular actions of individuals. We are at liberty to talk of the effects of the mob for two reasons. First, certain effects may come about because of the joint action of individuals. The barricades are breached because they were stormed by individuals acting together as a unit. If the joint action is broken down into its individual components, then the essential element in its effectiveness is lost – the jointness or co-ordination of the actions. Second, the particular individual actions through which a mob exerts an effect may (in part) be determined by the nature of the group as a whole. The individualist is committed to an account of an aggregate serial ordering and intermeshing of individual acts and intentional states that explains the flows and movements of persons, and the apparent co-ordination of their actions and attitudes in being directed together towards certain ends. Yet this seems at odds with the most natural way of talking about the mob, which is to treat it as an object exercising an effect on the world.

Broader and more enduring groups, such as a tribe or people, can figure in the explanation of the development, maintenance and transmission of practices, norms, standards and values. The prevalence of certain practices may be accounted for by the nature or character of a people. A group shaped through its history and encounters with others may foster and encourage certain standards, values and modes of thought to the exclusion of those common elsewhere. Such an understanding of groups may be discouraged by a wariness of creating 'ethnic myths' aimed at instilling hatred

---

in 2002 in London and other major cities. Such a body of demonstrators displayed the unity and played the role in explanation that warrants the ascription of grouphood.

or redirecting frustration and blame towards particular groups.[9] Nonetheless, the explanation of values and practices has often been given in terms of the character of the group, and deployment for racist or otherwise wicked ends does not rule out the possibility that the properties of a group and its causal impact on members might offer the best explanation of the values, norms and practices, particularly those which mark out a particular culture or people.

It is the influence of the group upon the attitudes, motivations and actions of individuals that plays a role in the shaping of the cultural and moral framework. Well, given that a group consists in interrelating individuals (according to interrelational holism), one may press the holist to shed light on how a group exercises such an influence. Few ontological individualists would doubt the significance of the engagement together of individuals in public space in the development of shared standards and practices. Both sides of the debate can agree that values and practices are at once embedded in the form of our interrelations, help to shape those relations and are in turn influenced by changes thereto.

If a group as an object is (at least) to partially determine the nature and transmission of cultural and moral norms and practices, then it must possess causally relevant properties salient in the explanation of such norms and practices. One avenue is to predicate a Geist or essence of the group, in which individuals somehow participate. This has an air of mystery in conjuring an occult property to carry the explanatory load. Less mystery attaches, though, to the notion that a body constituted of interrelating individual parts may have the causal power to determine or shape in part the attitudes and actions of those individuals. The properties of a people are not merely the aggregation of the properties of its individual members. Groups influence practices and standards because, from the potentially extremely complex set of interrelations between individuals, collectively held norms and practices arise which impose constraints and furnish opportunities on modes of thought and action. The influence is exercised by the group because standards, goals and practices gain currency with individuals through the totality of their interrelations, and these practices exert an effect on the individual as well as being subject to the influence of the individual's actions and attitudes.

Consider the group, G, composed of persons A, B, C. They share a belief about ways of living, such that engaging collectively in a range of activities is regarded as valuable. The group might be, for example, a people, a religious cult, a football supporters club, or a tribe. Each of A, B, and C through their adherence to certain beliefs and engagement in practices sustain the network of relations, practices and attitudes that tie them together as a group. Let us say that they engage in the collective practice of doing S (such as praying at a certain time or going to a football match), and that doing S constrains each one to also ϕ (for example to go through certain cleansing procedures, wear particular clothes, express certain beliefs). It is possible to imagine that C does not wish to ϕ, yet feels constrained to do so. It is not the

---

9   Stern (1984, Chap. 22) discusses the role of the creation of 'The myth of the Jew' in understanding how a leader such Hitler was able to emerge.

others' actions which constrain him, but his-plus-the-others', for it is his engagement in S'ing which creates the pressure to ϕ, and S'ing is the practice of the group.

In this small-scale case the group is constituted by their doing certain things together and sharing certain attitudes. In larger groups the participation of any single member in a particular activity may not be essential to the group's existence. Indeed, there may not be a single activity or belief that is constitutive of the group, but a range of practices, beliefs and values which characterise the complex relations in which large numbers of individuals stand. To continue to stand in that web of relations one must conform to their on-going demands. This is not a question of being affected by one's relations to the others only, for the form of those relations is partly determined by one's own actions and the outcome of one's reflections. Thus in a society which values certain practices, that valuing is a function of attitudes and actions of the individuals composing that society, and the impact of those valued practices on the further development and formulation of the relations between the individuals. In engaging in those forms of practices and espousing certain values and attitudes individuals are acting *qua* members. They are directed by ends which are expressible in terms of the group and constrained or empowered by what is acceptable to the individuals collectively. To be a member is to contribute to the formation and/or development or continuation of these practices through one's attitudes and deeds within a web of relations. Holism thus regards the individual as not simply influenced by others, but by the group that is constituted by those others and herself standing in a pattern of mutually affecting relations. I contribute to the impact others have on me. I am partly determined or shaped by the impact of the collective I form with others, and it is shaped in part by my reflections and actions.

The idea of progress being made is also sometimes explained by reference to a group. A people may be regarded as improving or developing in moral terms. Perhaps a people has developed in way that has seen the replacement of human sacrifice by alternative non-coercive modes of worship. It is natural to talk of the way in which the people has developed or progressed, and to identify changes within its culture and values that account for the changes in its impact on the world. The notion of progress within a domain of study or field of endeavour is also seen as a collective enterprise in which it is the properties of the group that account for the development. In discussing changes in science Kuhn has stressed the importance of the interplay between the characteristics of the traditionalist and the iconoclast. Although he talks about the successful scientist, Kuhn notes that '(S)trictly speaking, it is the professional group rather than the individual scientist that must display both these characteristics simultaneously'.[10]

A group can exert a causal influence on its members and the world in general, and in virtue of that causal power we have reason to treat it as an entity in its own right. In considering the causal impact of groups the discussion conforms to a naturalist view of the social sciences, holding the study of the social domain to be continuous

---

10 Kuhn (1977) p. 227. He adds that 'in a fuller account the distinction between individual and group characteristics would be basic'.

with the natural sciences. Set against this conception of the human sciences is the view that the study of man in his social context is an interpretative process, directed at the goal of understanding human action through an elucidation of its meaning. The debate between naturalistic or positivist approaches and interpretative or hermeneutic ones marks a fault-line in the practice of the social sciences and their conceptual analysis. It is beyond the scope of the current discussion to explore the relationship between these approaches, the way in which their different insights might be fruitfully connected, and the ontological status of groups. That debate is about the proper end and methodology of the social sciences. However, granted the importance of grasping the meaning and significance of certain actions and states of affairs to an understanding of the individual, it appears that our best understanding or interpretation of certain responses, situations and practices takes groups to be real. The holist must say more than our best understanding of the individual is as part of a group(s), in which the narrative of his life unfolds. That narrative could itself be amenable to a thorough-going individualistic analysis, so the holist should strive to demonstrate that the group is essential to or presupposed in the most plausible interpretation or analysis. In the remaining part of this section I propose that our understanding of the harm or badness in certain practices like bullying takes groups to be real.

A range of familiar sanctions support ontological realism about groups, because their force as sanctions derives from the imposition of a loss presupposing the value of one's membership of a group. A good reason to take ontological holism seriously is that it allows us to understand the peculiar harm or badness in certain kinds of sanctions and practices. Consider the punishment of exile. Here, an individual is driven from and permanently excluded from his community and its territory. Furthermore, exile begins from the time the sentence is pronounced. One may have to travel for a final time through one's homeland to the border or coast, but one is already 'dead' to the community. Contact and succour are typically forbidden. One must be careful not to sentimentalise or romanticise exile. It has been prevalent in cultures in which feuds are common and in societies characterised by political instability and a martial tradition. It serves the instrumental purpose of minimising disruption through feuding whilst satisfying a demand for justice. A reasonable way of dealing with rivals was to exile them. As warriors they would be able to fend for themselves, and exile may be calculated to raise fewer problems than killing them. As Campbell has observed, exile was a sort of occupational hazard for the ruling classes in Anglo-Saxon England and its continental neighbours.[11]

Nonetheless, exile carries with it a sense of irreplaceable loss. One's only hope is in the possibility of dramatically redirecting the course one's life has taken. There is no question with exile of 'doing one's time', for that is all the time one has. The punishment that inheres in exile is not simply the loss of participating in the ties of family and friendship; it is not just in the dispossession of one's property. It is certainly not located in being subjected to physical confinement. On the contrary, to

---

11 Campbell (1986) for example pp. 94–5; p. 137.

be subject to exile is to have the rest of the world, and only the rest of the world, as a potential haven. One can be denied the goods of family and friendship without exile. Indeed, their loss may be all the greater if one is permanently incarcerated close to them, but prevented from having any contact. With exile there is the resolution of a final farewell and the hope that the union of family and friendship can be restored by a return home or by their joining one abroad. If neither occurs there is the consolation of a 'fresh start' in the form of new ties. Consolation may also be found in the isolation of a cell, but this must come from one's reflections and exploration of one's self and history, not by restoring in part or to some degree what one has lost.

There is a further loss that motivates the use of exile as a punishment, and renders it distinct from other ways of isolating individuals. The individual remains free, but cast adrift of the community to which he belongs. It is the group in which he can no longer participate through which he has come to have an insight into his own nature; it is the practices and the values of that group that have in part shaped him and directed his own goals. It is to the group and the shaping of those goals that he has been able to contribute by his participation in the practices and public life of the group. It is the loss of engagement with the group in which the special pain of exile consists.

As a political or judicial sanction exile may have declined with the growth of nation states and with the greater capacity for individuals and information to move across borders. Today's exiles may count as many poets as politicians amongst their number, and the prospect of a complete exclusion from the life of one's own community may be less than in the Dark Ages. Nonetheless, there remains a spitefulness in exile that presupposes a loss of something beyond the ties one has to a circle of family, friends and associates. We cannot experience the absence of those we do not know 'one-by-one', the strangers who make up one's group along with oneself, but we can miss what we are together.

While exile operates at a level of tribes or peoples, there is a more commonplace form of exclusion in the practice of 'sending someone to Coventry'. This seems to be a sanction or way of attacking an individual which is typically employed in groups that are small enough for members to be able to identify particular individuals, not just recognise that they are also members.[12] Unlike exile, the individual is not ejected from the group, but completely isolated within it. He remains surrounded by its daily routines and life, whilst being prohibited from the kind of interactions, exchanges

---

12 It may be tempting to think that to ignore an individual, to refuse to have any form of dialogue with him, is likely to be a feature of face-to-face rather than larger groups. However, an individual can be excluded by the salient others – no matter how large the group provided the mechanisms for recognition and maintaining respect for the exclusion are in place. According to *Brewer's Dictionary of Phrase and Fable*, a possible origin of the phrase is in the legend that the people of Coventry once had such a dislike for soldiers that any local woman seen speaking to a soldier was instantly tabooed. Hence, when a soldier was sent to Coventry he was cut off from all social intercourse. The point here is that the sanction against talking to soldiers was supposed to be effective within a fairly large group – the townsfolk of Coventry.

and discourse that are central to his participation within it. The state of being sent to Coventry is illustrated in the film, *The Angry Silence*, in which a factory worker is ignored by his colleagues because of his refusal to join a wildcat strike. They do not speak with him, they refuse to acknowledge his presence, yet they continue to work together on the shop floor and to live in the same few streets. As with exile this manner of exclusion carries with it a harm or badness that presupposes there is an entity – the group. In part there is the loss of participation in the life of the group, the value of engaging with others. Crucially, in addition there is the sense that one is disgraced before the group. One has acted in a way that has brought down this sanction. It matters because membership is in part constitutive of what is good in one's life.

The point in sending someone to Coventry is that it is a joint exercise in excluding one of our own. This endows the practice with its particular edge. It can be contrasted with the situation in which an individual may fall victim to the singular prejudice, annoyance or malice of each of his colleagues so that each decides to ignore him. Here, the several actions of each bring about a situation in which he is excluded. Unlike the joint or collective exclusion from the group, this state of affairs is not marked by the sense that the group has turned against him. To suffer exclusion as a result of a series of individual decisions may be a terrible thing, but lacking is the disgrace before one's own group brought about by its judgement of one. This enables us to distinguish between a *de facto* exclusion from a group because one's fellow members decide individually to ignore one, and exclusion by the group. That is, a situation in which one's peers acting together impose the penalty upon an individual in order to shame and to force him to endure the harm entailed by his inability to participate in 'our' life together.

Exile and exclusion bite against those who are members.[13] Bullying, on the other hand, can be experienced by the non-member at the hands of the group. The problem is not one of exclusion, but of being singled out for special attention by an individual or a group. A victim of bullying in the workplace or school may find herself surrounded each day by a gang; they may taunt her or take things from her. On a broader canvass a minority people may face restrictions and be burdened by disproportionate demands by a state dominated by another group. The regular loss of resources, such as pocket money, and the physical harm suffered could arise from a group of five bullying a person or that person being set upon by five individuals acting separately.

Whether the bullying is undertaken by a group or individual the harm seems to be the same. In particular, an individual's personal integrity is abused and her self-

---

13 Refusal to acknowledge someone's presence and similar practices can be deployed to prevent or discourage new members. Of course, in responding to such an individual in this way an interaction of sorts is established between her and the group. The distress she feels may be best explained by the attitude of the others considered as a group – they together have excluded her, and this is different from being subject to their several expressions of indifference.

respect undermined because she has been singled out from others for this kind of treatment. The explanatory role of the group in bullying is not in shedding light on why its disvalue or badness has a certain shape. Rather, it is that the relation of being bullied is a dyadic one: it is a direct relationship between the bully and the victim. Whether faced by a single individual or a group comprised of many, the victim is subjected to the enforced dominion of another. If exclusion brings disgrace, then bullying carries humiliation to its victims. The source of the humiliation is in the wrenching away of the control a person has over his own life through the threat of violence, be it physical or psychological, and the helpless acceptance of that state of affairs. When a group bullies, the dominion over the victim is not distributed severally to its members, but is held by them together as a unit.[14]

The individuals in a gang typically do not bully its victim when they are alone, but do so as the gang. Proverbial and playground wisdom tells us to stand up to a bully, which in the case of a gang may, in practice, mean confronting the leader. It does not mean that the victim take on each of the members, for it is sufficient to demonstrate to them taken together that one is prepared to resist the claims being imposed upon him. The idea of bullying being a one-to-one relation between a victim and her persecutor is underwritten by the etymology of the noun, 'bully'.[15] It has an obsolete English usage as 'friend', 'sweetheart' or 'darling', and is thought to derive from the Middle Dutch, *boele,* meaning 'lover' and perhaps ultimately from the Middle High German, *buole*, a childish or diminutive variant of 'brother'. Etymology may be neither the first nor the last word, but it is suggestive of a two-place relation between bully and victim. The capacity of a group to act as a bully, as the counterparty with whom the victim must deal and to whom he submits, suggests that the group be identified as a distinct entity – an individual object in its own right.[16]

III   Individualist Objections

Reduction-In-Principle

According to the ontological individualist social phenomena such as the impact of mobs, the transmission and development of cultural norms, values and practices, and the significance of some sanctions can be explained in terms of individuals linked in sometimes extremely complex relations. The individualist sees no need to go beyond an understanding of, say, a people as a network of individuals linked through time by a series of practices and attitudes, which they both determine and by which they are in turn partly shaped. To talk literally of groups is just to indulge in the reification of these relations; to mistakenly assume that a description of often complex relations

---

14 A leader may often act as the focal point.

15 See Oxford English Dictionary.

16 I was interested to discover that the Norwegian noun for 'bully' is 'mobbing'. The word is borrowed from the English 'mob', and bullying is defined as physical or psychological group violence. I am indebted to Dr Eilert Sundt for drawing my attention to this.

between individuals as a 'web' or 'network' warrants a commitment to some *object* existing. Beware, the individualist will urge, of seduction by the surface form of our language: reference to the mob is merely a feature of the grammatical structure of language. The individualist criticism takes the holist not to have heeded the warning sufficiently, because the predication of a property or causal power to the group can itself be analysed in terms of the individuals-in-relations. As I shall explain this reductive analysis is to be rejected because the plural predication of a property to individuals-in-relations supposes that they together possess just the kind of unity underwriting the objecthood of groups. Moreover, the individualist commitment to the availability (in principle) of a reductive explanation means that she must sometimes offer an 'ultimate' or best explanation from which the (explanatorily) salient information has been lost.

To explain the fear of the soldier by reference to the charging mob approaching his post, the individualist can say that the individuals of the mob together instantiated certain properties, which induced the soldier's fear. Some properties such as size and volume are simply additive. A lot of small people may form an aggregate that occupies a large area. Other properties such as the fearsomeness or fury of a mob may only arise when individuals are interacting in certain ways: a bunch of frightening people may not add up to a frightening group. Indeed, together they may appear comical or merely strange. For them to be frightening they must interrelate in a way that brings it about that together they instil fear in others. The ontological individualist can hold that, for example, the fearsomeness of the mob is a property predicated collectively of a certain number of individuals. Together they have a certain property. Likewise, artistic endeavour may be encouraged within the culture of a certain people; or, a people may be said to be tolerant. In these cases, ontological individualism will maintain that there is no need to introduce a group. Rather, it is a property or propensity of the individuals collectively that they encourage the arts or are tolerant. The property of being tolerant need not be one that is possessed by each person, but it is instantiated through their interactions, which can take place in a complex network of cultural, political and economic relations.

A property or power is then being attributed to individuals considered together. The property is not held by any one individual, but is instantiated through individuals standing in certain relations. This kind of collective or plural predication seems, however, to be committed to an irreducible 'them'. They (the mob, the people and so on) are furious or tolerant. Rather than explaining away the introduction of a group *qua* object, this individualist strategy has in effect identified an equivalent in the form of a plural entity. Furthermore, the notion that a property is held by persons standing in certain forms of relations suggests that the property disappears from view if the relations undergo sufficient change. That is, it is the units held together (as a whole) which possess or instantiate or give rise to the property.

It might be helpful here to draw an analogy with the constitutive parts of artefacts and organisms. Consider the parts of a table or house or cat. When these parts stand in object-constituting relations, properties and causal powers are evident and attributed (at the level of everyday objects and experience) to the table, house or cat. The house may cast a shadow on my garden and its red wall annoy me; the family sit around the table each night to eat a meal, because the table can act as a load bearing device; the cat is a living organism. Alter the relations of the parts in certain ways and certain of the properties fall from view (alter the relations between the parts enough and the thing itself will drop out of the picture too). Therefore to offer an explanation in terms of individuals-in-relations carries with it a commitment to regarding those individuals as united, for it is the unity of those parts that bears the relevant property. Taking the individuals severally, one by one as it were, ignores the way in which they are related, and it is just in virtue of being so related that they together possess the property.

The holist response relies here on a purported difficulty for ontological individualism in the plural predication of (non-additive) properties. The holist wishes to argue that the predication of a property to individuals collectively is just equivalent to predicating it to a group. This assumes, though, that there are properties or causal powers which do arise from the interrelations of individuals. It is important to note that this need not entail a commitment to the emergence of genuinely new or *sui generis* powers or properties unique to groups, but to the view that such interrelations give rise to a property that would not otherwise be present. For example, a teacher and a group may each possess the property of inducing fear in others. While holism can escape the charge that it relies upon mysterious group properties, it is yet to address adequately the individualist insistence that we can ultimately explain the impact of the group in terms of the properties of each individual.

If civic duty and pride are encouraged within a particular culture, then individualism holds that the fact a person, P, pursues a career as, say, a policeman is not to be explained (even in part) by the impact of the group on his attitudes and array of choices. Rather the fact that P becomes a policeman is explained solely in terms of the properties of individuals, some close to P and others distant in physical and social space and time. Yet, against this individualist analysis one may insist that the reason (or at least a reason) P became a policeman is because such an activity or practice is encouraged within his culture. That looks like a good explanation. He pounds the beat because it is the kind of thing his group promotes. Further questions arise as to the mechanisms through which civic duty is encouraged, why it is valued, and the practices and attitudes through which it is expressed. However, the explanation of why he is a policeman appears to be lost if the question is answered with the enumeration of the properties of the individuals constitutive of the group.[17]

Or is this denial of the individualist analysis simply question begging? The holist maintains that the denial reflects the inability of individualism to deliver on its promise

---

17 I assume that it is not the case that every other member of the group is an 'encourager of civic duty'. If this were the case, then that fact might explain why P became a policeman. Although, it could be the case that such uniformity could produce a reaction against civic duty. The point at hand is that the individualist is aiming to provide an explanation conformable to ontological individualism of the fact that a culture encourages civic duty and the practices and endeavours it entails.

that reduction to individuals and their relations is in principle always an explanatory option. This is not, though, an option that is always in-principle available. It can be demonstrated that at least sometimes the identification of the *relevant* individuals must refer to the group, thereby leaving the group within the explanation rather than reductively analysing it away; or, the individualist must assume that *all* individuals are the ones relevant to a particular explanation. Let me explain.

The holist can escape the charge of begging the question by pointing to the requirement that an explanation be informative. An individualist explanation of the fact that a group encourages, say, civic duty or artistic endeavour takes the form of a list of individuals and their properties, which bring it about that individuals will be encouraged or disposed to encourage, for example, joining the police or engaging in art. The problem of plural predication is assumed to be addressed by the aggregation of the individual properties bringing about the relevant state of affairs. However, for the explanation to be informative it must go beyond a claim that the encouraging of civic duty or art can be explained in principle by reference to properties of individuals (considered singularly). It must be demonstrated that civic duty (or artistic endeavour or toleration and so on) is encouraged *because* of the aggregation of individual properties. Importantly, the claim must not be the trivial one that any social phenomenon depends on the possession by individuals of certain (explanatory) properties. The individualist needs to provide an explanation in which the salient properties of the individuals are not dependent upon the impact of groups. In the absence of actual explanations of this kind we have little reason to suppose that they are in principle always possible. An appeal to an 'in-principle' individualist analysis just presupposes the point at hand.

Such a presupposition does not rule out the possibility that given enough time and energy reductive explanations could be found. However, the kind of reductive analysis which would show groups to be eliminable faces a further problem as an explanatory schema. Individualism analyses groups away by showing them to be either reducible constructs of individuals-in-relations or fictions. According to individualism groups can drop without loss from our view, for all that needs to be said can be expressed in the language of individuals, their properties and relations.

In response to both reductionist and fictionalist approaches the holist may object that in order to pick out the relevant individuals it seems that we must look first to the groups of which they are members. This presents no special problem for ontological holism, since it individuates a group through its causal impact and properties: a group is picked out at a certain level of enquiry. As material objects the boundaries and composition of a group may be vague – in at least the epistemic sense of underdetermination. But, so are many other material objects at a sufficiently fine-grained or 'micro' level of investigation. The individualist by contrast owes an account of the principled basis for restricting the range of individuals and relations that might feature ('in principle') in an explanation.

The individualist programme is then the reduction of a group to its members analysed in terms of their relations or an account of the group-fiction in terms of individuals and their relations. The question for the individualist is which individuals

and relations are the right ones. Imagine a situation in which a town is set ablaze by
a rampaging mob. The individualist cannot explain the burning town in terms of the
rioting mob, but must offer an account referring only to individuals and their relations.
The obvious set of individuals is the mob's membership, but each member may
have his own set of relationships, distinct from those he has with his 'co-mobees'. A
reductive explanation cannot exclude these other relations on the basis that they are
not constitutive of the mob, because they may in part explain why that individual
participated in the rioting. Indeed, all the facts about each individual will contribute
to the fullest possible specification of why he participated in bringing about the
burning of the town. Yet not all the facts are salient in an explanation of why the town
is burning. The individualist needs a criterion in order to exclude those facts that are
in practice irrelevant. The obvious way of identifying the relevant individuals and
relations is to appeal to membership of the mob, or to those relations that brought
about the burning of the town. The first move is not available to the individualist
because it does appear to suggest that the group is on an explanatory par with the
individuals. The second is precisely what needs to be established. Individualism
is driven to the position of holding that in principle a particular social fact may
be explained by the totality of individual facts. Returning to an earlier example,
according to the individualist the fact that P became a policeman is explained only
in a shorthand way by reference to the nature of his group. In principle, though, it is
explained by the totality of facts about individuals. This hardly seems an informative
explanation, but rather reflects a view upon which both sides are agreed: groups, and
social facts in general, depend upon the existence of individuals.

The Causal Powers of Groups

There are then problems confronting the ontological individualist in offering a
reductive analysis in terms of individuals-in-relations. There is, though, a view of
explanation as the process of making something intelligible or clear by showing
how certain kinds of events or states of affairs or facts are connected by laws or law-
like relations. We can understand a law as a (near) universal generalisation capable
of supporting true counterfactuals and predictions. The social sciences are often
criticised because of their failure to identify law-like regularities, and in particular
their inability thereby to sustain a consistent predictive capacity. If there are no laws
at the social level, then one may doubt that there is any real explanation at that
level. A corollary of this view is that causation occurs at a lower level. When we
talk of mobs charging or a people's culture influencing individuals, then we are just
referring to an aggregation of effects which are to be explained by a causal story
at a non-social level. The individualist need not worry about providing a reductive
analysis, because we lack grounds in the first place for thinking that an explanation
is to be found at the social level.

One might object that if there are no laws at the social level, then there are no
laws about individuals in the social domain. The individualist can adjust the way the
claim is formulated to say that in the social world there are no law-like generalisations

about groups. On the other hand we seem to possess a rich and sophisticated model of our everyday psychology, which we deploy in explanations and predictions of the actions and attitudes of individuals. Even if it is granted that there exists a set of generalisations about individuals in contrast to the absence of any such set about groups, the ontological holist can dispute the inference from the lack of 'group-level' social scientific laws to the denial that groups therefore have any *prima facie* role in explanation.

A basic reason for resisting the inference is the implausibility in the suggestion that only law-like explanations are good ones. The identification of laws and the application of the 'covering law' approach have certainly been of tremendous importance in natural science. However, the significance of lawful explanation resides not so much in its explanatory as in its predictive value. A more modest form of explanation stops short of furnishing the enquirer with a predictive resource, but can satisfy the criterion of bringing clarity and intelligibility to the analysis of events or states of affairs. Such forms of explanation have been described by Elster as 'mechanisms', which are 'frequently occurring and easily recognizable causal patterns that are triggered under generally unknown conditions or with indeterminate consequences'.[18] For example, children of smokers may tend to smoke themselves or tend to be particularly hostile to smoking. We cannot predict which path (if either) a child will take, but the mechanism affords an explanation of the child's actions and attitude towards smoking. In the same vein it may be the case that the oppression of a group may cause it to break up or to consolidate into a more cohesive unit in which there is a more keenly felt and committed sense of belonging amongst its members.

If we wish to know why something has happened we want more than a (re)description of the occurrence of the event in question or the coming about of some state of affairs. Between description and laws there are mechanisms. An explanation of why the mob charged the barricades or why a culture is characterised by a high proportion of artists or warriors will be framed in causal language. A study of riots and mobs may permit us to recognise common patterns. If the mob is hemmed in and threatened it may quickly break up in panic or it may coalesce into a more co-ordinated body with a quickening momentum towards violence. Likewise social scientific generalisations about peoples and their cultures may be expressible in terms of mechanisms. A culture that values democracy and free speech may encourage both atomistic patterns of living, with, for example, growing numbers of small nuclear families and single person households, and provide the environment for a growth in religious bodies.[19] It is thus open to the holist to maintain that causal processes are triggered by, or dependent on, the properties of the group, without having to formulate law-like generalisations in which the group figures.

It can be pressed against ontological holism that more must be shown than that groups can feature as relata in causal mechanisms. If the appearance of groups in explanations is to afford *prima facie* reason to take seriously the claims of ontological

---

18 Elster (1999) p. 1.

19 Compare Elster's (1999) discussion of de Tocqueville's analysis of the United States.

holism, then the holist must indicate how a group *qua* entity can have causal powers. That is, when we talk about the barricades being destroyed by the mob or certain values or racist attitudes being encouraged by the nature of a group are we warranted in thinking of the group itself as exercising an influence through its possession of the relevant powers or properties?

Ontological individualism looks to the truism that it is individuals who charge during a riot and who hold and transmit values and beliefs. Causal congress in the social domain is between individuals, or between individuals and things in the world. Whether an explanation is to be understood in terms of a law or mechanism, it is individual persons who are acting on each other and the world. Talk of individuals acting together or in relations does not remove the fact that any event or state of affairs can be analysed in terms of the separate actions of each individual. Therefore, according to the ontological individualist, ontological holism cannot appeal to the role of groups in explanations when the explanation has a causal form, because the relata of causal relations in the social domain are individual persons (and artefacts and other organisms).

The priority of the individual over the group in causal explanations in the social domain as an argument against ontological holism (or, the narrower claim that social explanations lend credibility to the holist claim) can be resisted on several counts. First, the individualist must explain what model of the (social and natural) world affords this privileged position to the individual, without also undermining much of what the individualist holds to be true of persons. Crucially, the individualist is unable to deliver on this point. Second the individualist presupposes a view of nature we need not accept, and, third, individualist objections to the causal role of groups may arise because they attribute more to groups than holists.

To hold that groups do not figure in causal accounts because all of the causal moving and shaking in the social domain involves only individuals raises the question of how we should regard those individuals with respect to more basic or fundamental levels in nature. Assuming that there is a fundamental level of physical reality, described and explained by our best physical theory, then it seems reasonable to hold that it is at this level that the real causal commerce takes place. This view of nature finds a powerful way of being expressed when two theses are held together – *Materialism* stating that everything is ultimately composed of the same basic (physical) stuff and *Completeness* stating that every physical effect has a physical cause.

A commitment to this view of nature is consistent with recognition of the reality of higher level entities and properties. One may, for example, understand the higher levels as states of affairs at the fundamental physical level differently described. However, it is unclear on what basis the ontological individualist is distinguishing persons from groups in order to accord the former a priority in explanation which saves them from suffering the same reductive fate as groups. The priority is only one of being a level 'closer' to that of fundamental particle physics. There is no more (or less) 'real' causation at the level of individuals than there is at the group level. Since we do not engage cognitively and practically with the world at the level of fundamental physics, our ordinary conception of what is real is not determined by a theory about the locus of causation. The ontological individualist cannot preserve a robust realism about persons while excluding the possibility of realism about groups by appeal to a 'causal fundamentalism'.

An alternative individualist strategy is to show that individuals are causally relevant in a way that groups are not. Here there is a shift from talk of causal efficacy, a power or property evident at the level of fundamental physics, to a weaker notion of causal relevance. This holds that a state of affairs (or event) at one level can bring it about that some state of affairs (or event) is more likely to arise at a lower level, ultimately the level of basic physics. The occurrence of such a lower level state will then realise a new higher level state.[20]

Provided one is happy that the 'programming' of the lower level by the higher does not conflict with the monopoly of causation at the lowest level, this provides a model whereby we can save the appearance of much of our ordinary explanatory talk. For example, it allows that beliefs can be causally relevant and feature in explanation of intentional action, without committing one to the view that a mental state like a belief can stand in direct causal relations. The ontological individualist can say that persons *qua* minded entities are causally relevant in just this way. Our beliefs, desires, hopes and so on bring about (or make more likely) a neural profile that will realise further propositional states and sometimes issue in action by the individual.

This is not yet an argument against ontological holism, for it leaves it open that groups could be causally relevant in a similar fashion. The causal story of why the individuals forming the mob charged might have to be retold at the level of fundamental physics, but the fact that they together *qua* group possessed certain properties could have brought it about that each individual was disposed to act in certain ways at that time. Because the notion of the causal relevance of higher level states of affairs offers no causal account of how the influence is exerted, there seems no principled reason to say that groups can not 'program' for genuine causes at a lower level.[21] The question at hand reverts to the familiar one of whether our explanatory demands are best satisfied by reference to groups. For the scope of our explanatory interests is far wider than the causal account locatable at the level of fundamental physics.

The foregoing individualist objections presupposed the truth of causal fundamentalism, the thesis that causation occurs only at the level of fundamental physics. One may just not accept this doctrine. An alternative pluralist model of nature can recognise causation at many different levels as kinds of entities interact in diverse ways. Models of the world distinctly at odds with the hierarchy, determination and predictability (in principle) of reduction include an ontologically promiscuous realism of countless (cross classifying) ways of ordering nature and a patchwork of

---

20 Compare Jackson and Pettit (1990); Pettit (1996).

21 I must note that ontological holism ought to be cautious in drawing support from the program model, as it is arguably unsustainable or at best thoroughly mysterious. The arguments in chapter do not hang on a particular view of this version of non-reductive materialism.

laws governing local domains.[22] Our best explanation of, say, the distribution and density of life forms within an ecosystem may be due to identifying the properties and relations between different species and the impact of environmental features such as topography on them. A reduction to the level of basic physics loses the information that was explanatorily salient and may introduce probabilisation of event occurrence that is ill-suited to our specific object of enquiry.

Here I cannot hope to try to settle the question of whether we should conceive of the world in reductive or pluralist causal terms. Ontological holism as a thesis about the social domain is only undermined by an endorsement of the explanatory priority (indeed hegemony) of a causal fundamentalism so revisionary of how we think about the social world that ontological individualism also disappears as a substantive or interesting thesis. In our practical thinking the pluralist model seems to offer the more compelling picture, for it permits us to identify as causally efficacious just those entities with which we must deal at the social level. The pluralist model is consistent with the materialist thesis, for individuals and groups are ultimately composed of the same stuff and there need be no other kind of stuff in the universe. It is also consistent with the doctrine of completeness. However, as sketched, the pluralist model does not entail either doctrine and neither does the conception of groups and the social world defended here.

I suggested earlier that a rejection of the causal efficacy of groups might arise because individualists attribute more to groups than one need. I have in mind the concern that if groups can exert a causal influence over individuals, then this undermines or overrides the individual's free will and status as an autonomous agent. The explanatory holism described at the end of Section II does seem to entail a view of the individual as ultimately subordinate to the forces and powers of groups and social wholes. A view of groups as objects with causal powers in a world of like (material) objects, including individuals possessed of an agentive capacity, does not represent the same threat to individual freedom. Groups and individuals both constrain and furnish opportunities to each other. To be a part of a group does not undermine our freewill or agentive powers. It is one of the constraints we encounter and our membership of a group forms an element of what one is. Membership will explain in part the values, goals and attitudes of the individual.[23]

The Group Mind

The destruction wrought by the mob was because of its fury at being attacked by the police; a state's systematic oppression of a minority people is possible because the majority people holds that group to be inferior, unworthy and deserving of its

---

22 See Dupré (1993) and Cartwright (1994) respectively.

23 See James (1984) Chap. III for a discussion of the motivating role of individual freewill in individualism. If it is correct to diagnose this as a source of individualism, then in showing that ontological holism does not threaten individual freewill one source of objections may be stopped.

treatment. It is not uncommon to hear explanations in which the explanatory burden is taken by the idea that a group possesses a capacity for thought and goal directed action. A problem now seems to arise for ontological holism, since the individualist may insist that holism cannot draw any *prima facie* support from explanations in which the will, attitude, values or goals of a group feature. For in such cases the surface form of the explanation attributes a cognitive and affective capacity to the group. The appeal to explanation would lack the force the holist assumes, because the holist is yet to explain how a group can be minded.

The holist can say that talk of a group mind is just a way of speaking, which owes more to the misapprehension that groups are somehow person-like than to a proper understanding of their nature. The temptation to ascribe mental states to the group itself may arise if one has an antecedent view of groups as person-like. However, ontological holism has no commitment to any such prior conception of groups. For, in pointing to the role of groups in explanation, there is no need for the holist to accept that she is thereby taking at face value the mindedness of groups. The holist can acknowledge that groups do not have minds. Talk of the will of the people and the anger of the mob are ways of describing the nature or state of the group in question. The holist can understand a group's individual members as having certain beliefs, values, goals and needs in virtue of their group-constituting relations, and to recognise the group as helping to foster, sustain and develop those beliefs and needs. Groups are in this sense both dumb and highly significant in an understanding of collectively held beliefs.

It is open to the holist to employ metaphor and analogy in an attempt to make vivid certain aspects of a group's nature. The use of metaphor to talk about groups is quite distinct from talk of groups being metaphorical. Similarly a mountain is not cruel nor does it set out to kill climbers, but plays a causal role in their deaths owing to its nature, the conditions prevailing on it, and perhaps the attitude of climbers towards it. To capture aspects of both the nature of the mountain and our attitude towards it we may refer to it as if it were endowed with the properties of a cruel person. That a mountain lacks the cognitive capacity that normally underwrites the attribution of cruelty and the capacity to kill does not deter us from being realists about mountains.

The power of the metaphor of the group mind may also owe more to the emotional aspect or experience of individuals within a group, rather than to the beliefs, attitudes or goals they share. The idea that a group possesses a single and unified consciousness or mind seems most plausible when we think of the way in which the mood of a crowd can turn from being jovial to angry; a mob's joy switch to fear; or a nation become engulfed by grief. Of course it is individuals who are the loci of the emotional experiences, but it sometimes seems as if they are responding as one to some event or state of affairs. Scheler speaks of the 'phenomena of fellow feeling'[24] and identifies ways in which individuals come to be connected to one another through an immediacy in emotional engagement. For example, two parents

---

24 Scheler (1954) p. 12.

have an 'immediate community of feeling'[25] as they witness a car drive towards their child; they feel together the same fear and horror. Scheler puts this in terms of their *having a feeling-in-common*. It seems plausible to see in a similar way the fear that the members of the mob feel when the police dogs appear. Moreover, as Goldie has observed the 'sharedness of the emotion may serve to enhance and deepen (one's) emotional response'.[26]

I shall not here expand on an account of shared emotions, save for this brief suggestion. Within a group fellow-feeling may also come about through identifying with others so that one's sense of self is to some degree dissolved; or, an emotion may spread like an infection through a group – what Scheler calls 'mere emotional infection'. If one accepts that we can stand with others in a community of feeling, or be prey to contagion, then these phenomena point to a two-way relation between group and members. Just as our sharing a certain emotion may help constitute us into a group, so the group may exert its influence by encouraging our fellow-feeling.

Finally we should note that the possibility of a group mind should not be ruled out; at any rate, there has been no argument presented here to that effect. It has been suggested that a single self or consciousness could be 'stretched' over more than one human body.[27] I shall not explore this intriguing notion here, because if a group can literally possess a mind it may be best conceived in terms set out by Leibniz when he invites us to:

> (S)uppose that there were a machine so constructed as to produce thought, feeling and perception, we could imagine it increased in size while retaining the same proportions, so that one could enter as one might a mill. On going inside we should only see the parts impinging upon one another; we should not see anything which would explain a perception.[28]

We can imagine ourselves as parts of a group in the way that Leibniz's machine had parts. Through the interrelations of the parts a conscious, minded, entity may be constituted. As such it would be capable of interacting with the world and of being goal directed. It could interact with its parts, acting as a constraint on them and they would constrain it. However, even if its parts are themselves conscious, they would not perceive or experience the world as the group (the 'machine') does, because its mindedness inheres in the totality of their relations. The evidence we have for this class of minded entity would be its effects, not an ability as parts to share its cognitive processes or perceptual experiences.

Although there is conceptual space for a group to have a mind in this literal sense, there would seem to be no explanatory compulsion to attribute (literal) possession of a mind to a social group. Care must be taken, though, not to simply beg the question

---

25 Ibid.

26 Goldie (1999) p. 407.

27 C.f. Dennett (1991) p. 426.

28 Leibniz (1934) p. 5. *Monadology*, S. 17. Leibniz goes on to say that the explanation of perception must therefore be sought in a simple substance.

of what a mind is, and of what conditions something must satisfy in order to be aptly regarded as minded. The effects of groups can be explained in terms of their interrelational structure and their properties and powers as objects. Nonetheless, mindedness may come in degrees so that, short of attributing a mind (in some full-blown sense – whatever that may be) to a group, it may be appropriate to sometimes recognise that a group as such has some degree of cognitive-like capacity.

Ontological holism's motivating intuition – that groups are ineliminable from our social discourse – is not then undermined by considerations of reduction-in-principle, the attribution of causal power to groups or the notion of a group mind. Of course, more is needed to offer a full argument for ontological holism. In particular one must move from the identification of factors supporting the plausibility of ontological holism to a consideration of why we are committed in light of our taxonomic standards and practices to regard groups as material particulars. The holist can approach the remaining task without appearing to beg the question of why one would even think that groups as such are *real* objects. It is to a consideration of the holist thesis in light of our taxonomic practices that I turn in the next chapter.

Chapter 4

Objects of the Social World

I   Introduction

The state belongs to the class of objects which exist by nature.[1]

The Old Regime threw indiscriminately into the Third Estate all commoners from the wealthiest bourgeois to the poorest beggar, or some 96 per cent of the population, according to Sieyès. The Third Estate was a purely legal entity in which *the only real elements were social ones* - and of these the most important, the one which led and mainly benefited from the revolution, was the bourgeoisie.[2]

But in order for a social fact to exist, several individuals at the very least must have interacted together and the resulting combination must have given rise to some new production. As this synthesis occurs outside each one of us (since a plurality of consciousnesses are involved) it has necessarily the effect of crystallising, of instituting outside of ourselves, certain modes of action, and certain ways of judging which are independent of the individual considered separately. As has been remarked there is one word which, provided one extends a little its normal meaning, expresses moderately well this very special kind of existence; it is that of *institution*.[3]

Groups are ineliminable from our best explanations in the social domain. It makes no more sense to refer only to the parts of a group than it does to speak only of the parts of animals or artefacts. From their explanatory role we can analyse groups as real and independent. However, this does not entail the conclusion that groups are material objects. Social scientists may often just remain silent on the question of the ontological status of groups. Or, as with Durkheim, insist that 'we do not say that social facts are material things, but that they are things just as are material things,

---

1   Aristotle (1981) p. 59. He finishes by saying that man is by nature a political animal (*Politikon zoon*). That is, man is an animal whose nature is to live in a *polis*; men have 'a natural impulse towards this kind of association' (p. 61). In light of the narrower contemporary understanding of 'political' it is perhaps worth stressing the social or associative aspect to man's nature.

2   Lefebvre (1949) p. 41. My emphasis.

3   Durkheim (1982/1895) p. 45 For Durkheim the reality of social facts arose from the 'external' constraint they impose on the individual and from the causal efficacy of social forces or trends arising as emergent properties from the synthesis or interaction of individual (facts).

although in a different way'.[4] Clarifying his rejection of a materialist approach to sociology Durkheim explained that:

> In social life everything consists of representations, ideas and sentiments, and there is nowhere better to observe the powerful effectiveness of representations. Only collective representations are more powerful than individual ones: they have a nature of their own, and relate to a distinctive science. All sociology is a psychology, but a psychology *sui generis*.[5]

In arguing that the explanatory role of groups furnishes us with reason to be realists about groups I have been aiming to support the thesis that they are also material objects. If groups were non-material entities, then it seems thoroughly mysterious how groups as such could stand in the appropriate kind of relations with other kinds of things to exert the influence indicated by their role in explanation. Furthermore, if appeal is made to the emergence of *sui generis* social facts, properties or representations, then the question remains of whether the 'basal' interrelations and exchanges, the creative synthesis of individuals, give rise to a distinct object. Building on the arguments from explanatory role, the aim of this chapter is to further elucidate the view that groups are material particulars, thereby making clear the sense in which groups are most plausibly held to be real.

I shall explain that interrelational holism provides a model of groups, which is consistent with our concept of a material object and coherent within its own terms. I consider a number of objections and supposed problems, motivated by the belief that groups fail to satisfy the conditions necessary for, or behaviour characteristic of, material objects. Of course, the way in which we classify ordinary composite material objects is in principle open to revision. The argument for recognising groups as objects is ultimately grounded in a consideration of taxonomic consistency, rather than an appeal to the correct mapping of a world entirely independent of theoretical perspective or interests. I suggest that groups may be regarded as belonging to a kind marking a basic division in the social world, and I conclude this chapter by noting that interrelational holism classes together both human and non-human groups.

The defence of holism reveals interrelational individualism to be an undermotivated position. Interrelational individualism is unable to provide a principled basis for distinguishing the existential claim to material objecthood of, say, cats, tables and groups. It is undermined by the centrality to social theory and explanation of the relations in which individuals stand, and our everyday and theoretic views on the nature of objecthood. Cats, tables and groups are compositional and other-affecting objects. That is, all enjoy causal congress with other particulars. If ontological individualism is not acceptable, then by default we should endorse holism permitting existential recognition and explanatory role to groups and individuals. I shall not attempt to make the point 'by default' through an exposition of the failures of

---

4   Ibid., p. 35. Durkheim goes on to explain that a thing is 'any object of knowledge which is not naturally penetrable by the understanding' (ibid., p. 36).

5   Durkheim (1982/1908) p. 247.

interrelational individualism. A charge of undermotivation is only as telling as the alternative(s), and the burden of the argument remains with the holist to explain why groups are to be regarded as material particulars. In doing so the undermotivation of the individualist position becomes apparent, for the holist's starting point is precisely the recognition that individuals typically stand in a diverse array of relations with others at and through time. Putting matters rather crudely, individualism tells us this is all we need to say. The argument for holism consists in the elucidation of what remains to be said.

II   The Materiality of Groups and Interrelational Holism

What is it to say that a social group is a material object? Simply put, it is the view that a group is an individual entity with a unity of form and causal capacity through which it can be individuated and located in terms of its spatio-temporal co-ordinates. Objects respect the distinction between 'self' and 'other'. This distinction is expressible in terms of the difference between the way in which an object's parts interrelate and influence each other and the way in which external entities influence an object. The parts of, say, a cat interact to form that particular entity.[6] The unity of form characteristic of a cat is the organisation through time of an aggregate of parts, or a succession of aggregates, in such a way that they form some thing individualisable in virtue of its properties and causal powers. Everyday entities like cats and cars are tangible and visible. They readily satisfy the constraints of being locatable through the assignment of spatio-temporal co-ordinates (they have a definite location, at least at the macroscopic level), and the possession of (normally) sufficiently determinate identity conditions (or, more accurately, the capacity to have such conditions ascribed to them).

It is the organisational relationship between the constitutive parts that yields a whole, which can then stand in a relation to each of those parts. I speak of 'organisational relationship' with some care, since I do not wish to suggest that someone or something has necessarily organised the parts. Rather, in virtue of being related in a certain fashion (however that came about) the parts make or constitute an organism or body through being sufficiently orderly and systematically related. Some bodies, such as houses and dogs, are more readily perceivable as such in space. Others, such as groups, do not share that kind of physical 'solidity', but the contiguity of parts in our perceptual sphere has no *a priori* claim to figure in an

---

6   When a cat dies it may be argued that its parts are no longer interacting in the right way to constitute a cat, since the object now lacks the vital property of being alive. Its parts do though retain sufficient structural integration for some time to constitute a single object. It remains 'enough' of a cat to be accurately described as a dead cat. A dismembered cat does not constitute a single object; it has been broken down into a series of parts, no longer relating in a way constitutive of a cat. If we know enough of the cat's history, and sufficient biology, we can recognise that the parts did once form a whole.

account of objecthood. Indeed, it would serve to rule out groups as objects prior to consideration of their causal impact or their locatability in space and time.

With the exception of 'simples', material objects are composite. A house consists of bricks, tiles and assorted materials arranged in a certain way. A cat is an organisation of flesh, bones, blood and so on. Following Aristotle we can say that all objects consist of two logical parts - matter and form. Objecthood inheres in the relationship between these two logical parts. They can not be separated as if they were both physical parts of the object: we cannot divide a statue into its form and the bronze out of which it is made. An object consists in the way in which some 'stuff' is organised, the relationships that subsist between the parts that form it. For an object to survive is for its parts to continue to be organised in the relevant object-making fashion, even when those parts may be subject to replacement through time.[7] I do not necessarily endorse an explanation of something's form – the fact that this object is how it is – in teleological terms. Our concern for the moment is to elucidate in what objecthood consists, and one can say that in virtue of being related in a certain fashion the parts make or constitute an object or body through being sufficiently orderly and systematically related.[8]

A group is just a more or less complex organisation of individuals through time. The existence of a group is contingent on the patterns of interrelations being such that the individuals are united into a whole or body, which comes to exert an impact on the world – typical amongst which is an impact on the members themselves. Ultimately, then, the notion that groups are material objects rests on the view that individuals are related or organised in ways that give rise to a body with causal powers and properties.

---

7   If we take everything to consist ultimately in the fundamental physical particles (or perhaps 'superstrings') then it may be the case that the parts of any object are changing all the time. However, when we think of something's parts we usually have in mind its *proper* parts: those things that make it what it is at a particular level of enquiry (Here the notion of a 'proper part' is not being used in the technical sense found in mereology – compare Goodman in *The Calculus of Individuals*). Thus it is my limbs, organs, tissues and so on that constitute my body, and these in turn are constituted by molecules and atoms and so on. Again following Aristotle we could say that a hand or an eye has both form and matter. We should perhaps also beware of assuming that each level is well ordered, since order at one level could supervene on disorder at a lower level. That is there may be no, or no epistemologically accessible (and these possibilities amount to distinct claims), organisation amongst fundamental particles.

8   The classification of an object as being a certain kind of thing may depend upon its history. We may argue whether a 'swampman' formed through the chance assembly of atoms is a person, or indeed human or an animal, but would surely agree that it is an object. (See Davidson, 1987 for the idea of a swampman, a döppelganger down to the elemental level created in an instant by a chance of nature). A creature, which comes suddenly into existence with the material and structure of a particular human being, is postulated in order to consider the role of background and context in determining mental content and meaning). Furthermore, its continuity of form would be explained in terms of the relations amongst its parts.

Groups are compositional material particulars constituted by individuals standing in relations. The basic conception of a social group as the being and doing together of individuals, while highly schematic, is extremely capacious in that it allows a potentially indefinitely wide array of relations between individuals and their practices to constitute a social group. This reflects the diversity of groups we actually encounter. Nuclear families, work teams, gangs, mobs, tribes and peoples are all groups, and they are formed through relations which vary in form, content and complexity. All the details of the group-constituting relations need to be filled in on a case-by-case basis, typically within a (roughly) drawn framework differentiating groups by function, character and internal structure.[9]

This understanding of groups follows naturally from consideration of the role they play in explanation, and it is one that suggests why they have such a role. The way in which I can operate at my position on the assembly line is influenced and constrained by the way in which the line workers as a whole, *the-others-plus-myself*, have been operating. As a part of a rioting mob or crowd at a football match I may find my behaviour determined in part not (just) by particular individuals, but by the movement or mood of the whole. The opportunities and barriers I encounter, the way in which I understand and respond to the world, are partly shaped by both the groups to which I belong and with which I must deal as an 'outsider'. Likewise, within a culture I am likely to encounter norms, conventions and expectations that set limits on what I feel able to do or strive towards. These constraining factors issue from the nature of the people or culture of which I am a member, and whose nature consists in the on-going interrelations between individuals. Note, though, that just as the group I form with others can constrain any one of us, so each individual, through the way in which she interacts with others or with the group, has an impact on the group *qua* whole. I may resist the excitement of the mob or challenge the conventions of a culture. Equally I may respond to the exuberance of the charging crowd or endorse the values of the group. The key point is that the relationship between individual and group is a two-way one: each influences the other. The relationship between individual and group is a symbiotic one in which individual capacity for self-reflection feeds through to the shaping of the group, and in which the group in turn influences the individual.

III   The Scope of Groups

Interrelational holism analyses groups as a composite material particulars, with a group being constituted by suitably organised and interacting parts, which form a whole individuated over time through its causal powers and explanatory role. The non-intentionalism of the account suggests a symmetry between the concept of a group and that of a composite material particular.[10] Any such object can be understood

---

9   Likewise there are arguably necessary features of the group-constituting relations, which would need to be identified in a fuller discussion of the nature of groups.

10   See Chapter 2 for discussion on intentionalism.

as a group of parts or bits standing in a certain pattern of relations through time, which yield a whole at some level of theoretical and explanatory interest. A thesis about the nature of groups appears, then, to be the application of a general concept about the nature of composite material objects to a local domain - the social world.

It may appear that the treatment of all composite material objects as groups becomes possible with the rejection of the intentionalist thesis. However, all that rejection entails is that the parts of a group do not need to share certain intentional states. A global understanding of all composite objects as being groups (formed from appropriate parts) is reliant upon the principle that a group can be composed of non-mental entities. That is, if we are to analyse a table or a cat in group terms, then we must allow that a group can be constituted entirely of parts, each of which exhibits no mental properties. The metric of similarity between groups, organisms and artefacts is that they are composed of suitably interrelating parts, and all satisfy our conception of material particularity. There remains, though, at least an intuitive distinction between the ways in which different kinds of parts can interact. Entities with a cognitive capacity and some degree of intentionality need not share intentional contents, but *qua* mental entities they may be able to interrelate in ways that other kinds of parts cannot.[11]

Social groups are a class of objects which are composed of entities with a mentality. This has an air of stipulation, but it accords with the intuition that one of the ways in which objects differ is through the nature of their parts.[12] The rejection of the intentionalist thesis is significant because it reveals that group-constituting relations between mental entities are not characterised by a minimum requirement of shared intentional states. It does not show that the forms or pattern of relations in which the rowers or traders of Chapter 2 stand could also be instantiated between non-mental entities. Stipulation in accordance with an intuition is not an argument. However, to distinguish between objects in terms of the way in which their parts can interrelate does seem to be a principled basis (and almost certainly just one amongst others) for developing a more fine grained understanding of a very broad class of entities. Importantly, whether one makes this distinction or not does not undercut the basic claim that groups are composite material particulars. I take social groups to be constituted by entities with a mentality since this property determines a range of relations and interactions that other kinds of parts cannot stand in.

---

11 There remain the questions, unaddressed here, of what the domain of mental entities is and of how one should specify the hallmarks or necessary and sufficient properties of being such an entity. Being conscious is to be a mental entity, although this may only raise further questions about the nature of consciousness and the status of potential conscious things. Cats and human beings are examples of mental entities; rocks, trees and atoms are non-mental entities. Others, like insects perhaps, are harder to place.

12 That is an object's proper parts in the sense sketched in footnote 7 above. After all, there are strong grounds for thinking that all material objects are ultimately composed of or constituted from non-mental entities in the form of fundamental physical particles or wave packets.

Appeal to intuition reveals a further way in which groups differ from many other objects, and it may be thought that this establishes a disanalogy harmful to the overall project of showing groups to be material objects. When we talk about something's composite parts it is often the case that those parts do not figure at the same level of explanation as the object in question. Water is composed of atoms of different kinds standing in a particular pattern of relations; a pig's liver is constituted by an arrangement of molecules and so on. The constitutive parts of an object tend not to feature in our talk about the object itself. With groups, though, the individuals who form them do frequently appear in our explanations and descriptions. As discussed in the previous chapter we cannot appeal to the individuals in a reductive explanation of the group, but individual members of a group can feature alongside of it.

One may feel that if the constitutive relationship between a whole and its parts is to be conceived in terms of the whole (the object considered as such) and its parts being picked out at different explanatory and ontological levels, then groups do not behave in an object-like fashion. Levels, though, may be cut more or less coarsely according to one's theoretical interest and perspective. For example, in ecology and pharmacology eco-systems and human bodies are treated as wholes, conceived as dynamic systems linking many different kinds of object. Thus the body as a whole, its organs and molecular components all feature in the evaluation and explanation of the effects of chemical compounds on the body, and their effectiveness in remedying specific problems. An analysis of an eco-system looks at the impact of a pattern of activity on both the system as a whole and on specific parts or sub-components of it. Indeed, the focus of the study may typically be the way in which a change to a specific part or parts of the system impact on the whole, and how changes to the whole influences the nature of change to the specific part.

In support of their material particularity an analogy has been made between groups and individual organisms. However, one may have a nagging sense that the disanalogy between a group and an individual is rather stronger. In claiming that groups are like individuals one seems to be ignoring the obvious way in which a group composed of the individuals differs from any individual. For individual organisms possess a solidity groups do not. Furthermore, one can note the susceptibility of individuals to destruction through part loss, while groups seem able to survive such loss.

In the following sections I address a number of objections to treating groups as objects. Now, though, I wish to focus on the question of whether the disanalogy between individuals and groups is truly malign in undercutting the plausibility of regarding groups as objects. First we should note that the point of an analogy is to highlight a dimension of similarity, particularly one salient to the issue at hand. The analogy between individual and group shows that both are compositional wholes; and both are picked out in explanation in virtue of their causal powers and roles within a particular field of interest and enquiry. An investigation of quantum field theory is little concerned with either. A disanalogy with bite would arise if one were arguing that groups are individual organisms, or entities that are *just* like individuals. This is not the case, though.

It is also important to note that the purported difference between individuals and groups arising from part loss plays on an underspecification of the problem. Any object is at risk when it undergoes part change or loss, because with that change comes the danger of organisational disruption or destruction. If too many parts are lost or replaced in the wrong way, then the object-constituting manner in which the parts are organised may be destroyed, and with it that object. In this respect we can see that the removal of a person's body parts, the pillaging of a building for its bricks and material and a group's loss of members all carry the danger that the object will be destroyed. Different types of objects may be more or less resilient to such change and disruption, but this matter of degree does not provide a telling disanalogy between individuals and groups.

IV   Problems of Observation

The materiality of a group follows from the transitivity of materiality from parts to whole. It should be possible to locate the object in space and time, and the individuation of an object, x, has been characterised as its

> isolation in experience; to determine or fix upon x in particular by drawing its spatio-temporal boundaries and distinguishing it in its environment from other things of like and unlike kinds (at this, that and the other times during its life history); to articulate or segment reality as to discover x there.[13]

Now, an obvious objection to treating groups as objects is that we do not seem to readily draw a group's spatio-temporal boundaries in our perceptual experience. Even a small group such as a gang standing on a street corner may be difficult to locate precisely, its boundary seeming remarkably fluid as its members mill about. The problem is even more obvious if we consider larger groups such as a people. How do we fix upon the Welsh by drawing the spatio-temporal boundaries of that particular people? In the passage cited above Wiggins has in mind the individuation of everyday continuants, which he takes as the starting point for a serious consideration of the notion of substance. The claim that groups are like cats or cars in as far as all are material objects is not a commitment to the stronger claim that groups are just like everyday objects in every respect; a claim that would seem ill-judged in any case because it risks ignoring the ways in which these everyday objects differ in significant ways. We readily individuate objects such as cats and cars through our perceptual or other sensory experience of them. Our experience of groups can also be directly perceptual as when we witness a mob charging the barricades or an audience rising to cheer a performance. The boundedness of composite material particulars seems to be a feature of perceptual perspective, a consideration supported by the view that all non-simple material objects are composed of scattered parts, which are suitably interrelated and causally connected to form a whole. There is a

---

13 Wiggins (1980) p. 5.

sense in which groups are obviously scattered, but this does not in itself obviously count against regarding groups as objects. The dispersal of the Jews following the Babylonian and Roman conquests of Palestine does not undermine the intuitive sense in which there remains single people, whose members are scattered.

The experience we have of groups can occur through the transmission and maintenance of cultural or moral norms. Entry into a group may prove in practice to be impossible for an individual because she lacks certain properties, the significance of which or the acquisition of which arises through integration within the group. A system of values or set of practices can define the limits of entry to a community. The existence of a group such as the Amish[14] is indicated by the evidence of cultural difference in its forms of dress, transportation and agricultural techniques. The group can be recognised through the norms that prevail and the barriers to entry confronting those who are not already members of that community. We can pick out a group through the physical impact a group has upon its environment, for example through its agrarian practices or patterns of economic relations. We can individuate groups through the effects we note in the world and the collectively held attitudes, beliefs and goals of individuals. Even if one were to maintain that veridical observation is a sufficient condition of an object's materiality, knowledge of an object is not limited to its being observed.

Furthermore, we must beware of exaggerating the extent to which there is a problem in isolating a group by drawing its boundaries. In the first place we must ask for whom is it a problem? For our kind of creature it is certainly practically impossible to individuate a group such as the French people, for example, by identifying the spatio-temporal boundary of that group by simply seeing the group. However, the perceptual capacity of a kind of creature does not determine the objects there are in the world, merely the unaided epistemological access to a world for that kind of creature. We should perhaps look a little closer at any purported requirement that individuation requires the recognition or drawing of (complete) boundaries. Quinton suggests that social groups cannot be observed, contrasting them with bounded, concrete, and individualisable material objects.[15] For Quinton the problem with groups is that 'social objects are not, on the whole, effectively observed', being too large and scattered.[16]

Here one may wonder what in general it is to observe something effectively. It is certainly not to perceive every part of an object.[17] It is not just the case that I do not need to see the inside of an object to draw its boundaries, but I do not need to see all of its outside either. Perhaps I am only able to see part of a building from a distance,

---

14 A Mennonite sect in the United States and Canada. The Amish community has become well-known because it has maintained many of the practices and forms of cultural organisation brought to the New World in the seventeenth and eighteenth centuries. In doing so it has become readily distinguishable from mainstream American culture.

15 Quinton (1975).

16 Ibid., pp. 8–9.

17 Compare Ruben (1985) p. 12.

but still I can individuate it correctly as a tower block. Of course, I could have been mistaken, but veridical observation is prey to a host of defeating factors and this is not to say that something is normally incapable of effective observation. On the contrary, effective observation of an object is to identify it (at least the kind of thing that it is) on the basis of what is apparent to one.

A rejection of ontological holism because groups are not observable like medium-sized material particulars relies on what may be an ultimately self-defeating premise. An argument against the materiality of groups could begin with the premise that groups cannot be observed directly; that is, in an everyday or pre-theoretical sense, we do not see groups as bounded objects. In itself this does not rule out ontological holism, and it must be joined by the further premise that observability is a necessary condition of material particularity. Those entities, which we postulate in theory construction but cannot observe, are therefore to be treated instrumentally as elements in the theories we employ. At most we should remain neutral on whether to be realist or anti-realist about groups, treating successful theories in which they figure as 'empirically adequate'.[18]

It is ambiguous whether the test of observability is an epistemological or metaphysical constraint. If it is the latter, then the anti-realist argument is thoroughly unconvincing. We do not observe groups because they are the kind of thing that cannot be observed. Either this means there are no groups to observe, or observability is taken to be analytically part of materiality. In the case of the former reading the desired individualist conclusion is presupposed; with the latter, observing something cannot count as an empirical test of its materiality. Of course it is possible to stipulate that an object is material only if it is observable, but if, *inter alia*, locatability and causal impact are also hallmarks of materiality the stipulation looks arbitrary and lacking theoretical and explanatory motivation.

I take it, though, that anti-realism about groups does not begin from metaphysical presuppositions, but moves from the fact that groups are not observable to the ontological conclusion that they are not real. However, we can think of a possible world in which groups are observable in an ordinary sense. A sociologist in such a world would see groups as solid objects moving around in that world, and the individuals who compose the groups might not be readily individualisable as such.[19] In explaining the nature of the observable entities, and in the elaboration of successful theories, the sociologist might conclude that we have good reason to postulate individuals as their constituents. However, the sociologist would not have reason to be a realist about individuals, which perform the role of unobservable postulates in a theory.[20] An argument from observation relativises realism about a class of objects to an aspect of the perceptual capacity of

---

18 Compare van Frassen (1980).

19 Or, perhaps this is how things would seem to a Martian sociologist who has arrived on Earth.

20 The imaginary sociologist is in the same position as a physicist, and the philosophical debate about the ontological status of unobservables would take the same shape.

an observer, or a set of observers. Whatever merits this position may have, it is not one that ontological individualism can adopt. For it places individuals and groups on a par with each other, and thus fails to secure the priority demanded by ontological individualism.

It might be urged that because groups are not actually observable, there are no groups in the *actual* world. Even if one grants the non-observability of groups, if this were the argument against the materiality of groups, and as such taken to support ontological individualism, it would force the individualist to pay an unwelcome price. The possibility remains that there are worlds in which there are observable groups and in which individuals are merely postulated as their constituents. That is one of the ways in which things could have been besides the way they actually are.[21] An observation dependent reality of individuals and groups is indexed to a world or context of observation. The modality of this claim seems weaker than the individualist would want in her insistence on the priority of individuals to groups, if individualism takes that priority to be a metaphysically necessary feature of individuals and their relations. Reliance on observation would never allow the individualist to make good the claim that individuals-in-relations are necessarily prior to groups. Even in the actual world, the localised priority accorded by the observation of individuals and not of groups would be challenged by the Martian sociologist.

In any case, we should not grant too much ground to the alleged fact that we do not see groups. We do frequently perceive groups as more or less bounded objects. Let us return to the gang on the street corner. We can imagine the gang acting in a co-ordinated way to rob a passer-by and then taking flight as the police arrive. In observing the group we do perceive a unity of movement and action, enabling us to isolate that group from others. Likewise, as an army progresses through a valley, a lookout on the hill above does not observe the actions of individual soldiers, but the cohesive movement of a body; a body that happens to be structured through a chain of command holding together tightly integrated units.

V   Sharing Space: The Synchronic Identity of Groups

In this (long) section I consider a challenge to the thesis that groups are material objects. It is simply stated. Grant that the motivations sketched earlier furnish a *prima facie* case for realism. Yet, if groups are material objects, then they fail to behave in a significant way like the other kinds of material object we encounter in our everyday experience. For two or more groups can be in the same place at the same time, while it is ordinarily held that two objects of the same kind cannot be in the same place at the same time or coincident.[22] Material objects are regarded as excluding other material objects of the same kind from the space one occupies

---

21 The phrase is David Lewis's (Lewis, 1973, p. 84). Nothing here relies on his 'modal realism'.

22 Throughout I mean coincidence to be complete coincidence. Issues arising from partial coincidence or overlapping objects are left to one side.

at a particular time. [23] Groups, though, seem capable of being in the same place at the same time because distinct groups can have co-extensive memberships. The philosophy department football team and the university philosophy society possess distinct histories and exert their own effects. Each is individuated in its own right through time. Yet, we can imagine a period in their histories when the memberships are identical. If an object is located where its parts are, then during that period the groups are in the same place at the same time. Realism must explain why this capacity on the part of groups is consistent with the ascription of materiality to groups. Or, realism needs to show how the challenge is disarmed. For example, by explaining that groups are not coincident in any way that is inconsistent with an understanding of material objects in general – paradigms of which I take to be cats, trees and cars.[24] The realist thesis faces the challenge of reconciling the tension between the spatial exclusiveness of material objects and the spatial promiscuity of social groups.[25]

This challenge relates to a broader discussion concerning the coincidence of material objects. The problem of coincident objects finds expression in the well-known puzzle of whether the statue, S, is identical with the piece of metal, M, from which it is made. The 'standard account' of diachronic identity allows that the two objects, S and M, can indeed coincide while remaining distinct. The key to this view is that the objects differ in their dispositional and modal properties.[26] S can survive changes which M cannot – for example, the loss of arm – while M can survive change destructive of the statue – say, being beaten into a cube. The two objects are therefore discernible even though they consist of the very same matter so that they are for a period part-identical. A motivation to deviate from the standard arises from the puzzling claim that two objects whose fundamental, base

---

23 Compare Wiggins (1968; 1980) who defends the thesis that the occupancy by one thing of a certain spatio-temporal region excludes all others of the same kind. Leaving aside the possibility of metaphysical vagueness every material entity can in principle be located uniquely at any particular time. 'No two things of the same kind (that is, no two things which satisfy the same sortal or substance concept) can occupy exactly the same volume at exactly the same time' (Wiggins, 1968, p. 93). Of course, if one does not endorse that thesis, but understands materiality to permit such co-location, then there is no problem in the first place with respect to groups. Then of course the duty to discharge is that of explaining why we should reject the thesis.

24 For the purposes of this discussion I am restricting the discussion to objects at the level of the everyday 'macroscopic' world: the level of Austin's medium sized dry goods. The implications, if any, of quantum level phenomena (for example superposition) are not addressed.

25 One might object that no problem of material coincidence is generated because we should understand a group to be brought into existence when its individual members are collectively acting in a certain fashion. The football team exists when its members are playing football together. However, even if a group exists only when its members are collectively producing a certain kind of action, it could be the case that both kinds of action can be carried out at the same time: we discuss philosophy while playing football and so there are two groups in the same place at the same time. More importantly (and plausibly) ontological realism takes a group to exist when it is not engaged in its characteristic activity, but while its individual members continue to interrelate in the right ways. See discussion of the seminar group below.

26 The term 'standard account' is due to Burke (1997). Notable advocates of the standard account are Wiggins (1980) and Lowe (1995). Burke opposes the standard view.

structures are identical (i.e. they have precisely the same physical profile)[27] could differ in their dispositional and modal properties. The broader debate on coincidents moves forward on the supposition that the problem is to explain the coincidence of material objects of different sorts. The narrower issue concerning the coincidence of groups does not (at first glance) share that supposition. For, the problem appears to be one of two (or more) objects of the same kind (that is social group) being in the same place at the same time. One reason to care about the possibility of real social objects is this: if groups are real material objects which behave as our language suggests, then our understanding of the ontology of material objects in general must permit cases of type–type coincidence. A commitment to realism would be revisionary of the global scope of the thesis that two material objects of the same kind cannot be in the same place at the same time. The failure to support the possibility of type–type coincidence will point to the need to abandon or modify realism (in the latter case we would have to accept that groups cannot coincide notwithstanding the way we talk).

In outline I shall suggest first that two groups can be in the same place at the same time because the individuals constituting them can be organised in distinct ways. Sameness of parts does not entail sameness of fundamental structure. This is a strategy of dissolving the problem. In distinguishing the principles of organisation of parts (the ways in which the individuals interrelate) we individuate distinct groups. That is, individuals organised according to distinct sets of relations are constitutive of distinct groups possessed of their own properties and powers. The puzzle is (it is held) shown to be merely apparent, and the question of the coincidence of groups is addressed in the spirit of the standard account.[28]

However, this solution gives rise to a difficulty for the realist. The solution entails the view that whenever there is coincidence there are different kinds of group. However, our ordinary and formal employment of the term give us little reason to think two groups of the very same kind cannot be coincident. Groups may share the same kind of organisation, but be distinguished by extrinsic factors. In the face of this counter-intuitive consequence of the defusing solution the realist could distinguish cases of different kind coincidence from cases of merger. The latter would be instances of groups of the same kind coming together through co-extensive memberships and thereby merging into a single, 'new' group. Indeed, a defuser of the challenge might revise their strategy and suggest that all cases of co-extensive membership are to be regarded as mergers. Now, on both the narrower and wider appeal

---

27 As Levey (1997) p. 3 puts it. This leads to what Levey labels the supervenience problem: 'modal or dispositional differences among objects could only supervene on core differences that coinciding objects would necessarily lack [the difference thesis] ... Given the difference thesis, coinciding objects could not differ modally or dispositionally; and so it seems impossible there should be coinciding objects after all [supervenience problem]' (ibid.).

28 Levey (1997) appeals to the notion of a principle of composition to explain how different kinds of objects can share all of the same parts. It is important to note that Levey defends the possibility of coincident objects while rejecting the standard account. He opposes that account because of its commitment to an abundance of cases of coincidence. Levey doubts that there is a sufficient promiscuity of compositional principles for coincidence to be commonplace.

to merger, there is the counter-intuitive prospect of fleeting co-memberships giving rise to a new group. Furthermore, how are we to treat the 'reappearance' of the old groups should the new one split back into the 'originals'? Each of the arguments to disarm the challenge force the realist to amend her understanding of the nature of groups and the ways in which they figure in our folk and formal social scientific discourse.

Finally I propose that the realist need not attempt to respond fully in the spirit of the standard account. What that account helps render vivid is that groups possess their intrinsic properties in virtue of the interrelations between their parts – individual persons. Retaining this truth about groups, and in conformity with our use of group terms, 'social group' is to be regarded as (high-level) kind term in the manner of, say, animal or mineral. While the principle that things of the same kind exclude one another from the same volume at the same time has a wide scope, it does not express a necessary truth about the everyday world, and in particular of social groups. By appeal to certain thought experiments the realist can attempt to motivate an understanding of social groups concordant with the ways in which we talk about them (and other objects) such that groups are material objects capable of synchronous co-location.

The Problem of Co-location

Integral to our concept of a concrete material object is that such an object can be picked out as numerically distinct from amongst others of the same and different kinds. We can imagine that for a period of time the philosophy seminar group and the philosophy football team are composed of exactly the same individuals. On the face of it there does not seem to be a problem in treating them as distinct entities. Each has its own history and impact on the world, and we can develop theories and predictions in respect of each of them. The pattern of relations that form individuals into the seminar group are different from those that constitute them as the football team. The group-constituting interrelations can be sustained through changes in the membership. The groups are therefore discernible, possessed of distinct histories, effects and structures. Yet, for as long as they have co-extensive memberships they are also in the same place at the same time.

An objection to the materiality of groups takes the following form. Our intuitive or ordinary understanding of groups is committed to two principles:

(SP)   n-number of social groups can share spatial and temporal location.
(CP)   n-number of social groups can have co-extensive memberships at a time.

Taking another example, this year the village choir may be constituted by the full membership of the von Trapp family. At midnight mass the von Trapp pews are empty in the church, while the choir has taken its place and is busy singing. It seems reasonable to say that the family and the choir are both in church. Likewise, the university chess club and rugby club may have identical memberships. Both clubs are present when the complete memberships of all the university clubs gather for a rally in protest at declining funding. In both these cases it seems natural to say that different groups with the same members are in the same place at the same time.

Material objects are subject to two principles:

(MP) Two material objects of the same kind cannot be in the same place at the same time.[29]

(TM) If G is a whole and if $(i^1...i^n)$ are all of its parts and $(i^1...i^n)$ are material, then G is material.[30]

From (MP), (SP) and (CP) we can infer that groups are not material objects. Given the truth of TM we can also conclude that individuals are not constitutive parts of a

---

29 The occupancy by one thing of a certain spatio-temporal region excludes all others of the same kind. Leaving aside the possibility of metaphysical vagueness every material entity can in principle be located uniquely at any particular time. Wiggins (1968, p. 93; 1980) has defended the following principle: 'No two things of the same kind (that is, no two things which satisfy the same sortal or substance concept) can occupy exactly the same volume at exactly the same time'.

30 First, it is important to be clear that part is employed in (TM) in the sense of being one of the objects which constitutes (with others) a composite object. In the case of a social group its parts are individual persons who form the group by standing in certain relations. Simply believing oneself to be a member is not sufficient for membership. To be a member of a group is analysable in terms of being a part – a group-constituting part along with those others who stand in the salient set of relations (or stood in the group constituting relations. It seems plausible that there could be one person groups when there is just one member left). This notion of being a part of a composite object is not to be confused with the formal mereological concept of being a proper part or with being a member of a set (compare note 2 above). To be a compositional part is to be some object which actually makes up the object in question. To be such a part of some object as opposed to just some of the stuff of which it is formed it may also be that a part must be individualisable as some kind of object in its own right. While there is a mereological sum of objects and a set of objects which correspond (to put matters loosely) to the composite object in question (for example cat, football team), the very same mereological whole or set can exist even when the object *qua* object does not. Furthermore, the materiality of the members of a set is not transitive to the set, which is an abstract entity.

The question remains whether (TM), innocent of conflation with mereological wholes or sets, is true. A composite material particular occupies a certain spatio-temporal region. In reflecting upon the nature of such objects it seems that it can do so either because *qua* whole it is in some way spatially independent of its parts or because it is located where its parts are located. Whatever emergent properties an object might have, it is surely the case that there is (literally) no more to its constitution (its bits) than its parts (and the relations in which they stand). In the absence of a compelling rebuttal of that latter claim, considerations of simplicity and economy suggest that the best explanation of an object's location is the location of its parts (note, that I have restricted the present discussion to the level of everyday objects, so I eschew discussion of the quantum world). That explanation entails the transitivity of materiality from part to whole.

group.[31] Membership does not entail parthood, and realism about groups must regard them as non-material entities. In order to defend the materiality of groups one must motivate the rejection of at least one of (MP), (SP) or (CP), or to explain why the challenge is only apparent, thereby dissolving the problem it poses.

Dissolving the Challenge?

Groups with co-extensive memberships are in the same place at the same time, and they remain distinct entities in virtue of the different ways in which the parts are organised and related. For the period of co-location there is just one set, S, of individuals $\{i^1 ... i^n\}$ who constitute both groups, say the philosophy seminar society, P, and the philosophy department football team, F. We can thus say truly for that period that:

(P) $\{i^1 ... i^n\} = c$ P
(F) $\{i^1 ... i^n\} = c$ F

where $= c$ is read as 'constitutes'.

We can also state truly that:

(NI) $P \neq F$

where $\neq$ is read as 'not numerically identical to'. The conjunction of (P and F) and (NI) is also true. The trio of statements is consistent because of the distinct ways in which the members of S interrelate in order to constitute P and F respectively. We can elaborate P and F as follows:

(P*) $\{i^1 ... i^n\}$ interrelated ϕ – wise $= c$ P
(F*) $\{i^1 ... i^n\}$ interrelated ψ – wise $= c$ F

The difference in the constitutive relations gives rise to distinct groups.[32] The groups possess different capacities and survival conditions. Were F to be disbanded (perhaps because of poor results, a collapse in the confidence the rest of the team has in its defence ...), then P could nonetheless continue to flourish.

---

31 Compare Ruben (1985). The membership relation between the individual and her group would therefore need to be analysed in terms independent of any appeal to members being parts of the group.

32 A counterfactual test for distinctness is to ask whether there would be a group, say P, in a world in which the only salient difference from the actual world is that members of S are not organised ψ-wise so as to constitute F. I set aside difficulties arising from cases in which one mode of interrelations is dependent upon another. For discussion on how one coincident object can survive changes fatal to another see Levey (1997) pp. 6–7.

Parts of a group – its individual members – are organised and stand in the relations constitutive of that group through time. That there is a co-incidence of memberships does not entail that those individuals are organised in a single fashion. On a Wednesday afternoon individuals who constitute the philosophy seminar group may be engaging in the regular philosophy seminar. However, they do not just constitute the group at that time; they are not the seminar group just when they are actively engaged or primarily conceiving themselves as such. The group exists over time through the relations in which the individuals stand, amongst which might feature the commitment to exchange papers, obligations to keep the group informed of one's intention to miss a session, perhaps to behave in a fashion supportive of the group and so on. For the period when the seminar group and the philosophy football team have co-extensive memberships the seminar group exists when just those individuals head off for a match, the team being, so to speak, present during the seminar.[33]

Now, in order to hold the four principles consistent it is necessary to render explicit an assumption central in the foregoing argument. That is the view that P and F are objects of different kinds. Well, surely, one might urge, they are both groups. However, given that they have been distinguished by the ways in which their (coincident) constituent parts interrelate, it seems that it is just such an organisational distinction which marks a difference between kinds of groups. And for the purposes of (MP) that serves to distinguish them as falling under different kind concepts. The challenge facing realism is dissolved. We were wrong to think that groups of the same kind could be co-located. Our mistake was to fail to recognise the fine-grainedness of the distinctions between kinds of group. Properly speaking, then, the term group ought to be recognised as a high order kind term or taxonomic division. On this way of considering matters we modify (SP) so that it reads 'n-number of social groups of different kinds can share spatial and temporal location' and the problem of coincident social groups is answered in the spirit of the standard account.

Problematic for this approach is the possibility of cases in which groups of the very same kind are coincident. A difference in organising relations is not the only way in which groups (objects in general) can be distinguished. Extrinsic properties are also important such as the relations in which a group stands and the causal role and effects the group has. Taking first the case of non-coincident groups we can individuate groups of the same kind by their causal effects and relations in which they stand. Two gangs may have the same internal structure, but differ in terms of, say, their impact and character. One gang may inhabit a city of timid folk and few rival gangs and enjoy great success, while the other gang may struggle in a city with an aggressive population and many rivals. Back in the academic world with a juggling of term times and/or really good transport links we can conceive of

---

33 This analysis can be extended to deal with situations in which the membership of one group is a subset of the membership of another. The former is not necessarily part of the latter, but simply sharing part of its space. For one group to be part of another they must be related in organisational terms, not merely through shared memberships.

the King's London philosophy department being coincident with, say, the Munich department for a period in their respective histories.[34]

The realist could insist that they are different kinds of groups, notwithstanding the fundamental similarity in the ways in which they organised. A difficulty with this first response is that we have no reason to think that two departments, football teams, gangs and so on are really different types of group. Indeed, that we gather different groups together under such concepts in our best explanations and descriptions of the social world suggests otherwise. The realist could instead suggest that we *do* attend to the extrinsic properties of co-located groups as well as their organising relations in distinguishing the groups. Now, though, there are two groups with the same organising principle so as to count as the very same kind which can *only* be distinguished by their effects and relations. Why, the critic of realism may ask, should we think there are two distinct entities here rather than one group which exerts distinct kinds of effects and stands in a variety of relations? We would in effect have a case of the same thing being picked out under different names or descriptions.

An alternative strategy for the realist is to hold that cases of synchronous co-location be restricted to cases of different kinds of groups sharing memberships. In the case of same kind co-membership we should properly say that the groups have merged to form a single entity. This appears somewhat *ad hoc*, and perhaps insufficiently attentive to the claim that the groups can be distinguished through their extrinsic properties and relations. [35] The idea of merger could, though, be extended to dissolve the problem of co-location in general by holding that whenever there is co-extensive membership, there is also merger, thus giving up (SP) and (CP).

In the recent example there is not the King's and Munich department*s*, but a single, new group resultant from their merger. The temporal duration of the coincidence of membership may vary a great deal. Should we say that a fleeting

---

34 Why these departments? A version of the paper on which this section draws was given at a conference in Munich in 2004. There was also a football match between the King's and Munich departments in which the latter group triumphed.

35 A worry might also arise in cases in which distinct groups are in one sense the same and in another different. The philosophy department and the prison warders of jail X football teams are both teams, and under this kind term, the same kind of thing and yet they are different kinds of groups in that they are representatives of different institutions. It is, of course, entirely to be expected that a higher order kind term allows us to pick out different objects in respects in which they are at once the same and different. Paul and Peter are both animals; Paul is a small vole, Peter a human being. With groups the question arises as to whether a period of co-extensive membership brings about a merger with respect to one kind of group, but not the other. Imagine that the philosophers are recruited to the prison football team, so that after a time the philosophy department and jail teams come to have co-extensive memberships. To say that the groups are in the same place at the same time (and are the same and different in the ways described) would need to be analysed in terms of the two football teams being in the same place at the same time through their co-extensive memberships, and each continuing to represent its respective institution through the relations in which the team(s) stand to the different institutions.

overlap of members gives rise to a new group? Let us imagine that departments share members for a week. What are we to say when this new entity divides back into a King's department and a Munich department? Well we could maintain either that the very same group can survive a gap in its temporal path or history. Or, that in spite of appearances the new Munich department really is a new entity, standing in some kind of successor relationship with its predecessor. Alternatively one can avoid postulating gappy identities and preserve the strong sense that the group now, which looks to all intents and purposes like the group seven days ago, is indeed the very same one. Rather like roads that come together for a short stretch we could say that both groups are always present in the period of merger.³⁶ The plausibility of regarding groups as merging into a single entity and then reappearing at some later point will be determined in part by whether one understands persisting objects to endure as continuants or to perdure as occurrents or four-dimensional wholes. This is a dispute about which I shall here merely note that I shall say nothing. Save, that for my part I am inclined to regard persisting objects as continuants, being wholly present through the time they exist.³⁷ I say more in the next section on how we might understand the diachronic identity of groups which have merged or divided.

The attempts to defuse the problem of the problem of the synchronic co-location of groups reveals a wide ranging challenge to the very notion that groups are material. In our talk of groups, and presupposed in the approaches adopted, we have taken 'group' as a higher order kind term which embraces a wide range of exemplars, 'group' seeming to function as do terms like 'animal' and 'artefact'. Yet, in our experience of those latter kinds we find that particular animals or artefacts compete for space. The scope of (MP) appears to be very wide; and the solutions offered in the standard account do not typically allow individuals picked out as belonging to such high order kinds (for example two dogs or two statues) to be coincident. Now, *this* is not an argument against the possibility of groups being co-located, but it is an appeal for further reasons to think that it is possible. Rather than seek to dissolve the problem the realist can attempt to motivate the view that (MP) is not universally applicable, and that in particular it does not rule out the co-location of groups. It is to this attempt that the final part of this section turns.

Possibilities

(MP) may express a truth about the nature of certain kinds of material objects, and in particular medium sized artefactual and natural objects and organisms. Chairs,

---

36 Compare Lewis (1976, repr. 1983, p. 64). As David Lewis has observed, 'by crossing the Chester A. Arthur Parkway and Route 137 at the brief stretch where they have merged, he can cross both by crossing only one road. Yet these two roads are certainly not identical'.

37 Lewis (1986) p. 202 explains that an object perdures iff it persists by having different temporal parts or stages at different times, though no one part of it is wholly present at more than one time. An object endures iff it persists by being wholly present at more than one time. For criticism of Lewis see Lowe (1987; 1988).

rocks and cats do exclude other objects of the same kind from the space they occupy. Some things, which are locatable and causally efficacious, do not exclude others in the way demanded by (MP). A room can be filled by oxygen, laughing gas and mustard gas. All are in the same place at the same time and each has a distinct causal role. We know why the man dies laughing. We can imagine in the case of gases that as a heavy gas sinks it passes through a level occupied by a lighter gas, so that for at least a moment the two are in the same place. Odours can also be in the same place at the same time: the aroma of freshly brewed coffee and of burnt toast can both be present at the same time in the kitchen. However, perhaps we should not place too much stress on such purported counter-examples. Gases and odours may be better thought of as aggregates of particles of the same kind, and as not being suitable candidates for undercutting (MP) as a claim about objects. Nonetheless, the fact that many objects do respect (MP) appears to be a contingent one. While Locke notes that 'whatever exists at any time excludes all of the same kind, and is there alone', Leibniz suggests that Locke relies on the presupposition that 'penetration is not conformable to nature ... but we see two shadows or rays of light which interpenetrate, and we might invent for ourselves an imaginary world in which bodies would act in the same way. But we do not cease to distinguish one ray from another by the very rate of their passage even when they cross each other.'[38]

We can indeed imagine two billiard balls which are able to pass through each other.[39] We are able to individuate them in terms of their properties and trace their movements. For a period the balls occupy a single space, and then emerge as they continue along their paths. For the spell during which they have interpenetrated we are unable to distinguish them by location, but we have good reason to talk of two balls being in that spot because we have traced two distinct histories. Or in more prosaic terms we have followed the balls up to the point of merger and we can continue to trace them after they separate. Moreover, we can tell if the interpenetration has changed a ball in some way because, knowing its pre-penetration properties, we can track the ball through change resultant upon or coincident with the interpenetration.[40]

One might reject this approach because one understands the meaning of material when applied to an object to entail *impenetrability*. This is certainly how Locke regards materiality. Perhaps the concept of an extended material body just is of something which (i) fills a precise three dimensional region of space and (ii) is in

---

38 See Locke (1975/1690), Eassay II.xxvii.1. Leibniz's remarks are in his New Essays Concerning Human Understanding. Both are cited in in Sanford (1970) p. 75.

39 See Sanford (1970).

40 It might be noted that the interpenetration of the balls can only be understood in terms of the respective (micro) structures somehow overlapping completely. The balls do not acquire just the same parts through merger. In the case of groups interpenetration arises as a result of co-extensive memberships. The point of the ball thought experiment is to suggest that the materiality of objects does not rule out the possibility of synchronous co-location.

some manner impenetrable to other classes of space occupiers.[41] If this is how we understand the meaning of materiality, then we might see the objection as amounting to this. In the actual world an object is material just if it is impenetrable, but this does not rule out objects which are material in one world interpenetrating in other possible worlds (the *de dicto* sense of materiality). This leaves conceptual space for the materiality of groups, but denies that groups are actually material. The understanding of materiality has a *de re* sense. For an object to be material is for it to possess essentially the property of impenetrability. Again groups are ruled out of the class of material objects.

The realist can challenge the apparent presupposition that our concept of materiality is fixed. Even if materiality turns out be an essential property of certain things, we should not think that we have nothing further to learn about the concept and its extension. Through a consideration of social objects we find reason to deny that impenetrability is a necessary feature of materiality. *If* groups are causally efficacious entities composed of material parts, then to exclude them from the class of material objects would require an explanation of how a non-material entity can exert a causal influence and of why there is a failure in (TM).

A defence of realism and the materiality of groups cannot quite leave matters at this point. In granting the realist the transitivity of materiality a problem is also generated. The parts of a group are impenetrable. The realist has argued that groups are material but can be penetrable. Why is the impenetrability of the individual persons not inherited by the group they compose? The answer is that groups interpenetrate by having the same members. The Leibnizian thought experiment shows there is nothing conceptually incoherent in the notion of interpenetration and that co-location itself does not rule out the possibility of individuating the objects in question through time. In the particular case of groups we do not have interpenetration involving two distinct sets of parts, and so there is never any question of distinct individuals *qua* parts having to meld together.

Finally, in support of the view that groups can be material objects it is worth noting that certain organisms do actually have a capacity for fusion and separation, which appears very similar to the behaviour of the imaginary balls. David Hull has noted that 'when presented by a prey too large for a single individual to digest, two amoebae will fuse cytoplasmically in order to engulf and digest it. However, the nuclei remain distinct and the two organisms later separate, genetically unchanged.'[42]

In their capacity for synchronic co-location groups do not behave in the fashion of many other material objects. Nonetheless, this is not a difference that in itself threatens the materiality of groups. Or we should not be inclined to treat it as a threat if we are to admit the relevance of the thought experiments illustrating how objects can interpenetrate one another and be spatially co-located. The admissibility of these examples hangs on whether one regards conceivability as sufficient for possibility. Hume noted that nothing we imagine is absolutely impossible – 'to form a clear idea

---

41 Zimmerman (1996) p. 2.
42 Hull (1978) p. 346.

of anything, is an undeniable argument for its possibility, and is alone a refutation of any pretended demonstration against it'.[43] Whether we should indeed accept this Humean dictum is open to challenge. Whether something is conceivable or not might be said to be a question about our psychological and cognitive capacities. It is a further question whether or not it is possible. Here, of course, there is a parallel with the relationship between the *a priori* and the necessary to which Kripke drew attention.[44] If one thinks it imaginable that Hesperus is not Phosphorous or that Gold does not have an atomic number of 79 (even though these propositions are not possibly true), then the Humean test of possibility should be rejected. After all, one might believe there are many things one can conceive which turn out to be metaphysically impossible. Drawing on a classic example, we know that water is H_2O. Following the approach developed by Putnam and Kripke we can say that upon being named (or baptised) the wet, watery stuff of our acquaintance, 'water' always picks out or refers to H_2O: that is what it means. Water cannot be anything other than H_2O. Now, I might nonetheless conceive of a world in which the watery stuff flowing in rivers and so on is named 'water' and is composed of another combination of elements – say (inevitably) XYZ or whatever. In this way I am able to conceive of water as other than it actually is. Water just denotes the wet watery stuff at a world. Depending on which world is taken as the actual world and on whether I am considering counterfactual hypotheses across worlds there are different senses in which I think of 'water'.[45] While I can conceive of a world in which 'water' picks out something other than H_2O, I cannot (on the supposition that our world is the actual world) conceive of water as anything other than H_2O. *That* thought turns out to be impossible given the function of water as a rigid designator. Whenever I pick out water in a counterfactual context my thought is of a certain kind of stuff in the world, namely H_2O.

On the other hand a critic might retain the Humean test, but deny that the examples are really conceivable at all. On a careful analysis they turn out to be impossible or mock thoughts, and so ought not to be taken to indicate the possibility of co-location.[46] The opponent of realism could look to formulate a compelling argument to explain why interpenetration is either not conceivable or is not metaphysically possible. The former is difficult to motivate for we do seem to be able to imagine it while remaining sensitive to the need to keep other things as they normally would be. The latter – the possibility of interpenetration – is exactly the issue at stake. On this issue

43 Hume (1978) p. 89.

44 See for example Kripke (1972/1980). The distinction between the capacity to conceive of some state (or entertain as true some proposition) and the possibility of such a state is discussed in for example Tidman (1993).

45 For related discussion on two-dimensional modal logic and meaning see for example Chalmers (1996) and Jackson (1998).

46 An explanation of how we can have genuinely impossible thoughts will be required. Papineau (2002) in his discussion of consciousness and the rejection of dualism about the mind suggests one such account.

the opponent of realism is yet to deliver a decisive or compelling explanation of the necessity of impenetrability.

VI   Identifying Groups Through Time

A group can undergo change through time, while remaining the same group. The most obvious form of change is in a group's constitutive membership. For most objects the very same thing survives change in its parts, provided its parts continue to be organised in the form characteristic of that kind of object. A second form of change is in the character or nature of the object. For example, an animal typically changes as it matures and comes to shed the bonds of neoteny. The character of a person develops through her life, so that there is a sense in which the very same person may be said to now possess a very different personality: that person may no longer be her old self because of the experiences she has endured. A third mode of change is metamorphosis, the transformation of an entity from one form to another.[47]

There can be practical difficulties in determining whether the object before us now is numerically the very same one as before, and in keeping track of an object through changes of the foregoing types. We may, for example, be uncertain how to regard an object which has undergone extremely rapid and substantial part replacement. An individual can undergo changes in personality or suffer damage to her cognitive capacities so that there is a question as to whether she is to be classed as a person. A radical change in an object's form can render it practically very difficult to trace the history of an individual. A group can develop in these ways, and be prone to problems with re-identification which can potentially arise for any composite material object.

Groups can also change in other ways. A group can merge with another(s), and a group can divide. We can imagine two tribes which become progressively more integrated over the years. Previously isolated by poor communications, the tribes are now able to contact each other with ease thanks to a new road or environmental changes removing the previous natural obstacles. The practices of each will be exposed to the influence, criticisms and endorsement of the other. The practices will become subject to the intervention of the other through such criticism, the impact of trade, the unforeseen consequences of external activities (for example the introduction into one tribe's valley of the other's agrarian practices), aggression and so on. Over time a single pattern of relations may develop amongst the individuals and a fusion or merger of the groups may occur as practices come to be shared and their effects can no longer be attributed to one or other of the old tribes, but to the single entity that occupies the territory. At the level of specific practices the merger could take place by adjustment or compromise in, for example, religious practices. One tribe may have been Christian – a result of missionary work – and the other

---

47 A fourth kind of change is for an object to cease to exist as such. This is not a change through which identity can be preserved, unless one believes the very same object can come and go out of existence.

practising a form of animism involving blood sacrifice. Through dialogue between the groups and the inability to establish the superiority of either of the old ways a new form of religion could develop over perhaps a few generations. Thus, the Christian sacrament of mass could be infused with sacrificial practices, thus giving a literal dimension to the wine and wafer.

After a certain point there is just a single group – the merged tribe, which has been produced through increasing levels of contact, cultural interchange, intermarriage and co-operative action. Their respective practices and beliefs develop through this contact and exchange of ideas and goals, so that the two groups come to establish a new, merged one with its own goals, values, and practices. Later still, a new group may begin to develop away from the tribe, perhaps through engaging in the abandoned practices and endorsing the goals of one of the 'original' tribes. Individuals would constitute a group that is a distinct entity from the 'main' tribe. Membership of both may be compatible, but the two groups exert their own effects upon the world and their members.

The merger of groups here is not just a case of co-extensive memberships. It is the integration or fusion of groups so that after a period or process of merger there is just a single group – one entity counted by reference to causal powers and explanatory role. I have in mind groups which come together to establish a single entity, individualisable as distinct from each of the merging groups. As opposed to merger one group can absorb another, so that it continues recognisably as itself, while the other fades from view. A minority culture may come to adopt the practices, goals and values of its dominant neighbour to the point where there is just a single entity, as the smaller group increasingly engages in those practices. In the case of division two or more new groups may be the result, or the original group may continue, while another(s) group has emerged as a result of splitting off or pulling away. Below I consider the relationship between the merged and earlier ('original') groups, and of that between new and old groups when a group divides. First, though, it is worth stressing that in determining whether a group(s) has merged or divided, we may need to defer judgement until we have seen how matters have progressed. The question of, say, whether two groups are now merged may only be answerable in retrospect – once we see how things have developed.

Merger and division are hardly unique to groups. The fusion or merger of distinct entities occurs when germ cells unite to form a zygote; in the case of sexual reproduction parts of separate organisms merge to establish a new organism. An amoeba can divide and hydras produce buds, which are distinct organisms in their own right. The relation between the old and new groups is not one of identity. They are not stages in a single historic individual. Rather, they are numerically distinct objects linked by an ancestor relation. Again, we may face problems of epistemological underdetermination. It may just not be clear whether there is a new group because of limits on the information we are able to obtain or handle (There may even be a metaphysical indeterminacy about the matter, although I shall leave this as an open issue and remain neutral on the question of metaphysical vagueness. If there is metaphysical vagueness, then it could just be indeterminate whether groups have merged, or whether a group has divided). Nonetheless we are able (roughly) to track the history of a group and to recognise when that group joins with another to produce something new, or when a new group emerges from it. The question of identity gives way to one of historic connection and influence. To the problems which might arise with tracing a group through part change, character development, and transformation from one kind of group to another, we can thus add an understanding of groups as typically temporally limited individuals, from which new ones arise as a result of mergers and divisions.

When groups merge, then, a new body is established, historically related to the merging groups, but not identical to them. Claims advanced identifying a group today, particularly a people or culture, with one in the past can be powerful because of the symbolic and emotional significance of that past group. The understanding sketched here suggests that groups can be diachronically connected, with the later group being dependent on the earlier one, without the groups being (stages of) a single entity.

The position outlined is one in which a group which has merged with another is no longer picked out or individuated as the very same group post merger. That 'original' party to the merger is no longer an entity which we identify as exerting an influence or playing a role in explanation. We would only refer to it in as far as its pre-merger activities continue to be relevant to certain of our explanations and descriptions. Post-merger *that* group disappears from the on-going historic record. After the merger there is just the one (new) group to figure in our explanations and descriptions.

An alternative holist position (canvassed briefly in the previous section) is to maintain that groups survive merger, so that a group can re-emerge from the fusion of groups. Here it is no use thinking of the emergence of a people or culture after a period of subjugation, because in such cases there was never the kind of fusion or integration characteristic of a merger. We cannot look to merely subjugated groups, but must appeal to the notion that a group is somehow latent within another. However, if previously distinct groups have fused to form a single one, then it appears mysterious how more than one group can survive. Unlike cases of shared memberships a merged group is formed through a single pattern of interrelations and individuated in virtue of its properties and causal role. Either a single dominant group survives the absorption of other ones or an entirely new merged entity springs from the fusion of groups. Yet, returning to the example of the two tribes, it is conceivable that a group with all the practices and goals of one of the original tribes could develop and split off from the merged group. Rather like Lewis's roads which come together for a stretch, one could say that both tribes were always present in the merged entity. Or, one seems in a position to endorse that view if one is also committed to a four-dimensionalist or perdurantist understanding of objects. Against the plausibility of distinct groups somehow continuing to exist as such during a period of genuine merger one might note that when groups merge several loci of causal power and objects with explanatory role are fused into a single entity. There is insufficient reason to hypothesise constituent groups into existence in the absence of identifying their (own) causal and explanatory role.

I have not offered a clear-cut argument against the possibility that groups can survive merger. Rather, I have taken as problematic the idea that an entity can survive a gap in its historic record. The problem with merger is not that an entity's form or organisation has been disrupted, as when a vase is smashed into a thousand pieces or an individual dismembered. It is rather that its parts (and their successors) are organised in just the same way so that a new group of the very same kind is formed from the merging groups. Or, that groups come together through a new form of organisation to merge into a new kind of group. In either case there is no longer any role for the 'original' groups to play; there is just the 'new' group.

While an appeal to one entity being latent within another seems mysterious, it is perhaps more plausible to hold that a group can be reconstructed. In the case of both the re-emergence of pre-merger groups and the reconstitution of a group that ceased to exist upon division,[48] the notion of reconstruction could be employed to explain how the identity of a group can survive a gap in its narrative record. A familiar form of reconstruction, in the philosophical literature at any rate, is the re-assembly of an artefact's original parts after they have been replaced by new parts. Just as the question of whether the original planks of Theseus' Ship re-assembled in exactly the original way constitute a ship now, which is identical with the one on which Theseus departed, so the re-assembly and organisation of a group's original members gives rise to the question of whether this group is identical with the original one (and of what relation it has with the group that has continued, developing over time partly through the replacement of parts). I shall not attempt to address the identity puzzles raised by Theseus' Ship, but note the fact that Theseus style problems can afflict groups indicates that they are material particulars, about which in general questions of re-assembly and continuity arise.

A group can be said to have been reformed without any of the original members being parts of it. By engaging in the practices and endorsing the attitudes and goals constitutive of a group, which had ceased to exist (for example through division) one might claim that the very same group is now reformed. The identity claim appears unnecessary to explain the way in which the groups are linked through the adoption or revival of practices. More significantly, one of the ways in which we individuate objects is through their histories or narratives. An end of the story looks to be the end of the object. If a group divides with the formation of two new groups, distinct from the original one, there are now two fresh narratives to trace. That tells us that the old group is no more, although it figures in the explanation and understanding of the new ones.

---

48 A group G divides into distinct groups G1 and G2 at time t. After some time has elapsed G1 and G2 merge at t^1 to form a group which has all and only the practices, properties powers, and even members of G. Calling the group formed at t^1, G*, the question is whether G = G*: is it the very same group?

The question of whether groups survive merger or can be reconstituted as the very same one after division has a certain grip on us because we view identity questions through a uniquely human or personal lens. Questions of identity are frequently framed by our concerns about the grounds for personal continuity and by the sense that the question of identity is significant in evaluation and judgements of a certain kind. In particular the moral attribution of praise and blame and the identification of the object of the policies flowing from our judgements. As shall become clear in discussing the moral status of groups we make an error in taking groups to be evaluable in just the same way as persons, an error within the terms of the ontological analysis of groups and an error within the terms by which we measure our standards of judgement.

VII   'Social Group' as a Kind?

In this section I shall suggest that there is good reason to employ the notion of grouphood in making well-grounded taxonomic divisions. In taking 'social group' to be a kind term, it is necessary to adopt a theoretical model of kindhood, which is more concessive than an essentialist basis for ordering the world into natural kinds. Different kinds of objects may be more or less prone to the acquisition of new, and sometimes very different properties, through the course of their existence so that re-identification can be problematic. To individuate this thing before me now as the very same cat I saw yesterday, it must be a cat. While, it is not enough to just recognise that the same kind of thing is in front of me, it is a start. To pick a thing out in terms of its being a certain kind of entity seems a necessary, but not sufficient, condition in re-identifying it. For this thing now to be Basil, the very same cat who awoke me yesterday, it must be a cat. In order for the cat to be Basil (i.e. the same one as yesterday) he must exhibit the continuity appropriate for an object of that kind.[49] His parts must remain interrelated in the appropriate cat-forming fashion. There must also be a narrative chain to Basil's existence consistent with the kind of thing he is, and the life this token of its kind is actually leading. In principle one should be able to relate his story, to give his history.[50]

---

49 It can be objected that the unity of an object's identity does not depend upon it continuing to be a particular kind. Caterpillars become butterflies; we can imagine a world in which dogs change into cats at the age of three, and cats into dogs, while each individual retains its character, memories and cognitive capacity. Rather than seeing such cases as challenging the way in which objects are categorised in terms of kinds or as threatening the way in which we may claim to have knowledge about something's identity, we should regard some kinds of things as being characterised by a tendency or capacity to change form through their life history. In the case of cats and dogs changing form at a certain age a question would arise as to whether there were just a single kind of animal. If not then we should need to confront the epistemological difficulty of differentiating dog-cats from cat-dogs.

50 Strawson (1959) has argued that reference is possible only if an object can be re-identified through change, and so criteria of identity assume a central importance. Such criteria

The re-individuation of a group as such suggests that we employ grouphood as a kind term. At a minimum 'group' is a sortal or kind term operative at a high level of generality like animal or plant (a detailed charting of the different kinds of group is an empirical matter to be left to the social sciences). A sortal is a universal providing a principle for individuating and re-identifying some thing. Locke notes that,

> it being evident that things are ranked under names into sorts or species only as they agree to certain abstract ideas, to which we have annexed those names, the essence of each genus, or sort, comes to be nothing but that abstract idea which the general or sortal ... name stands for. [51]

Sortals then mark off kinds of entities as what they are, and do not just characterise or qualify them in some way. It might be urged that 'group', like 'thing', does not single out any thing in a sufficiently determinate fashion to qualify as a sortal term. To say how many things there are in town appears a hopeless task, for we must first individuate what there is according to their kinds. If we give an answer in terms of things, that answer is entirely derivative on the sortal(s) we employ. Group, as understood in terms of an interrelational whole, does enable us to distinguish and count those entities which exhibit a certain form and activity as groups. Like 'animal' the class of groups may be enormously varied and be subject to further sub-division. It may also be the case that the availability of the concept 'group' as a higher level or general individuative concept follows consideration of its instances and generalisation therefrom.

The view that groups (or different sub-kinds of group) represent an explanatory and descriptively significant division within the social world is captured in the idea that 'group' (or particular types of groups) is a natural kind term. If we are to take group, or perhaps different types of groups, as natural kinds then we must obviously be clear about what is meant by natural kind. The simple idea is that a natural kind represents a real division or cleavage in the world to which our taxonomic scheme must conform if it is to accurately report the ordering of things. A natural kind records a real distinction in nature around which theories are constructed. It would seem then that natural kinds are to be contrasted with categorisations produced through convention or to serve some interest or function. Note that the distinction between natural and non-natural kinds recalls Locke's distinction between real and nominal essences. The former is whatever it is that accounts for the characteristic form and nature of some kind of thing, while the latter is merely the set of properties by which we distinguish objects belonging to that kind. Diamonds may be characterised in

---

are available only if we locate 'basic' particulars in space, which provides a frame of reference through which an object's history can be traced. Strawson identifies medium sized everyday particulars as 'basic', located in space and time, and securing our linguistic practices since reference to them affixes discourse to the world. The arguments set out in this chapter suggest that groups would pass the test to be recognised as basic particulars in this Strawsonian sense, reinforcing the view that our talk of groups is metaphysically well-founded.

51 Locke (1975) Essay, III, iii, 1. 5.

terms of their hardness, transparency and clarity, but their real essence is given by their microstructure, which reveals that they are carbon.

While our capacity to segment the world according to natural kinds is contingent on empirical work, the conceptual framework for an essentialist taxonomic strategy is evident in the work of, *inter alia*, Kripke[52] and Putnam.[53] In Putnam's theory the meaning of a natural kind term, such as gold or cat, is analysed into four components: a syntactic marker, a semantic marker, a stereotype and an extension. The term 'cat' may have as its syntactic marker, 'noun', as its semantic marker, 'animal', a stereotype of 'small, furry, often domesticated animal with whiskers, tail, distinctive miaowing and purring sounds and so on', and an extension determined by the microstructural or other theoretical facts about cats. Once we have the facts about something's microstructure we can class it together with other individuals of that type, and the question of whether something counts as one of this kind becomes answerable by whether it bears the appropriate sameness relation with respect to its essential (microstructural) properties. In virtue of the nature of a kind predicates about things of this kind can be formulated and (successful) predictions made possible; a kind's real essence underwrites the lawlike possession of properties and the characteristic behaviour of tokens of that kind.

It is by no means clear that groups would count as natural kinds in the sense outlined. It may prove to be the case, of course, that groups share certain common essential structural features, which may be revealed by the social sciences. A systematic ordering of the world in accordance with kinds which we have good reason to recognise can proceed ahead of the empirical discovery of the details of a kind's essence. We must simply move forward on a provisional basis, prepared to revise our classifications in light of fresh discoveries. Although a case can be made for taking groups to be a kind determined by essence, the essentialist conception of kinds is itself subject to criticism as a global template for taxonomy. An alternative account of kinds is available, and it is one with which the treatment of group as a kind marking a real division in the world is consistent. Furthermore, it presents a more plausible ground for regarding groups as being a kind of object, because it does not appeal to an as yet undiscovered true essence.

Leaving aside for the moment all considerations about groups, let us consider why it is doubtful that the essentialist account succeeds in providing a general way of ordering the world. It does certainly appear to work with the chemical elements such as gold, the extension of which can be cashed out in terms of atomic number: anything with an atomic number of 79 – any atom with 79 protons in its nucleus – is a specimen of gold. We might pick things out in virtue of their stereotypical properties as certain kinds, but there is a fact of the matter provided by the microstructure. Two distinct objects are gold if and only if they share the intrinsic and explanatory property, which defines what gold is.

---

52 Kripke (1972).

53 Putnam (1975). I shall not attempt to give a detailed exegesis of Kripke's or Putnam's accounts, nor do I consider the ways in which they differ.

However, an essentialist approach has been widely rejected by, for example, zoologists seeking to systematically order the natural world into kinds of species. Kinds of organisms are taxonomised according to their membership of historic breeding populations, a species being understood by most biologists as an historic individual rather than as kind, a universal instantiated through organisms structured in a characteristic fashion. A species is a spatio-temporally restricted entity constituted by (non contiguous) parts, which causally interact in a characteristic fashion, and which are diachronically linked through an ancestor relation.[54] Unlike the ordering of chemical elements as a result of atomic theory, species exist as a result of the contingent nature of evolutionary pressures and outcomes. Mutant cats and the descendants of today's cats, which may possess a very different internal structure, can all be classed as cats because of breeding potential. Furthermore, there seems little reason to suppose that all valid distinctions in the world must correspond to the kinds suggested by science, and ultimately physical science, which plays the role of final arbiter in determining extension. A less narrow conception of natural kindhood is available, and it is one that is aligned to an understanding of taxonomic practice driven or constrained by realism about the world and theoretical interest and perspective.

Such a view relies on a rejection of the categorisation of natural kinds as 'the most fundamental categories of nature, to be contrasted with categories which are useful but superficial. Instead natural kinds are non-arbitrary categories, to be contrasted with arbitrary, nominalistic schemes of classification'.[55] In this respect a category gathers together a class of objects with correlated properties, such that those properties will hold across new instances. On the basis of the categorisation a range of predictions and predicate attributions are projectible. The nature of the object as a certain kind, K, provides a basis for prediction and a means of explanation, so the 'function of categorisation is to allow extrapolation from observed to unobserved instances. Useful concepts represent projectible categories'.[56] A theory of natural kinds can be

---

54 See discussions in for example Hull (1978), Ghiselin (1987), Dupré (1993). Hull (1978) p. 335 observes that 'species have been treated traditionally as spatio-temporally unrestricted classes. If they are to perform the function which they do in the evolutionary process, they must be spatio-temporally localised individuals, historical entities.' Defending the individuality of species Ghiselin (1987) and Sober (1993) compare a species to a nation or corporation. Thus the individuality of species is taken to be supported by the fact that 'Alaska is part of the United States in virtue of the nexus of political interaction that unite the 50 states; the fact that Alaska does not spatially touch the lower 48 is immaterial' (Sober p. 150). An individual cat is therefore not an instantiation of a kind in virtue of its possession of certain essential features, but is an object individuated as such in virtue of its membership of a group (in which the relevant group constituting relation is breeding potential); and that group is treated as an individual because of its explanatory role and causal impact. As I discuss below the talk of kinds ought to shift from an essentialist framework to one concerned with the drawing of non-arbitrary divisions.

55 Griffiths (1997) p. 6.

56 Ibid., p. 187.

detached from essentialism dividing the world at the level of microstructure. The properties which unify objects as a kind are relative to a theory and the theoretical domain of the observer. A category is non-arbitrary when the relevant correlation of properties has an underlying explanation that makes it projectible. In this respect then the 'essence' of a kind is:

> its causal homeostatic mechanism – whatever it is that explains the projectibilty of that category. A microstructural essence is only one kind of causal homeostatic mechanism. Other possibilities include external forces like those produced by the ecological niche of a species and the 'design niche' of an artefact. Yet another possibility is the shared history that holds together the members of a biological taxon.[57]

Now, it may be that one would wish to reserve the term 'natural kind' for those kinds that mark absolutely objective cleavages in nature: that is, schisms in the world, distinctions between things, which are completely independent of human psychology or convention. In locating these distinctions we would find entirely mind independent distinctions between things, and perhaps discover there entirely natural properties.[58] The question arises as to the level(s) of enquiry at which these forms of distinction are to be found. If there is to be reserved a special use for the concept of a natural kind, the more concessive notion of kind outlined can be preserved by talking of kinds located between these perfectly natural ones and merely conventional ones.[59]

Consider the sculptor who groups together different stones as 'ornamental marble'. Marble is a crystalline form of calcium carbonate, while other 'ornamental marbles' such as onyx is an oxide and porphyry a silicate. Prior to the development of modern geological science and the employment of chemical analyses and microscopy, all three may have been classed as a single kind of stone by science. Now, there is reason for the geologist or chemist to class them as separate kinds. A more fine grained taxonomy has not affected the sculptor because his needs are driven by the practical requirements of his craft. He continues to treat the different rocks as a single kind, since they all satisfy the criteria of being suitable for carving and polishing, and possessing a certain fitness of grain and translucency. The taxonomy of sculpture is constrained by the nature of rocks, but within that constraint its different perspective (the aesthetic rather than the division of the world at some level of chemical or

---

57 Griffiths (1997) p. 212.

58 But compare Barry Taylor (1993) p. 81 and his criticism of David Lewis's use of natural properties on the grounds that the doctrine of natural properties as markers of nature's joints is 'utterly mysterious'. He recommends the metaphysician forego natural properties by relativising 'key concepts – laws, causation, events – to human perspectives on things (theories)' (p. 99).

59 Kitcher (1979) talks of kinds located between natural and conventional which are governed by empirical generalisations. A body of generalisations, empirically verifiable and predictively reliable, as found in, for example, folk psychology and folk social sciences, can function with respect to the determination of kind membership in much the same way as natural laws govern natural kinds in Putnam's theory.

micro composition, and the predictions derived therefrom) organises the things in the world according to its own interests and practical demands.[60]

The division of the world according to non-arbitrary kinds is a taxonomic practice, which suggests that there is a plurality of warranted non-arbitrary descriptions of the world yielding a series of potentially cross cutting classifications. Taxonomy addresses the question of how entities in the world be ordered or organised, and a taxonomy of any domain or field of enquiry aims to be informative. In particular, a goal of taxonomy is the articulation or mapping of the underlying structure of the diversity that may be characteristic of a certain area of study, such as ordering the diversity of living organisms, chemical elements, or patterns of human interaction and behaviour. Here we should note that we do not merely strive for a classification, but for one that is informative so that something of the nature of the object before us is revealed through its classification. In ordering objects we are applying certain principles, and empirical discoveries, in order to create a structure or framework. Equally, through the development of theories, principles and empirical findings we may find that we have reason to acknowledge that there exists a certain class of object.

The question arises as to how such a division and ordering should proceed. An 'extreme' realism holds that there is an entirely objective and independent (of human interests or perspective) set of criteria by which to determine the classificatory structure of the world, or some relevant domain of interest. Yet, our interests in and ways of approaching the world are multiply diverse. If the way in which the world is divided is to be informative, and useful as a mapping of reality, there seems little reason to anticipate that a single set of distinctions awaits discovery 'out there'. For a single set of real divisions may just not be able to bear the burden of the array of potentially cross-cutting classifications which are actually employed. Why should the botanist, ecologist and tribal shaman make the same distinctions? For the taxonomies they each employ may prove powerful in their informational content and role in the formulation of successful predictions. This is not to deny that there may be distinctions that apply globally, and around which there is taxonomic convergence. For example, it seems likely that the description of the world at the level of fundamental physics is constrained by the nature of particles at that level, leading to a convergence of our best theories in an agreement about the structure of the world at that level of enquiry.

A mind-independent world determines what there is, but not (entirely) how we conceptualise or order it.[61] The world is not neatly ordered 'before us', but neither

---

60 Scruton (1994) pp. 241–2 employs the example of ornamental marbles also.

61 At this point I should stress the separation of two issues. First the question of taxonomy – the division and ordering of the things in the world according to a classificatory scheme. To order the world we must pick out things as being a certain kind. To individuate that thing as a dog does require possession of the concept or sortal term 'dog'. Whether any kind of conceptual content is required in order that one be able to pick it out (*qua* thing or object) simpliciter is the subject of the second issue – a debate on the conceptual content of

can it be described or carved in a merely arbitrary fashion. The individuation of entities in the world is not simply given by how the world is, nor is it just a question of conventionalism. There is space between the extremes of a world structured in way susceptible to a determinate taxonomisation – waiting to be carved at the joints – and one in which what there is depends only upon the conventions established by the observer. The individuation of entities in the world should be regarded as the outcome of the relation between two constraints: what there (really) is in the world and the perspective or theoretical interest of the observer. A plurality of true descriptions and explanations are available across different modes of enquiry, because 'how things are' is amenable to a number of different cuts. This is not to relativise what there is, but to note that the way in which the world is taxonomised and individuated is partly driven by the interest and questions possessed of the observer.

It is reasonable, therefore, to regard 'group' as a kind that marks a non-arbitrary division within the domain of material objects, and as a category of particular significance in the social sphere. The division is not merely conventional or arbitrary because we have good grounds to take groups seriously as causally efficacious and explanatorily relevant objects. Furthermore, the impact of the group – the charging of the mob or the development and transmission of cultural norms – can be explained in part by its internal organisation or structure.[62] Ontological holism underwrites a taxonomy featuring groups and individuals, an ordering of the world reflecting our best explanations and the kind of constitutive and other-affecting relations in which individuals and group stand with respect to each other.

VIII Animals

The model of groups outlined in this chapter is not limited in its application to human groups. At least some kinds of non-human animals can form groups through their interactions just as we can. The distinction between us and other animals is in our cognitive, conceptual and affective capacities; in particular our possession of language, our self-awareness and capability for reflection. Many of our groups do possess a different and distinctly human character, setting them apart to a lesser or greater degree from primate colonies, packs of wolves and flocks of birds. To talk of animals in social or group terms is not a metaphorical extension of a concept that has its application centrally to the human world. Rather (self) conscious creatures of many kinds seem to be able to interact in ways that form and maintain other affecting bodies or units. The pack of wolves or flock of migrating birds interrelate in ways that constitute a

experience and whether the individuation of an object requires the possession of some sortal (like) concept. I shall not address the second issue.

62 Note this is not tantamount to admitting that a reductive analysis is possible. The properties and powers a group possesses may be explained in terms of its structure or organisation. The properties and powers are not reductively analysable to individual members, but emerge from the totality of the relations. It may be that social science will discover a striking correlation between kinds of structure and the character and powers of a group.

group. The individual members of, say, a wolf pack might recognise that there are others with whom each is engaged and there is a directedness of the individuals towards a common goal. Of course, the pursuit of food or flying south may not be conceived by dumb creatures in propositional form, but it does not need to be for them to constitute a group.

In drawing distinctions between our groups and animal groups, and especially, morally relevant ones, we cannot just appeal to the fact that we live in social groups. Rather, the distinction between our groups and animal groups must appeal to either the character of the groups or their constituents, and the question remains open of whether the morally salient features draw a sharp line between human and non-human. Furthermore, given the possibility that groups can be entities in virtue of or towards which we may have obligations and duties, both human and non-human (and mixed) groups could figure in our practical and evaluative thinking and judgements.

In summary, then, groups are material composite objects constituted by interrelating individuals. As such we are faced by both practical and conceptual difficulties when addressing questions of identity and in trying to set out the properties or characteristics which distinguish one type of group from another. In recognising that the concept of a group marks a non-arbitrary division in the world we can note a way in which naturalism in the social sciences can be preserved without a commitment to reductionism. The continuity of the natural and social sciences is, though, attained through the rejection of the priority or dominance of the physical world-view, in favour of potentially cross-cutting taxonomies constrained by reality and theoretical interest. With these comments at the end of a long chapter I conclude the principal argument that groups are material objects. The next chapter explains why we must draw a difference in kind between groups and corporations, a distinction which runs counter to the standard view in philosophical and social scientific discussion that corporations are a paradigmatic type of social group.

Chapter 5

The Corporate Soul

I   Introduction

Corporations, such as companies, universities and churches, are usually seen as social groups. Indeed, in illustrating the ways in which we interact to form bodies with their own causal and explanatory role it is unsurprising to witness the realist about groups quickly turning to such entities. For it is just such corporations from which civil society appears to be woven, and it is their presence and character which shapes important aspects of the lives of individuals. Ontological holism draws support from the ease with which we talk of the personality or character of an institution, and from our ability to trace its narrative and anticipate its future conduct. Realism about corporations has been a way of marking either a useful distinction amongst groups or, more radically, as marking the distinction between social groups and mere aggregates of individuals.

In this chapter I shall sketch why we should recognise corporations as possessed of great significance within the social domain. However I shall also explain that within our taxonomy of the social world there is a distinction to be made between social groups and corporations. There are of course distinctions to be drawn between different types of groups, but the differences I have in mind suggest there is a difference in kind between corporations and groups. In particular, unlike groups, corporations are existentially dependent on a set of rules and can survive changes a group is unable to withstand.

At a high level of taxonomic generality one can hold that both groups and corporations are material entities, and so share in a very high order kindhood. However, a stronger claim is also possible, which denies that groups and corporations are distinct (sub) kinds within the class of material entities. The stronger claim maintains that corporations are better understood as non-material entities capable of standing in relations with material ones such as individuals, groups and artefacts. Under this latter view a corporation is attached to or intermingled with the material entities through which it exerts an impact on the world in a way reminiscent of the relationship between soul and body postulated by substance dualists. While noting this view, the weaker claim suffices to motivate an important, and generally unrecognised, distinction in the taxonomic classification of the social world.

A corporation typically consists in the organisation of individuals and groups according to a recorded and referable set of rules and procedures.[1] In this respect a corporation is an instantiation of a set of potentially open-ended series of rules determining goals, values and procedures. Through these rules the corporation can be thought of as animating individuals and groups as parts of the corporation to act in certain ways, to hold particular attitudes and reach certain judgements. The distinction between a corporation and a group is to be drawn with respect to the essential role played by rules within a corporation and the survival conditions of a corporation. The three key ways in which groups and corporations differ are:

i.   A set of recorded and referable rules is essential to a corporation, but not to a group.
ii. A corporation can have active and passive phases during its existence as that (the very same) corporation, while a group cannot.
iii. A corporation is not existentially dependent on individuals, but a group is.

These differences underwrite the distinction in kind between groups and corporations. The modality of each claim entails that if it is true, then a group cannot be the same kind of entity as a corporation. Each claim alone is sufficient to underwrite the distinction in kind. To these can be added the view that corporations are minded in a way that groups are not, and in virtue of which corporations are more suitable candidates for moral agency.[2] Thus:

iv. A corporation is minded and (potentially) a moral agent.

We must beware of overstating mindedness as marking a general or typical difference between groups and corporations. Perhaps, some kinds of groups and some kinds of corporations are minded to some degree while other kinds of groups and corporations are not. For the moment I shall note that even though corporate mindedness may inhere in the rules and structure of the corporation, rather than the practices of a group, and even though mindedness may be a general feature of corporations and a rare one amongst groups, it may not strictly mark a difference in kind between corporations and groups.

The relationships between a corporation and the individuals and groups acting for it will often be complex. In particular, by distinguishing between a corporation and the groups through which it operates, practical judgements about the moral responsibility of the corporation may demand an exact and subtle approach. For

---

1   I say 'typically' because a corporation can exist in the form of a computer programme, and operate via machines it controls. I discuss below the possibility of an 'electronic corporation'.

2   The operative understanding of a group could just be extended so that corporations are included within that class, although this would do nothing with regard to the differences that exist.

example, when a company makes a decision to flood the market with its excess stock, regardless of its likely dire social consequences, it acts through individuals and groups. The way in which they act is partly determined by the corporate rules, and perhaps partly by the internal nature of the group – say the solidarity of the factory workers – and character of individuals – for example, the ambitions of the directors. In recognising the separation of corporation, group and individual a complexity may be added to our judgements, but with the benefit of being able to measure and target with greater accuracy our judgements and actions.

II   The Significance of Corporations

Corporations are first sources of value, guidance and help to shape the character of their members. Bradley put this in terms of acquiring a station in the social world. Such a reference brings with it the baggage of 'pre-ordained' places in the natural organism that is the state, and echoes of Plato's Republic. However, one's 'station' is not mysteriously 'given', but is acquired by the individual in the conduct and shaping of his life through the many forms of fellowship experienced. We become what we are through the immediate ties of family, the bonds of association forged in, *inter alia*, schools, churches and firms. Moreover, the cement of obligation, the normative primitive which commands our actions and binds values to deeds, may only evolve within the self-identifying group, and probably the corporation. This is not just a rehashing of the truism that as a matter of fact we are social creatures in the sense that we do live in communities in which we generate values and ends. Rather, it is that 'corporations exert a kind of tutelage over their members, demanding the recognition of objective rights and duties'.[3]

The objective obligation is one that is both independent of any consent and integral to a person's status as a member. It is partly how a person is a member, in that a failure to recognise that she owes something to, say, the gang or church is fatal to the claim of membership. To return to a kind of Hegelian metaphor, we acquire a sense or capacity to recognise and be moved by obligations in our journey from neoteny to adulthood. We come into being as moral agents through the ties of membership, which demand the acknowledgement of the 'personality' of certain groups and institutions. It is only in virtue of this sense of what obligation is that we can enter into contractual arrangements.

Second, corporations unite generations, and individuals or groups which are distant in space. Corporations unite those who otherwise could not interact. For example, to belong to the Catholic Church is to share a membership and, to some extent, attitudes in virtue of that membership. Strangers are united through their participation in the life of the corporation. Furthermore, a corporation can endure beyond the span of mere human lifetime. Both its goals and the commitments it can make may reflect this, so that its call for respect or obligations is underwritten by

---

3   Scruton (1989) p. 255.

its capacity to deliver the promised protection or goods beyond one's own life for the benefit of future generations. Equally, a corporation can stand accused today of betrayal of those unborn or still young who should be in the embrace of its concern. In the UK of the late 1990's some of the hostility towards the conversion of building societies from mutual to listed status may have arisen because the converting institution was neglecting the interests of future members, through the monetisation of building society reserves in the form of windfall or bonus payments to current members in the process of incorporation. Indeed, it may be more than neglect, but behaviour which shatters the bond uniting members through time and in which bond each successive 'current' generation finds in large the measure the security of the institution.[4]

The third way in which corporations appear to be significant in the social world is in their apparent capacity to possess moral agency. This places them beyond the domain of those things to, or in virtue of which we may merely owe obligations and duties. We may have a duty with respect to beautiful objects or to dumb creatures, but they are not on a moral par with us in the sense that they (unlike us – persons) cannot bear the ascription of responsibility and the attendant burdens of praise and blame.[5] There may be strong reasons to doubt that a corporation can be a full moral agent, that a corporation can be just like a person. Nonetheless, it is the case that corporations enjoy that kind of agency to a certain degree through a minded capacity for goal directed action, reflection and revision.

Corporations are held to account for their actions and intentions in law. In both the civil and criminal courts corporations are taken to be legal persons, capable of sustaining evaluation and of being the proper objects of punishment. In England, for example train operating companies and building contractors have been held responsible for the deaths of passengers and employees. The purported difficulties in securing convictions against corporations prompted the UK government to amend existing legislation with the introduction of a corporate manslaughter bill in 2006. Beyond the scope of the law a corporation may be deemed to display or possess a certain character or property. A corporation may be racist or benevolent. Corporations can be loved or reviled. Corporations seem to stand in relations structured by their possession of obligations, rights and duties.

---

4   There is a certain awkwardness in this example as a building society converts from mutual status to being a limited liability company. One might want to hold that mutuality is a form of group-constituting interrelatedness. However, today's building societies possess the organisational structure of any other retail financial services company; the difference between mutual bodies and incorporated ones resides in the ownership structure.

5   The grounds for being apt to be judged or held morally accountable are the subject of much debate, and as I observe in Chapter 8 it is not a debate to which I can make any substantive contribution here. I take it, though, that if a corporation is a minded entity of sufficient sophistication and capable of acting in an appropriate fashion that it is at least a candidate to be regarded as a moral agent.

They do not simply invoke a moral responsiveness in us, but they are presupposed to enjoy the capacity to respond in a like fashion to others.

Realism endorses a literal understanding of such judgements, actions and attitudes: ontological realism about corporations is the view that a corporation is an entity capable of sustaining certain judgements, acting in appropriate ways, and being the warranted object of affective states.[6] This has suggested to realists about corporations that we understand the corporation in terms of its personality; that is, we see corporations as persons. I shall explore below the plausibility of ascribing (moral) personhood to corporations. In summary the thought behind the ascription of personhood to corporations is that if we take a corporation to be a 'fully fledged member of the moral community of equal standing with the traditionally acknowledged residents: human beings',[7] then the equivalence arises in virtue of both being the same kind of entity – persons.

One realist view of corporations takes as its core position the rejection of the doctrine of legal fictionalism. This doctrine holds that that all persons recognised by the law, those entities which are granted recognition or status before the law and powers within it to defend or pursue one's (or others') rights and/or interests, are creations of the law. The characteristics necessary and sufficient for legal status are determined by the law itself.[8] In essence all persons *qua* legal persons are extensions or creations of the state. The realism opposing this understanding maintains that the 'law does not invent its subjects, but recognises the non-legal existence of persons'.[9] The task remains of showing that corporations are real in the right sort of way. A reality theory of law specifies that way in terms of corporations being *persons*.

There are, however, good reasons to reject the attribution of personhood to corporations, while also maintaining that their individuation in law does follow from a recognition of their extra-legal reality. Within the law this leaves unresolved the tension that follows from the denial that corporations are persons, but nonetheless real, and the law's treatment of them as persons. I shall not offer a reconstruction of a reality theory of law, but focus on the ontological nature of corporations as

---

6   I assume that we are mostly warranted in loving or reviling the things we do, and that we have a particular attitude towards them because (at least in part) of their properties or actions.

7   French (1984) p. 32.

8   This doctrine has its roots in Roman Law and is continued in Canon Law and Natural Law theories. Corporations can only be created through the authorisation of the state. Its identity is just that contained within the terms of the law enacted by the legislature. The Roman law concept of a *persona ficta* emerges in Canon Law in the thirteenth century as a means of clarifying the legal status of bodies such as monasteries. That they were regarded as being comprised largely of dead persons raised problems for (living) abbots in the enforcement of their property claims. Under Pope Innocent IV such bodies came to be regarded as fictional persons. Ownership of the property resided with this legal person, while the abbot and monks stood in the capacity of guardians. See French (1984 and 1992, Ch. 13) for discussion of this point.

9   French (1992) p. 137.

instantiations of (probably open ended) sets of rules, which typically organise the activities of individuals and groups.

There are of course alternative, anti-realist, views of a corporation, understanding it as an entity capable only of 'secondary agency'[10] or as a 'nexus of contracts',[11] which I shall not consider as I am concerned with elucidating a realist understanding of corporations in light of the earlier discussion of groups. In particular I attempt to disentangle the (unhelpful) ascription of personhood to corporations from the grounds we have for recognising them as *bona fide* residents of the moral world. The reason to regard a corporation as a moral agent is that corporations are minded. They possess the capacity for decision making, the formulation, review, and revision of goals, and responsiveness to criticism and praise of their goals.

Much of the discussion on corporations has concentrated on their moral status, concluding either that they have the necessary and sufficient hallmarks of personhood to count as persons in their own right;[12] or, that they are merely vehicles for, or constructs of individuals who are ultimately morally accountable and the proper objects of our judgements – even if they may be put beyond our reach by the law.[13] Standing behind these discussions is the ontological question: what kind of entity is a corporation? A pressure to address the question arises because the moral analysis can be tested against its ontological commitments; whatever a corporation *is*, it must be (the kind of thing) capable of acting in the fashion demanded by its (alleged) moral standing. In the next section I turn to the ontological bases for distinguishing corporations from groups.

Thereafter I focus on the third aspect of the corporation's role in the social domain, its role as a moral agent, and in doing so address head on the question of corporate personality. As with social groups I reject the notion that a corporation is a person, and eschewing a looser deployment of 'personality', I arrive at an ontological view of groups that accommodates all three dimensions of the corporate role in the social world. I explain why we should not treat corporations as persons, while defending their status as moral agents – or more tentatively as having a *prima facie* claim to be such. Recalling the sense in which groups can be 'dumb', and anticipating the discussion of their moral status, the agentive capacity of corporations marks a significant way in which they differ from groups.

III   The Ontological Status of Corporations

The distinction to drawn between corporations and groups is by no means apparent given our everyday understanding of corporations and the way in which we define the term. Definitions of a corporation identify three key features, specifying a corporation as: (1) a group of people authorised by law to act as an individual and having its own

---

10 Werhane (1985).
11 Kilpi (1998).
12 For example French (1979; 1984).
13 For example McMahon (1994).

powers, duties and liabilities; or, (2) the municipal authorities of a city or town; or, (3) a group of people acting as one body.[14] A wide range of organisations or institutions intuitively count as corporations, including companies, churches, clubs, organised crime syndicates, voluntary associations and states.[15] Some corporations we join voluntarily, others we are born into.

It is immediately obvious from (1) above that a corporation is defined by reference to a group of individuals, a group which enjoys a certain status in law; (2) is a particular restriction on the general view expressed in (1); (3) does not distinguish a group, as I have analysed the concept, from a corporation. Leaving open the question of whether corporations are groups, unless (3) is elaborated so as to require that individuals must be recognised in law to act as a body, it indicates that corporations need not be legally empowered or recognised within the law. It seems correct to allow that a corporation can exist independently of legal recognition or even in opposition to the law. Consider outlawed or proscribed organisations. The Irish Republican Army, for example, is formally structured through a series of rules and procedures, delineating its goals, methods and processes, in the same kind of way as a multinational company or legally recognised army. Furthermore, just as we might speak about the values, goals or attitude of British Airways or the French Army, so we refer in the same way to the IRA, or to other illegal entities such as Tong or Triad gangs.

If a corporation just is a group endowed with legal powers and duties, or is simply a group which acts as one body, then a distinction in kind would be difficult to motivate. The sketch in the previous section of three ways in which corporations figure significantly in the social domain indicates that it is the individuals and groups organised by and acting for the corporation through which an effect is exerted on the world and ideas and values transmitted. It is therefore understandable that corporations have been treated as groups, because social scientists and philosophers have focused on their impact. Nonetheless, there are sound reasons to distinguish between the corporation and the group(s) through which they typically operate.

A corporation is an instantiation of a set of rules through which its values and goals are identified, its decision making structures formed and the reflexive relations between values, goals, outcomes and responses articulated. The corporation is structured through the way in which individuals and groups are organised in accordance with the rules; rules which may develop through time with the practices of the groups. A corporation is individuated in virtue of its impact on the world, not through the set of rules organising its actions. After all, the same set of rules could be multiply realised. The identity of a corporation is indexed to a particular realisation of such a set of rules. Depending on the character of the corporation it may employ, dismiss, kill, buy from and sell to individuals and other corporations. A corporation

---

14 This definition is derived from OED and Collins dictionaries.

15 Partnerships are like corporations in many respects, particularly given the existence of partnership deeds and documentation. However, a partnership's reliance on there being partners seems to deny it the open-endedness of a corporation.

acts in the world, and its actions are typically best understood as being in pursuit of its ends. Since a corporation is individuated in virtue of its causal impact we have reason to regard them as material entities.

The rules, procedures and processes of a corporation can develop through a responsive or reflective capacity to assess goals and procedures in light of information. The rules of a corporation determine the way in which individuals and groups operate within it, or perhaps more accurately *for* it. The rules and organisation of a corporation must be set out or laid down in some form. Typically, a corporation will have a legal form through its documents of incorporation. A company, for example, will be registered and its form and goals set out in its Articles and Memorandum of Association. Its general goals and form will acquire greater specification and detailed working out in its procedures manuals, policy statements and the like.

There is likely to be a wide variety of ways in which the corporate rules can be set down and procedures specified for their implementation. The important point is that the rules determining the nature of a corporation are recoverable and referable. Given that there is an indefinite number of sets of rules, then one might say that any activity at all is an instantiation of a particular set of rules.[16] Furthermore, any uninstantiated or unimplemented set of rules could come to be instantiated, bringing us to the cusp of a kind of Platonism about corporations, which regards all possible corporations as existing in conceptual space. I do not object to the coherence of either of the foregoing views. However, within the social domain a corporation exists because a set of rules, which are actually specified and recoverable (in the sense that the rules can in principle be accessed) organise individuals, groups and artefacts in activities specified and developed in accordance with those rules.

Thus far I have not demonstrated the distinction between corporations and groups. The description of a corporation might seem as if it is just specifying that a corporation is a group, or assemblage or 'federation' of groups and individuals organised in accordance with a set of rules. This seems amenable to the view that corporations be identified with groups or reductively analysed in terms of groups. However, three ontological differences do motivate the distinction I have alleged ought to be respected. Note that I take each of the following points to stand alone. To the extent that one is inclined to agree with all of them, their effect may be cumulative, but each individually marks a point at which a corporation is characterised in way not conformable to regarding corporations as groups.

First, the set of organising rules or principles of a corporation are external to the groups they are co-ordinating and whose practices and goals they may determine. By external I mean just that they are recorded in some way and are independent of the groups organised. This is not to say that they cannot be developed or changed because of the way in which those groups implement or interpret them. It is to note that the rules governing the corporation are not irretrievably embedded in the practices of the organised groups. Rules-of-thumb or working practices may inevitably spring up in

---

16 Here I set aside consideration of problems relating to whether we can know that a particular rule is being followed or not.

the working of the corporation, but these are always testable against and defeasible in light of the formal or official rules structuring the practices, goals and values characterising the corporation. With a group there is no such external set of official rules. The rules, such as they are, of the group are embedded in and worked out through the practices of the group itself. The family of practices, values and goals characterising the French people or the Jones family or the philosophy department seminar group are internal to those group-constituting practices, values and goals; they are not framed or calibrated by an external set of rules. There is no recorded set of rules and procedures to which we can refer as a people to check if we remain true to our character.

It might be accepted that groups and corporations do often differ in this way, but that this does not mark a conceptual difference. Corporations may require essentially a set of organising rules, and groups may in fact for the most part lack them. However, to mark the distinction in kind between groups and corporations it is necessary that a group could not have such a set of rules. On the face of it we as a group could establish a set of recorded and referable rules determining our practices, goals and values. Now, in this case it seems to me arguable that we have established a corporation. It is a corporation constituted by *us*. Here constituted can be understood in the sense of being established by us through the creation of something like a constitution defining the nature of the corporation and in the sense that the corporation acts through the rule governed relations in which we stand. This does not entail that the group we constitute is identical with the corporation. For the set of rules organising the group does not seem to be internal to the group in the way in which our constitutive practices and goals are. That the rules may express our current group-constituting practices is a contingent fact about the way in which we are presently related to the corporation. As a group we may develop and move onto new ways of being. If the corporation is to remain active, its rules must change or it must come to be constituted by individuals who organise themselves to pursue its goals and engage in the practices it specifies. The group can become detached from the corporation in a way that indicates it was never identical with it. One should therefore resist the temptation to hold that corporations are analysable *as* groups, where this is taken to mean that they are identical with a group.[17]

Second, corporations can survive even though they are inactive or dormant. The set of rules, the values and goals can be set down, ready to be activated, as a specific legal entity. There are countless shelf companies available for purchase from all good legal outlets. These are companies with standard articles of association and memoranda, individualisable only by name and company number. They are waiting in a more or less literal sense to come to life. At the other end of the corporate lifespan are those companies which have just avoided liquidation. They inhabit a limbo of inaction. Their assets have typically been fully depleted in paying off creditors, and

---

17 Corporations can thus share space with groups. Should one hold corporations to be a kind of social group, then such cases could be analysed as instances of space sharing and subsequent division by groups.

remaining liabilities have been written off or lurk, awaiting the company's return to action. Corporations in this kind of state can still be picked out, but they are passive. Strictly speaking the corporation does have a physical realisation because its existence is recorded somewhere. For example, we may be able point to the legal documents setting out the details of its incorporation. Nonetheless it does nothing *qua* corporation and stands in no kind of causal relations with anything else.[18] Moreover, there is no (non-arbitrary) limit on the period of corporate dormancy.

A dormant or passive corporation might not be regarded as continuing to exist, just because it is no longer active. One might stipulate that a corporation exists when its essential rules are actually organising individuals and groups. Here we can find a parallel between the corporation and organisms if we are inclined to view both as being constituted from matter organised according to a characteristic form. Under this view, a dormant corporation is not properly understood as a corporation at all, but as more like a record of the corporate form.

A difficulty with this view is that there is nothing odd or incoherent in talking about the past actions of a now dormant corporation, and in projecting into the future plans of what it will do. In the past the corporation developed a large number of office developments, and this is what it will return to doing. For the moment, though, it is inactive. If a permanent peace settlement is maintained in Ulster we can imagine that the IRA will slip completely into inactivity. It is also easy to imagine that at some further point it will become active again as the very same organisation. The university origami society may have once flourished, but its once abundant numbers have declined to the point at which there are none. It continues to be listed as a university society, and to render it active new members would need to follow the procedures and rules set out in its terms of establishment. When Bob becomes chairman of the society and begins to seek recruits it is the very same club appealing for paper folders as the one that once thrived. To hold that it was not really in existence while inactive or dormant makes this intuitive view of the continuity in the club's identity difficult to hold. The more natural way of understanding matters is to regard the corporation as surviving periods of dormancy.

A group does not seem to have the capacity to have this mode of passive existence. A group consists in the engagement together of individuals through time. As discussed in the last chapter, members of a group do not spend every waking moment engaging in the relevant practices of the group, but over time they do sustain the group by their forms of interrelations. If the group-constituting practices cease then the group ceases to be. There is the question of whether the very same group can be reconstituted later, an affirmative answer to which may commit one to a 'gappy' view of diachronic identity. That is, to maintaining that the very same object can cease to exist at one point in time, while coming (back) to exist at a later point. With a

---

18 I deliberately oversimplify the details here. In fact to maintain registration of a company it may be necessary to pay fees and have individuals nominally serving as directors. This is, though, a contingent feature of certain jurisdictions.

corporation, though, there is no question of its passive phase being one in which it ceased to exist. It was just passive.

Now, it might be objected that I have contrasted the potential passivity of a corporation with the 'death' of a group, while ignoring the possibility that a group could be passive in much the same way as a corporation, or at any rate inactive without ceasing to exist. A group can do nothing in the sense of not engaging in any activity: this inactivity may be purposive in the sense that doing nothing is the goal of the group, or it may be incidental in that doing nothing is entailed by the goal of the group. For example, we might form a group with the express purpose of engaging in no activities *qua* group. Of course, we would be co-operatively engaging together in the common pursuit of maintaining an inactive state. The group has the property of being inactive because this is a goal of the group-constituting interrelations. Alternatively, the group may be inactive because it is waiting to spring into action. The gang of robbers or squad of soldiers before an assault may remain motionless for some time as they wait for the moment to strike. In neither case is the inactivity of the group the same as the dormancy of the corporation.

The main point of contrast between the corporate capacity to survive a dormant phase and groups is not found in instances of a group doing nothing. As a protest (against say a majority group's oppressive government) a minority people may decide to do nothing for a minute. Each member just stands still. There is a sense here in which the group is inactive as a group. The contrast is in the fact that a corporation can be out of action indefinitely. In the case of a group its members must interact over time in order for the group to be constituted. A group that does nothing for a long time is inactive in virtue of the continuing relations between its members. A group, though, cannot survive the termination of its group-constituting relations. A group may be doing nothing, but it cannot be dormant in the sense that it has no members who are interrelating in ways which constitute it. Vagueness may infect our judgements of when a group has gone out of existence, but it is clear that a group does not survive (non-gappily) through an indefinite cessation in activities. Yet, it is just this indefinitude which is the hallmark of corporate passivity.

The third way in which corporations differ metaphysically from groups is in the fact that an active (non-dormant) corporation need not be composed of individuals: it has no need of individuals. It is existentially independent of persons. As noted at the end of the previous chapter, groups may not be restricted to human beings, but be constituted by other kinds of animals. Even on this broader notion of a group there is a constitutive dependence on entities which form a body through their interrelations.[19]

We can imagine a corporation set up by entrepreneurs with the goal of making profits from the manufacture of certain goods. It establishes itself in its line of business and has become involved in the public life of its society by supporting

19 At this point I do not restrict the ontological dependence of groups to interrelating organisms. I see no *a priori* reason to rule out groups constituted by intelligent robots if such entities are possible. The point is that a group is formed through things which do interrelate.

charities, political parties, contributing to debates and consultation documents and so on. After a number of years the board of directors, acting in light of corporate policies and procedures, decide to utilise accumulated earnings to buy back its (publicly listed) shares, perhaps as the best way of generating shareholder value. Its future capital needs can be met by internally generated cashflow. Later still, the whole operation is mechanised and the running of the company comes to be handed over to computer. The directors gradually retire and the workforce runs off through retirements and voluntary departures, so that the company comes to be controlled and run by a computer operating via its control of the machines. The output of goods, marketing and relationship with customers, suppliers, regulatory authorities are handled by the controlling computer.[20]

The computerised corporation acts in accordance with values and ends identifiable through its policy pronouncements and actions. The corporation, which started off being dependent on people standing in certain relations, is recognisable as the same entity in its later form through the continuity in its activities and through the traceable development of its goals, operational procedures and attitudes and actions towards customers, community, government and others with which it must deal.[21] Dan-Cohen's aim is to show that legal personality is compatible with enjoying the status of an intelligent machine. The thought experiment also suggests that the corporation can exist as a minded entity without the participation of any human individuals. Furthermore, the corporation has the capacity to flourish because it has values and ends towards which its efforts, resources and policies are directed. To the extent they are realised, its values affirmed or developed in the light of experience it can be regarded as flourishing. This is to echo the ancient sense of flourishing whereby one realises one's nature to the fullest extent.

IV   Corporate Personhood

A further way in which corporations would be distinguished from groups is if corporations were regarded as persons, for groups are not persons. In particular corporations would have a claim in virtue of that personhood to moral agency. Now, arguments for the personhood of corporations have typically assumed that corporations are social groups, and that their personhood distinguishes them from aggregates or other less interesting kinds of groups. For our present purposes the failure of that assumption does not impact on the argument for corporate personhood. Of more significance for the notion that corporations might be classed as persons is the understanding one has of the concept of a person.

On one influential view of persons it is impossible to see how corporations could be persons. On an *animalist* account of persons only an animal can be person. As David Wiggins has put matters:

20 This is a summary of a thought experiment set out by Meir Dan-Cohen (1986). French (1992) p. 140, also refers to this tale in defending a reality theory of legal personhood.
21 Compare French (1992) pp. 140–41.

(P)erhaps *x* is a person if and only if *x* is an animal falling under the extension of a kind whose typical members perceive, feel, remember, imagine, desire, make projects, move themselves at will, speak, carry out projects, acquire a character as they age, are susceptible to concern for members of their own or like species...[note carefully these and subsequent dots] conceive of themselves as perceiving, feeling, ... On this account *person* is a non-biological qualification of *animal*, and, potentially at least a cross-classification with respect to zoological classification across the grain, so to speak, of the evolution based taxonomy.[22]

The animalist approach can be strengthened by the claim that the only firm grasp we have of a person is expressible in terms of a human person. The advocate of corporate personhood must reject this notion of personhood (or argue that a corporation is an animal?).

An alternative approach is suggested by Locke, who defines personhood in a way that does not presuppose an answer to the traditional question of the ontological status of persons. Locke regards person as 'a thinking intelligent being, that has reason and reflection and can consider itself as itself, the same thinking thing in different times and places'.[23] Whatever is to count as a person will satisfy these conditions, and the determination of the domain of persons is thus an empirical rather than a conceptual matter. In this section I shall outline an argument offered by Peter French, which he claims shows that corporations are persons.[24] I doubt that he succeeds, because it is uncertain that he demonstrates corporations possess the intentional and agentive capacity which he takes as the hallmark of personhood, without already presupposing that personhood. Rather than try to settle this matter, I suggest that it may not be full-blown personhood which underwrites aptness for moral agency or provides one of the ways distinguishing corporations from groups. Rather it is their mindedness, and French's account does suggest how a corporation can be taken to be minded.

If corporations are persons, then they have the same moral status as individuals, unless there is a further distinction between 'personhood' and 'moral personhood'. Peter French argues that corporations (in the form of firms) are moral persons. They are to be held accountable, blamed and praised for their actions. They are included in the extension 'person', and as such qualify automatically for the further ascription of 'moral'. French's main concern is to 'examine the sense ascriptions of responsibility make when their subjects are corporations'.[25] It is argued that we do not have a sound grasp on such an ascription unless we take corporations to be moral persons, nor do we have the required remedies against the unjust acts of corporations unless we are prepared to recognise that they have rights and duties *qua* corporation.

---

22 Wiggins (1980) p. 171.
23 Essay, II, xxvii, 2.
24 French (1979; 1983; 1984; 1992).
25 French (1984) p. 32.

Contrasting the identity conditions of corporations[26] with aggregates of persons such as crowds, French argues that the crucial element of a corporation is its internal corporate decision making structure. This permits us to regard it as a noneliminable subject of a responsibility ascription. It is this feature that makes a corporation a moral agent.

> A responsibility ascription ... amounts to an assertion of a conjunctive proposition, the first conjunct of which identifies the subject's actions with or as a cause of an event (usually an untoward one) and the second conjunct asserts that the action in question was intended by the subject or that the event was the direct result of an intentional act of the subject. In addition to what it asserts it implies that the subject is accountable to the speaker (in the case at hand) because of the subject's relationship to the speaker (who the speaker is or what the speaker is, a member of the 'moral community', a surrogate for the aggregate).[27]

To be a moral person, to bear an ascription of responsibility and to stand in responsibility relationships an agent must be an intentional actor. For French 'to be a moral person, the subject must be at a minimum, what I shall call a Davidsonian agent. If corporations are moral persons, they will be non eliminable Davidsonian agents'.[28] To treat a corporation in this way it must be the case that some events are redescribable in a way that make those sentences true which state that the corporation's doings were intended by the corporation itself. Now, if one holds that the actions of a corporation supervene on the intentions and actions of the human agents who compose it, French must locate just such a device of redescription. French claims that the corporate internal decision (CID) structure is precisely the redescription licence of the right sort. At the core of his argument is the referential opacity of attributions of intentions. Thus within the life of a corporation and the lives of its executives the same event (say a board vote and a corporate decision) can be described non-synonymously:

> The referential opacity of intentionality attributions ... is congenial to the driving of a wedge between the descriptions of certain events as individual intentional actions and as corporate intentional actions.[29]

---

26 More exactly he speaks of 'conglomerate' collectivities (1984 p. 13), which are organisations whose identity is not exhausted by the conjunction of the identities of the persons in the organisation. Moreover, conglomerates have characteristics which licence the ascription of responsibility statements to them, which are absent in mere aggregates. The most significant is the possession of an internal decision structure and the adoption of roles within the terms of the conglomerate by individuals. Corporations are paradigm conglomerate collectivities.

27 French (1979) p. 211.

28 Ibid.

29 Ibid., p. 212.

The CID structure enables us to regard the corporation as acting in its own right because it structures the framework of values, ends and intention formation in which executives can operate. It provides this framework and articulates goals because it possesses two elements:

> (i) an organisational system that delineates stations and levels of decision making; and (ii) a set of decision/action recognition rules of two types, procedural and policy. These recognition rules provide the tests that a decision or an action was made for the corporate reasons within the corporate decision structure. The policy recognitors are particularly relevant to the attribution of corporate intentionality ... the organisational structure of a corporation gives the grammar of its decision making, and the recognition rules provide its logic. The CID structure provides a subordination and synthesis of the decisions and acts of various human beings and other intentional systems into a corporate action, an event that under one of its aspects may be truthfully described as having been done for corporate reasons, or to bring about corporate ends, expectations, purposes and so on. [30]

The actions of individuals as members or parts of the corporation are in this way determined by the ends of the corporation, and it is the corporation to which we attribute agency.

Carl Wellman[31] has suggested that it looks as if the action of a corporation is just assumed by French to be the cause of an event. To demonstrate this French needs to show that the cause is an event in the life of a subject. However, it is plausible that Davidson should be understood as stating that intentionality implies personhood only in the sense of presupposing it. While Davidson presents a thesis that agency can be defined in terms of intentional acts, he takes it as given that actions are the doings of persons. Thus Davidson asks: what events in the life of a person reveal agency; what are his deeds and his doings in contrast to mere happenings in his history; what is the mark that distinguishes his actions? To which the answer is: in the case of agency, the proposal might be put: a person is an agent of an event if and only if there is a description of what he did that makes true a sentence that says he did it intentionally.[32]

Wellman's criticism of French concludes that it is insufficient to point to the redescription of a corporation's acts as intentional in order to reveal corporate (moral) personhood, because it must first be shown that a corporation is a person in order to utilise Davidson's conception of action and 'thereby infer the existence of a Davidsonian agent'.[33] In response one may insist that it just leaves open the question of what one means by 'person'. For a person to be a (moral) agent (s)he must exhibit intentionality, evidenced through the way in which the life of that person unfolds. Now, if we assume that a person is also a human being then our question is limited to establishing what makes a human an agent. More strongly,

---

30 French (1992) p. 213.
31 Wellman (1996).
32 Davidson (1971 repr. in Davidson (1980, pp. 43–61)).
33 Wellman (1996) p. 162.

there might be the underlying assumption that only humans can be persons, and that the marks of intentionality can only be recognised as such when exhibited by a certain kind of creature or biological entity. Establishing the domain of persons is precisely the question being investigated, however. Intentional action (as exemplified by, but not necessarily restricted to, human beings) is taken as the salient feature of personhood.

Rather than pressing the point that a corporation is a person in virtue of its CID structure, one should ask what it is about individual (human) persons that endows them with moral agency. Hardly a small or uncontroversial point, but if it turns out that corporations can at least share with persons a necessary property (short of full-blown personhood) of moral agency, then the possibility arises of detaching moral agency from being a person. Or at any rate, it becomes possible that a corporation can be regarded to some degree as a moral agent.[34]

Abstracting to a high level of generality it is clear that a capacity to formulate and adjust goals, to recognise values,[35] and to reflect upon them in light of, say, one's commitments and the state of the world (especially the reaction of other individuals) sets a necessary (and perhaps sufficient) condition for something to be treated as a moral agent. An agent is held accountable for her deeds and proclamations, and in being held accountable she is taken to possess a capacity to respond appropriately to praise and blame. Now, it may be that much more than this is required for personhood. We shall leave that matter to one side, for it would appear that the kind of internal decision making structure French has in mind is capable of organising the flow of information and the formulation of policies and directives in just the way that would warrant an ascription of goal directedness and reflective adjustment to the corporation. In this respect the corporation is minded, and it will structure its activities in a way that permits the ascription to it of intentions, undertakings, and perhaps even of lying and forgetting.

In being minded corporations find another dimension of difference from groups, and the idea of corporations as moral agents is considered further in the next section. For the moment, though, we should consider an aspect of the argument that corporations are minded in virtue of the way in which they are organised. It sounds as if a corporation is a system for handling inputs and issuing appropriate outputs, with a capacity to adjust or revise its organisation in order to maintain its goals and ends. As a model of mindedness it seems to suggest that anything with this information-handling and responsive capacity counts as minded. A thermostat becomes a minded entity, albeit a minimally sophisticated or complex one. Amongst corporations the model does not distinguish between highly complex corporations

---

34 See Chapter 8 for related discussion. Of course, an advocate of corporate moral agency will prefer an argument to show that a corporation can (or does) possess a property taken to be sufficient for the ascription of moral agency.

35 This is meant in a wide sense and is not committed to a 'realist' view of values; whatever one's view of the nature of values, and the status of values within our process of evaluation, we can consider them and their role, whether as, say, Platonists or as Fictionalists.

and those whose sole function is to engage in a single simple operation, such as to own a property or receive dividend payments.

To respect the intuition that neither thermostats nor very simple corporations are minded the model of mindedness needs to be developed to explain that mindedness is a function of the sophistication and complexity of the system. Perhaps, in additon to a functional responsiveness to inputs from the world it would explain mindedness as characterised by a richness in the array of qualitative or phenomenal experience enjoyed by a minded entity. Alternatively, we could allow that thermostats are minded, but that the significance of being minded depends on the sophistication and complexity of the mind. I shall not attempt to flesh out either of these alternatives, nor connect these brief observations to a wider discussion in the philosophy of mind. Rather, I shall move forward on the basis that some corporations are minded in a way that has moral significance.

V   The Character of Moral Experience

Corporations need not then be persons in order to enjoy moral agency, if mindedness is sufficient for that status. Or, if this claim is too strong because mindedness is not on its own sufficient, we can hold that corporations are at least candidates to be regarded to some degree as moral agents.[36] In virtue of a corporation's capacity to act in accordance with goals and to be responsive we are able to locate a corporation in networks of obligations and duties. A corporation has certain aims and acts in order to realise them; criticism or failure, for example, are 'inputs' into its decision making and deliberative structure. They can be assessed and responded to in light of the original aims and the way in which they have shaped that structure. Yet, it may be objected that an essential aspect of moral experience – evaluating, judging, reasoning – is the internal character of that experience. Acts of praising, blaming, admiring, or condemning are typically accompanied and characterised by being experienced or felt by the evaluative and practical thinker in a certain way. States such as guilt, remorse and shame are marked by an affective character. To be subject to that kind of emotion is to be in a complex state of connected beliefs, attitudes and feelings. An act of atonement must be carried out in a true spirit of repentance if it is to be meant: to atone for a wrong, for the destruction of that which was of value, is in part to hold certain beliefs, possess particular attitudes and to be in a distinctive phenomenal state.[37] It would seem that a corporation lacks the affective array required to properly engage in the moral domain.

---

36 We treat children and people who suffer from some kinds of cognitive impairments as capable of bearing moral responsibility to a degree. They are apt for blame and praise, punishment and reward, up to a point. We do not judge them to the same standard as a full-blown moral agent, but we do judge them to a degree appropriate to the ways and extent of their differences, impairments and incapacities.

37 Or so I stipulate here, galloping over virtually the entire debate on the nature of the emotions. What I say reflects the kind of non-reductive account of emotions as complex

One could just deny that corporations are lacking in this way. A 'mad' view allows corporations to share with us the felt emotional experience of judgement and action.[38] A second view is that the phenomenal or affective aspect of moral experience is inessential to the capacity to stand in the relevant forms of relations and to the capacity to respond in the appropriate fashion. The capacity to obey the moral law is enough.[39]

An inner life, partly characterised by moral emotions, is one of the hallmarks of a person. For one of the ways in which a person is attached to a world of others is through her sentiments. At the same time morality imposes certain requirements on how we respond to each other, sometimes regardless of how we may feel. That is, there is an obvious external dimension to our moral relations in the form of action, which is appropriate in light of our values, practices and expectations. If one has been justly criticised or one is rightly remorseful, then it is not enough to experience the appropriate emotion. One's goals and actions must be calibrated in light of that criticism or remorse, lest one fail as a morally responsive agent. The lack of an inner life does not prevent a corporation from responding in the right way in as far as it is engaging with others.

The criticism that corporations cannot possess the proper moral emotions can be generalised. A corporation lacks the inner life of the subjective viewpoint, rich in its beliefs, pro-attitudes qualia and affective states. This may be a telling criticism of a thesis of corporate personality, but the more restricted notion of mindedness, with its commitment to goal directedness and reflective capacity, does not seem prey to it. Corporations are not persons, but they can respond to judgements. They can undertake the burdens of obligations and duties because they act within the framework of goals, responsive to and adjustable in light of the content of the commitments they have taken on. We should also note that a corporation may also be insincere. In the pursuit of its goals it may be structured in a way that means it systematically seeks to mislead those with whom it deals. A terrorist organisation may state that it regrets certain actions, but such a statement is just a strategic move dictated by its goals, commitments and the way in which these are articulated through its organisational

---

(psychological) states due to for example Goldie (2000). On an alternative view emotions can be analysed as cognitive states which contingently are accompanied by certain feelings.

38 Compare the possibility of a group mind discussed in Chapter 3. If corporations are distinct from groups in the ways noted, then one could not rely on that account to explain the corporate experience of emotions. Taking a corporation to be an instantiated set of rules, one would just stipulate that it can *feel* particular emotions, perhaps through the way in which its rules and organising principles are structured in relation to each other. For as long as we are talking about the felt experience of an emotion as we understand it, it is difficult to grasp how a corporation would be able to *experience* it. One might respond by analysing emotions in terms of inputs to a system and function within it.

39 For certain kinds of creatures it may be necessary that they have a certain affective dimension, array and responsiveness in order to recognise and be motivated by the moral facts.

structure. The statement of regret may be a response to criticism, but it does not reflect an actual adjustment of goals, values or policies.

Finally, we should consider whether a corporation is the kind of thing that can be punished. Moral agency means that one stands in reciprocal relations with other agents, an aspect of which is to bear the burden of just retribution, or at any rate measures aimed at reforming or correcting attitudes. An inability on the part of, say, a church or business corporation to respond to warranted criticism and to bear the punishment of its wicked actions seems to rule it out as a moral agent. We may continue to have duties towards it and it may have rights, but we judge it as we would a person who is impaired in some way that prevents her from engaging with us in practical and evaluative reasoning.

Such a failure of responsiveness defines an extreme, though. We are often reluctant to acknowledge the nature of our deeds, goals and attitudes and must be brought to see their disvalue. As persons we can be conducted along a route by an appeal to our sentiments; we may be brought to share with an interlocutor an evaluational perspective from which we are able to adjust our attitudes. A corporation may lack the internal affective array through which, say, the experiencing of the feeling of shame can bring it to fresh moral insights. However, if its decision making structure is sufficiently responsive, then its failure to achieve certain of its goals, or the inconsistent commitments entailed by its goals, or the gap between goal and actions can figure within its decision making structure as inputs imposing certain pressures within its (logical) structure and internal relations – we might say as reasons – to adjust and develop goals or systems. A corporation may lack the fluttering of sentiment in its breast, but in being responsive to the failings and inconsistencies that provoke certain affective responses in us, there appears an analogue in the moral dialogue one can sustain with a corporation.

The attribution of personhood to corporations has sometimes been taken to enable one to explain their status as moral agents and, suitably qualifying their properties *qua* persons, the role of corporations in the transmission of norms and values and the unity of generations. However, if the capacity to sustain judgements and to be an appropriate target of criticism depends on (some degree of) mindedness – goal directedness, reflective capacity and responsiveness – then the pressure to regard corporations as persons diminishes. Strip the corporation of its putative personhood, and we shall be left with its mind and the character of that mind. I have suggested that the cognitive and affective array that mark us out as persons, as perhaps do certain biological and evolutionary properties, are not necessary to be regarded as a moral agent – at least to some degree (although they may explain why for us certain reasons acquire a priority within our practical reasoning). It may be that the denial of corporate personhood brings us closer to a conception of metaphysical personhood due to Boethius: a person is an individual subsistence of a rational nature. The corporate soul is then its minded capacity, and this is a soul devoid of the inner aspects that define for us the personal standpoint. Nonetheless, the corporate soul is the source of the organising principles, goals and values that shape much of our lives, inspiring, *inter alia*, love, hatred, devotion and the pained indifference of lapsed membership.

Chapter 6

The Moral Status of Social Groups

I   Introduction

Social groups are composite material particulars individuated in virtue of their causal and explanatory role, and this understanding and treatment of them is consistent with our general taxonomic practices. In the remaining chapters I turn to a consideration of the way in which groups figure in our evaluative and practical reasoning. I do not attempt a comprehensive analysis of the appropriate way to understand the role of groups in our forms of moral discourse, a task too sweeping in scope to accomplish within the present context. Rather, an examination is undertaken of how we might begin to go about making sense of our references to groups in moral discourse. The starting point is our everyday, legal and social scientific talk in which groups are often treated as if they are the kind of things to which we can owe obligations, which can possess rights, and which we can evaluate and judge as being morally responsible. If we are to take this talk at face value, then we must show that groups are indeed apt to be treated in such ways.

The ontological holism defended earlier does not entail any commitments about the moral treatment or analysis of groups. Only if materiality were a sufficient condition for an entity to be an object of moral consideration in its own right would the materiality of groups compel us to take at face value the appearance of groups in much of our moral discourse. Materiality does not seem to be such a condition with respect to moral consideration, not least because of our moral stance towards material objects such as tables. Equally, if it is determined that groups are not apt to be regarded as proper sources of obligations, the holders of rights, or the bearers of moral responsibility, then this would not undercut ontological holism. The consideration of the moral status and role of groups does presuppose holism in the acceptance that groups exist *qua* bodies, but the arguments for groups being regarded as apt for moral status, rights and responsibility are independent of that ontological background presupposition.

The dialectical relationship between ontological and moral parts of the analysis of groups is one of illumination and support. Ontological holism provides the background and framework in which moral questions about groups can be discussed. Ontological individualism simply rules out any prospect of saving the appearances of a significant swathe of our moral discourse. Allowing that there are groups for reasons independent of our moral considerations, permits an examination of the status, treatment and role of groups within morality to be conducted in terms of moral theory. To the extent that ontological individualism is motivated by an abhorrence of according moral status or dignity to collectives, particularly when this constitutes a threat to individuals, then that motivating reason needs to find a more effective vehicle than a flawed ontological thesis. For on the face of things it does seem natural to expect morality to protect individual persons, and amongst the threats an individual encounters in the pursuit of her life are the demands of groups upon her and others. This is merely a rough statement of an intuition. However, it is an intuition ontological holists and individualists can share, and one which the former are in a better position to delineate because they can recognise groups. The relationship between the ontological and moral claims is also supportive, because the analysis of plausible bases for recognising groups as sources of obligations, the holders of rights and the bearers of responsibility rights relies upon the identification of relations between individuals, which are also group-constituting ones.

Just as the truth of ontological holism carries no entailments with respect to the moral status of groups, so the denial that groups can have moral status, rights or responsibilities does not reduce or undermine the plausibility of ontological holism. After all, I owe no obligations or duties to the desk at which I am writing, it can sustain no moral judgements, nor can it possess rights. Nonetheless, I am committed to its material reality, and although I have no moral connection to it through my writing, the desk certainly figures in an explanatory account of how this passage has come to be produced. Our best explanations, for example, of why the governance of early modern European states was characterised by (say for the sake of argument) the consolidation of elite power around the institution of absolute monarchy, or of why the Nazis rose to power, may cite the role, character and practices of social groups. Thus in explaining the development of absolute monarchy in France we may need to look at the values and practices of the emerging bourgeois class in seventeenth century France as the best account for the availability of mechanisms and background conditions for certain states of affairs or events. Perhaps a truly evil individual, or a saint, can only emerge from a culture in which there are certain forms of practices and concepts available. Such a man is in that sense very much a product of his group. However, from explanatory and descriptive indispensability we cannot infer a moral capacity to generate obligations, bear responsibility or hold rights on the part of a group. If we were to become convinced that our moral references to groups were systematically in error,[1] then an explanation for this might be located in a conflation of the causal and explanatory role of groups with the kind of role that can only be attributed to entities capable of sustaining certain kinds of moral predications and judgements.

Nonetheless, we have no reason to assume *ab initio* that this kind of systematic error is being made, or that there is implicit knowledge that talk of obligations to a group, group responsibilities and rights is really decomposable into the obligations, responsibilities and rights of individuals taken apart from their membership(s). The

---

1   Except when functioning as shorthand.

task of this and the next two chapters is to suggest reasons why it is at least plausible to take our moral references to groups at face value. This treatment of groups depends upon presupposing certain positions in moral theory, which are supportable but by no means uncontested. In line with the restricted scope of the investigation I do not argue for these presuppositions against rival positions. Rather, to the extent that the attribution of moral status, rights or accountability to groups depends on a certain position within moral theory, acceptance of that moral position indicates (part of) the price one must pay to hold a particular view of groups.

In the present chapter I argue that groups can possess moral status. A group is the kind of entity towards or in virtue of which we can have obligations or duties. The primary reason for this is the importance and value to a group's members of irreducibly social goods, prominent amongst which may be the practices through which the group is constituted and the good of membership itself. To maintain that groups can possess moral status is a relatively weak claim, since many other entities may be said to have moral status – for example, beautiful paintings, eco-systems and the dead. To possess moral status is to gain entry to the moral domain, but it does not necessarily undercut the priority of individual persons in our practical reasoning. The issues of whether and in what sense a group may possess rights and be held morally accountable in its own rights are addressed in the next two chapters. Building on the notion of irreducibly social goods to be elucidated in the present chapter, I go on in Chapter 7 to suggest that a harm-based account of rights can make sense of the claim that a group has a right against coercive intervention. The loss of some goods can be so destructive to what is of value in the lives of a group's membership, that they together *qua* body have a claim on others in the form of a right. Next I ask whether, given that groups are not persons, nor obviously minded to any significant degree, there is any intuitively plausible basis for regarding groups as apt for assessment in terms of moral responsibility. I suggest that a group can possess a capacity for collective deliberation, which may provide a basis for ascribing some degree of moral responsibility to a group.

II   Moral Status

A group can possess moral status: a group can figure in its own right in our moral evaluations and practical reasoning, being amongst those things towards or in virtue of which we may have obligations and duties. A group enjoys moral status because of the role of the group-constituting relations, practices and ends in the formation of the character, goals and well-being of its members. It therefore follows that moral status is not entailed by grouphood, since there can be groups which do not stand in the appropriate kind of relationship with their members. I defend the view that groups can have moral status against moral individualism, which holds that there are moral reasons for considering only individuals as being the sources and objects of obligations and duties. I have employed the notion of a group being recognised or treated 'as such' or as an entity 'in its own right'. Now, one might ask what exactly does it mean for a group to have moral status in *its own right*? For a group to possess moral status others' concerns, evaluations and policies are directed at individuals considered together – as *them*. Furthermore, some of an individual person's own claims can only be made (or are only claimable) as *ours*. Concern for the needs, values, or well-being of an individual group member can sometimes only find expression by taking *their* – the member and her peers – needs and values as linked, as coming as a single package, in which some of the needs or goals of any one person are identified with those which are only expressible collectively. *My* demands can sometimes only be expressed as *our* demands. Sometimes it is not possible in practice to avoid harming others, but, *ceteris paribus*, it is possible to give their interests and needs consideration in our practical deliberations. It is in being considered in the balancing of obligations and duties that something's moral status finds expression, not only in its *prima facie* legitimate claims on others actually being honoured and acted upon in practice.

As noted earlier, the account of the moral status of groups is modest. Many kinds of things might possess moral status. Mary Midgley, for example, has provided a list of seventeen entities to which persons may be held to sometimes have moral obligations.[2] Her list begins with 'the dead', takes in all living (not just sentient) entities, artefacts (including works of art), groups (including families and species), countries, ecosystems and the biosphere. It also includes (at number two) 'posterity', suggesting (along with the dead?) that non-material entities can also have moral status. The case for the moral status of any particular kind of entity must be made on its own merits. Nonetheless, the very weakness of the nature of moral status does support the view that its possession could be widespread. It is weak in the sense that its possession is defined in terms of being the kind of an entity *towards or in virtue of* which one may have obligations or duties. This is, so to speak, just an entry pass into the moral domain, bringing objects of a certain kind as ends in their own right within the scope of evaluative and practical deliberation. It does not, though, obviously undercut the liberal presumption of basic individual rights possessed by persons, and the special place they have in practical reasoning, nor does it inform our judgements on whether something can be held morally accountable. An entity with moral status does not necessarily have, say, rights nor must it be capable of sustaining evaluations such as being 'praise or blameworthy'. After all, we may have duties towards infants and severely mentally impaired human beings, and in respect of beautiful paintings, without considering such things to be rights-holders or moral agents.

In talking about morality in a very general way, I make no attempt to draw any distinction between 'morality' as rule based and 'ethics' as a way of being or outlook. Broadly speaking, I regard morality as constructed through our interactions, our reasoned scrutiny of values and principles for consistency, the evaluation of new standards and information, and as embedded in our practices. Morality is indeed a

---

2   Her list is noted in Warren (1997) pp. 173–4, who endorses the diversity of the moral domain as part of her of a multi-criterial approach to moral status, in which a range of considerations are brought into play and balance.

practice, or perhaps a complex family of practices, in being what we do in making particular forms of evaluations, such as whether that person or thing or state of affairs is 'good' or 'valuable' or 'praiseworthy' (or not). To engage in this practice one must be sensitive to the law-like dimension of morality. We not only possess standards of evaluation, but act under the constraint of commands or injunctions. We act appropriately in responding to these 'laws' by respecting them when they enjoin us to do what is possible; and by calibrating our responsiveness to them in light of our evaluative standards. Through the practices of morality we exhibit a moral or ethical attitude. I take a primitive feature of human interrelations to be the capacity to feel, and the tendency to exhibit concern for other persons, albeit circumscribed by context, the proximity of the others and self-interest. Such sympathy is, of course, a crucial element in Humean moral genealogy, and if fully explored amounts to a sophisticated thesis in moral and social psychology. The point here is that our main focus in arriving at judgements and decisions to act is on the needs of others. While the notion of having a concern for others certainly includes being concerned *for* their well-being, it should also be taken as a concern that the evaluation of and response to the individual be appropriate. Given this essentially 'anthropological' view of morality, it may be argued that one reason to respect groups is that the law, custom or tradition tells us to do so. This will not suffice, however, because laws, customs and traditions do not stand outside of our practices but are elements within them. Even if we are called upon to obey or value our groups, we can only find reason to justify our respect if it is consistent within the body of our practices.

I take it, then, that sympathy, a responsiveness to the situation and needs of others, albeit partial and imperfect, is central in our evaluative and practical thinking. Granted this, a reason to respect a social group in its own right is located in its capacity to endure suffering or experience value distinct from that suffered by any of its members alone.[3] The assault on (or promotion of) the institutions and practices of a group generate harms (goods) for each of the members. Each may endure a personal pain or see new opportunities arise for her. In addition to all of the isolable harms endured by each member, there may be one common to them all, producible in virtue of their being together as a group. The harm or good can only arise when the group – its practices, traditions, language and goals – is targeted or marked out (intentionally or not) for 'special treatment' by others.

In considering why a group can possess moral status, I presuppose the centrality of a responsiveness to the needs of other persons in a moral or ethical attitude. When we think of attacks on particular groups it is commonplace or natural to talk of the harm done to such groups. We identify the needs of the groups, consider the obligations others may have towards or in respect of them, and even frame discussion of the groups in terms of their rights. Consider, for example, the periodic expulsions

---

3   There is a parallel here with aesthetic judgements and judgements about the value of non-persons. Each flower in a bed of flowers may be valauble in itself, and perhaps even have moral status. At the same time the flowers *qua* bed may also be valuable and possess moral status.

of Jewish communities in the Middle Ages, the pogroms directed against Russian Jewish communities in the late nineteenth century, and the genocide of the Jews and others in the Third Reich; the forced conversion of the Moslem population in sixteenth-century Spain; the systematic discrimination of Apartheid South Africa; the claims made by, and on behalf of, Blacks, Hispanics, Whites, Women, Men, Homosexuals, Heterosexuals and so on in the United States. I suggest we are not disconcerted when, say, a religious body claims it has the need to establish schools because *it* makes the suggestion. Nor does it appear unusual to talk of the demands made by ethnic or cultural groups or gender or sexual orientation based groups for cultural or political autonomy, or for a distribution of resources or the allocation of legal rights and entitlements. We may not agree, but nothing seems out of place with this 'group-talk'. It prompts the sense that there are harms and needs in addition to those of each individual considered alone, that a group can have needs, wants and goods. The tenability of this kind of claim is not guaranteed by the failure of ontological individualism. The attribution of moral status to groups is opposed by a distinctly moral thesis, moral individualism, which maintains there are moral reasons to deny that we have obligations or duties towards, or in virtue of, groups. I suggest that this thesis be rejected because a moral or ethical attitude sensitive to the needs and claims of individuals leads us to recognise the *sui generis* needs of their groups.

Imagine that a decent, democratic liberal government terminates the economic and infrastructural support necessary for the survival of a rural community. It may no longer feel able to justify to its other citizens the disproportionate *per capita* expenditure. The village dies and its folk move to the towns and cities. The mixture of personal suffering at the loss of the way of life and the hope of new opportunities varies across individuals. It is not clear that they have been wronged, perhaps merely unfortunate that consideration of overall fairness has stemmed the flow of resources to this particular community. Yet a dimension of the way in which each individual has been harmed or benefited relates to the dissolution of the group constituted by a particular way of life, a network of practices. There is a sense in which *we* are no more, and that this is a harm or good which can only be produced and experienced in virtue of one's membership of a group. To care or exhibit concern for an individual in certain contexts requires us to take her and her peers together as a unit; to understand that *her* needs, values or demands are *theirs*.

III   Moral Individualism

Moral individualism is a thesis about which entities deserve moral consideration, eliminating groups (and other non-persons) from the domain of those entities which can have moral status. The tension between the group and individual in our thinking can be dissolved by regarding talk of the moral status of groups and policies directed at them as metaphorical in form and instrumental in intent. Thus the individuation of a people as worthy of self-determination or the levying of reparations from a nation come to be justified by moral concern for individuals considered severally.

There is a reasonableness to the inidividualist claim. For it seems to express the importance of the individual in our moral deliberations without forcing us to abandon the recognition of non-persons in those deliberations. A representative statement of moral individualism is found in Kant, who believed that:

> A human being can [therefore] have no duties to any beings other than human beings; and if he thinks he has such duties, it is because of an *amphiboly* in his *concepts of reflection*, and his supposed duty to other beings is only a duty to himself. He is led to this misunderstanding by mistaking his duty *with regard to* other beings for a duty *to* those beings.[4]

Under this view it remains possible for a person to be under a duty to act in a certain way with respect to non-persons, such as animals or groups (as far as I know Kant does not talk about groups in this context). However, such a duty would be neither to nor (solely) in virtue of the nature or needs of the entity in question.

A differently motivated case for moral individualism grounded in a concern for individual well-being is illustrated by 'welfarism', which has been characterised as the claim that '(M)orality is fundamentally a matter of the well-being of individuals'.[5] It is held that welfarism comprises three theses:

> Existence Thesis: there is such a good or value as individual well-being. Significance thesis: some individual well-being has moral significance, *qua* individual well-being. Exclusiveness thesis: individual well-being is the *only good or value which has basic moral significance*.[6]

Christopher McMahon has addressed directly the question of whether groups can have moral status, and, in arguing against such a position, suggests that:

> organisations, and other social entities – viewed as distinct from their members – are not appropriately accorded moral consideration in their own right … over and above that accorded to the human beings who are their members.[7]

Such a view does not mean that coherent moral questions about the group *qua* entity are exhausted by the prioritisation of the individual over group in our practical reasoning. We may still ask about the needs of the group, balancing its considerations against those of the individuals, but inevitably deferring action until the satisfaction of the latters' needs. According to McMahon, moral individualism maintains that 'even if there are no metaphysical objections to talking about the good

---

4   *The Metaphysics of Morals* Episodic Section, section 16.
5   Moore and Crisp (1996) p. 598.
6   Ibid. My emphasis.
7   McMahon (1994) p. 62.

of an organisation or social entity, it can have no bearing on what morality requires'.[8] For McMahon the only morally relevant properties a group could possess supervene on the properties of its members, as do its other properties. Consideration of the individual person rules out according groups moral status. As he sees matters:

> (T)he central fact about organisational morality is that even if organisations are distinct moral agents, their actions supervene on the behaviour of agents of another sort *who are also moral agents*. But the direction of necessitation in a supervenience relation is from the bottom up. What happens at the lower level determines what happens at the higher level. The moral analogue of this is that what ought to happen at the lower level determines what ought to happen at the higher level ... the principles that apply at the lower level determine how the system as a whole should or may behave. This is because the individuals in the supervenience basis are appropriately guided by principles which apply to beings of a different kind, and what they do determines what an organisation does.[9]

What a group may do reflects what individuals are permitted to do; a group can only be said to have interests and goals to the extent that they cohere with its members'. Moral individualism is characterised by the assumption that the moral standing of the individual is not altered or influenced by the engagement together of individuals in, for example, certain practices, the sharing of particular attitudes and the endorsement of common ends or values. That is, being a member of a group plays no morally salient role in how one ought to regard that individual, and in particular how one ought to regard the individual in relation to her fellow members. But this is precisely the point at issue, and the focus of my disagreement with moral individualism.

There are needs, harms and values which individuals can only experience, suffer, enjoy and claim together. They have an irreducibly social character or shape. A concern for the individual partly consists in recognising the moral status of the groups of which she is a member, as well as respecting her status as simply a person. Moral individualism presupposes that the (group-constituting) interrelations in which individuals stand possess no moral import, save in the way in which they might contribute to some set of basic moral criteria already understood in individualistic terms, or affect means-end reasoning through the capacity of a group to do things an individual can not. The interests, goals and character of the individual may in part be determined or shaped by those interrelations and her relationship with the group as a whole – with the practices established and maintained by her and the others. To respect the individual may sometimes entail that our response is directed at the group. The force of moral individualism rests on an assumption that individuals have a unitary and atomistic moral status. That is, the individual can always be considered in isolation from others in a way that captures what it is to respect her. Moral individualism begins from a commitment to the moral significance of the

---

8   Ibid.
9   McMahon (1994) p. 68. (McMahon's emphasis). McMahon makes it clear that by organisation he is referring to social groups in general.

individual person. That commitment is not in dispute. What is at issue is how we substantiate that commitment in our practices and attitudes.

IV   Irreducibly Social Goods and Harms

A group is morally considerable when it is the necessary locus for the production and the source of the enjoyment of values (or the suffering of disvalues), which are irreducibly tied to the interrelations of its members. Some of the ways in which individuals interrelate in the formation and maintenance of a group both generate values and depend upon the enjoyment and recognition of those values. The proscription or destruction of a group's practices and institutions can produce a harm that can only be suffered as a member. The nurturing and encouragement of such practices can furnish a good, enjoyment of which depends upon membership of the group.[10] It is only within or through a group that certain goods and harms can arise to enrich or blight the lives of the individuals who constitute that group. In such cases, for a practice or its loss to be a good or harm for me, it must also be a good or harm for my fellow members. It is in its collective production and enjoyment (or enduring) that the goodness or badness of a practice or its loss inheres.[11]

Charles Taylor identifies a class of goods or values as 'irreducibly social', rather than merely 'convergent',[12] and Jeremy Waldron a 'deeper' kind of public good, a communal good.[13] Certain goods such as the provision of utilities, a clean environment and a secure defence of one's home are public by being non-excludable, non rivalrous and jointly produced. They cannot be designed or delivered so as to benefit some to the exclusion of others. The enjoyment of the good by one or some persons cannot compete with its enjoyment by others; and the good can only be produced through the co-operation, agreement, or at least passive acquiescence of most of its potential subjects. Here we can think of the benefits produced by the operation of a dam, which provides a community with power and water. Indeed, the presence of the dam may be the crucial factor in allowing a community to exist in its particular form. Yet these goods are public merely in the sense that if any one enjoys them then all can. An individual acting alone could in principle secure such goods for herself. Their generation does not require (of logical necessity) interaction between individuals. They are as a matter of fact jointly produced, not necessarily

---

10 Of course other harms or goods may also be generated which are not social.

11 Sometimes the destruction of certain institutions or practices, though painful to the members of a group can be a good thing. A group may perpetrate evil, for example by valuing the oppression and exploitation of others.

12 In the discussion that follows I have in mind the arguments Taylor sets out in his analysis of the resources of 'mainstream' anglophone liberalism to address the diagnoses of so called communitarians and the challenges of multi-culturalism. In particular, 'Irreducibly Social Goods'; 'Cross Purposes: The Liberal Communitatrian Debate'; 'The Politics of Recognition'; all repr. in Taylor (1997).

13 Waldron (1993).

constituted through the engagement together of individuals in certain practices or ways of life.

Some practices and goals, which are generated collectively, depend for their enjoyment or recognition as goods on individuals participating as members of a group. In a case such as the conviviality generated at a party, to cite an example of Waldron's, 'the individual experiences are unintelligible apart from their reference to the enjoyments of others. For me to enjoy the conviviality is partly for me to be assured that others are enjoying it too'.[14] This is a feature also true of the fraternity and solidarity of shared membership of a tribe or religious congregation, the value of shared cultural practices experienced in the context of a wider group such as a people. The enjoyment of each individual is isolable, in the sense that the enjoyment is experienced by this particular person, and that experience has for its subject a directly accessible subjective quality. However, the character or nature of the enjoyment is as an instance of, say, conviviality or fraternity. The source of the experience, its basis and the grounds upon which we would regard the individual as warranted in having it, is the form and nature of the group practices. In particular, it is how things are with the group, with the membership as a whole, that determines how things are with the individual in certain contexts. There can be no account of the worth of the good without reference to its worth to everyone together. For example, the pride or satisfaction a person may feel at observing a road sign in his (e.g. minority status) native tongue refers beyond the individual experience to 'the fact that there is something whose nature and value make sense only on the assumption that others are enjoying and participating in it too'.[15]

An irreducibly social good is not merely brought about by collective action, attitudes and goals, but is partially constituted by its being the subject of a common understanding of its value and meaning. Moreover, the enjoyment or value of the good is not decomposable into its several enjoyment by a disjunction of individuals. Each member of a community may value the dam which protects it from flooding and provides power, or the provision of roads, but the value is not something which resides in a common space between individuals. Its value is not understood as something that is valuable for us together, but rather for each individually. This contrasts with a social good, such as friendship or fraternity or cultural membership. For with this kind of good, 'it exists not just for me and you, but for us, acknowledged as such'.[16]

That a good is *ours* is linked to its possessing value at all. Relations such as those of love, friendship, fraternity, equality, being part of the same people or cultural group, can be valued as goods in themselves only where such a relation is the subject of a common understanding of its nature. As Taylor notes we cannot stand on an equal footing with one another unless there is some common understanding and recognition of what this is and why it is of value:

14 Waldron (1993) pp. 355–6.
15 Ibid., p. 358.
16 Taylor (1997) p. 139.

The footing does not exist unless there is some common sense that we are equal, that we command equal treatment, that this is the appropriate way to deal with each other.[17]

The practices of a group can thus be expressive of a range of goods, the production of which reflects a common understanding of their value.[18] Now, of course, it is the individual person who enjoys the value of fraternity, or the practices of being a member of a congregation, tribe or people. Yet, it is something that the individual can only generate and/or enjoy with others, either directly engaging with them or through the mediation of ceremony, institutions, conventions and so on. Indeed, I cannot, for example, be a friend nor participate in a culture if I am not engaged in some fashion with others.[19]

(Having stressed their distinctiveness, one nonetheless ought to be wary of overemphasising the distinction between irreducibly social and convergent goods. Very often the value of a convergent good (for example security) is in part identified in its value to us together. It can be valued by us together because of its role in preserving our way of life. Of course it might also be valued on a several basis by each agent because it affords him (alone) protection for his singular schemes. Individuals can hold a plurality of motives and values, shaped in the constant interplay between the individual and the groups of which she is a member. However, by recognising the distinction between the kind of goods one avoids a confusion which leads to a presupposition in favour of moral individualism – the position that is at issue in considering the question of the moral status of groups).

In identifying this class of goods, we find a reason to consider the group as such in our moral thinking. The production and enjoyment of irreducibly social goods are integral to the engagement together of agents in certain activities or practices which are expressive of the value of those goods, or presuppose that value. As a member of a group the goods and ends which we value figure as important with me. To accord

---

17 Ibid.

18 Taylor in 'Irreducibly Social Goods' talks of two ways of defining irreducibly social goods. First is by reference to their role in making certain actions, practices etc. conceivable. Second is by reference to their incorporation of common understandings of their value. He goes on to note that both features are probably mutually dependent, with neither perhaps being able to survive the demise of the other. There may be a stronger connection between the two dimensions of the irreducibly social good. Certain ways of living or practices or feelings which irreducibly social goods make conceivable are *our* ways. The individual values them at least partly because they are constitutive of his being part of the group. It is valuable to him to participate in the life of the group, not merely for any instrumental purpose, but, partly, just because that form of engagement is valuable in itself. There is a direct connection between the conceivability of an action or practice and its being valued.

19 One can ask whether the last member of a group belongs to or participates in the practices or culture of the group. If a person really is the 'last of ... ', then one remains connected to the group through the attitudes, practices and values which have been transmitted to him through his past contact within the group. One may no longer be engaging with fellow members, but one has engaged with them in the past, and through the continued influence of practices and beliefs one remains attached to the group and its past membership.

me moral respect, it must be recognised that *qua* moral subject I am tied to other persons through membership of the group in a web of relations spun by and around the goods for which we (may potentially) demand recognition. If I make a claim that we be permitted to, for example, enjoy a measure of cultural autonomy, or that referees treat my team fairly, then that demand cannot be respected or evaluated as a series of individual demands, each of which is capable of being discretely satisfied. In so far as each person is to be accorded consideration in respect of this kind of claim, the members must all be taken together. The irreducibly social nature of certain goods and their production by individuals standing in relationships aimed at and fostered by those goods give us reason to regard the group, and not only each individual, as the appropriate focus of moral consideration.

I have suggested that a group has moral status when it is the source of irreducibly social goods and harms. It may be objected, though, that this is to misunderstand the relationship between judgements and policies citing the group and irreducibly social goods. It may be that we are only justified in treating groups *as if* they had moral status on purely instrumental grounds. Groups are treated as if they had moral status as a means of securing for individuals the needs which respect for each person demands.[20]

It is my concern for her, which motivates recognition of the group. Does this not sound like an instrumental relationship between individual and group? Yet, for the role of the group to be instrumental it must be the case that the goal aimed at in using the group could in principle be achieved in some other way.[21] In respecting the individual's needs and the significance to her of certain group practices, goals or values, one cannot eliminate the group, for the practices which we recognise as important are irreducibly connected to it, in being partly constitutive of it. The needs and values important to the individual are only produced or realised through his engagement with others. To respect or respond to these needs of an individual one must respond to the individual and his peers together – to them. The moral target at which we aim is to respect individuals appropriately. In certain contexts we respect them *qua* members. Respect for an individual person partly consists in recognition of the group's moral status. For example, to accept or reject a group's claim that it be accorded a degree of cultural autonomy in the form of language rights is to treat its members together by giving or denying them the relevant resources and entitlements. My need to be part of certain form of community is respected by acknowledgement of that community.

Of course, I may love my friend and respect her membership of a group, but deplore its values and ends. It hardly seems to be the case that I only respect her

---

20 The criticism that assignment of moral status to a group is only ever instrumental assumes the burden of explaining the end or goal being secured by such a treatment of the group, and of showing that it could be attained in some alternative fashion.

21 In practice there may only be one way known to achieve a certain desired end, but it remains instrumental since one would replace it if a more efficacious alternative were available.

through recognising her group. Yet, my concern, praise or criticism cannot attain an appropriate shape or direction if the group does not figure in my judgement. My understanding of her incorporates my judgement of the group. Of course, sometimes love or faith or loyalty can be blind. This does not mean that I cannot, or do not, judge the group, but that my relationship provides reasons to undermine judgements I make of her in virtue of that membership. Moreover, because of the bond with her I may come to fail to act as I ought with respect to the group, but this does not deny it moral status.

V   The Explanation of Harms

Moral individualism appears a counter-intuitive doctrine when one considers the way in which it must explain the apparently warranted claim of an individual to have been harmed or neglected morally because of the way in which her group has been treated. A person, *P*, may feel that she has been harmed if another member(s), *Q*, of her group is attacked or ill-treated when the attack is motivated by the fact that the victim(s), *Q*, is a member of that group. Moreover, the sense that a harm has been endured by *P* need not have as its correlate the likelihood of *P* suffering the same kind of attack or treatment as *Q*. For example, Kurds living in liberal democratic states in which the rule of law is firmly established would have no grounds to feel personally endangered by the state by reports that Kurds are suffering state repression elsewhere because of their group membership. Nonetheless, the Kurd in London may claim that he suffers when Kurds are attacked and practices proscribed in say, Turkey. Practices and ways of being which are valuable, a group of which he is part, are placed under threat and as a member he suffers.[22]

A natural way of explaining why a person regards herself as harmed when there is an attack on one or more of her group, even though there is no direct threat to her, is because the attack is against her group. It is directed at the group because the individual(s) attacked is singled out for that treatment in virtue of her membership. To attack this person(s) is to signal (at a minimum) hostility towards the group as such. An attack on an individual can be at once a personal misfortune and an assault on his group; the harms generated are personal and collective.[23] As members of a

---

22 It does not appear necessary that he need have family or immediate links there. Groups can be dispersed and yet retain a sense of being *this* group through practices and traditions which both maintain the values of the group and provide a common basis for membership and interaction. The idea or goal of a homeland can play a significant role in these practices – consider Judaism and the Jewish Diaspora, but it need not – consider the Roma as a culture or people.

23 Part of being a member of a particular group may be to care about fellow members in a way, or with an intensity, that one does not direct at non-members. Partiality of this kind may underpin a concern for members, so that even when there is no (real) danger to me or to the group, I experience the discomfort of concern and even anguish for the fate of others, because we are together members of the group.

group we have a claim on others not to impose that kind of harm onto us as a group, in addition to the claim each of us has as an individual not to be assaulted.

Moral individualism does not explain why an individual feels she has been harmed as a member. Moral individualism cannot allow that a person can suffer *qua* member, because then it is no longer able to establish a basis for holding that a group – the members considered together – cannot possess moral status. If a Jew in London claims to be harmed when Jews in Russia are attacked, then moral individualism cannot appeal to the fact that the Londoner's harm is grounded in shared membership. As a Jew he suffers because the group is being picked on. If he is harmed as a member, then we/they are all (potentially) harmed. The group becomes the object of moral concern. The abuse of members of a group, *G*, in country *A* is a harm endured by members everywhere. It may be that we should be concerned first to attend to the persons in country *A* suffering direct personal abuse. There remains, nonetheless, the harm that we all can endure because our group, its practices and values are being subjected to attack. It is plausible to look to duties or obligations owed to a group in virtue of the harms its members can endure collectively as an appropriate response, but this is exactly the path blocked by moral individualism.

Moral individualism could just deny that a person, *P*, does experience any harm when a fellow member, *Q*, is attacked for being a member in a context in which there is no direct threat to *P*. I doubt that such a flat denial accords with experience. People do express concern and profess to suffer harms when other members of their group are singled out for hostile treatment elsewhere. Granted the implausibility of a flat denial, individualism does better to argue that a person suffers harm, but that it is not grounded in her membership of the group. Rather, the suffering of a harm is just a matter of the subjective feelings of the individual. A Jew in London suffers on learning the news that a Jew has been attacked by anti-Semites in another country, but this is just an emotional response to a particular piece of news. Moral individualism does not acknowledge the moral significance of individuals constituting a group, and the values attached to its practices and plain existence, and therefore it is unable to rationalise the emotions the London Jew experiences. He is just upset or worried, but individualism cannot explain his state in terms of his membership.

Of course there may be a story about the particular individual which would explain his emotional response as rational. However, that individual story would not obviously generalise into an explanatory account of how individuals can come to be exposed to a certain class of harms. Not all Jews will necessarily be upset on learning of attacks on fellow members, but a membership account of certain harms provides a mechanism through which individual experiences can be explained. Furthermore, the individualist account of the harm may be likely to fail to accord with the individual's own explanation. The individual may explain his being harmed in the following way. 'I am harmed as a Jew. My distress has arisen because I am a Jew. The attack on this stranger, who is a Jew too, is also an attack on us – the Jews'. Individuals are not necessarily the best source of explanations for their motivations, attitudes and actions. Nonetheless, the account I favour of the moral status of groups allows this *prima facie* rational explanation to be just that: an individual making a rational assessment of why he feels exposed to harm.

In fact, moral individualism would seem to suggest that a self-understanding framed in terms of one's membership is mistaken. For moral individualism the only harms that are morally salient are those that befall individuals. The London Jew may have a well-grounded concern for an individual who has been the victim of an unwarranted attack, but he is in error to think that there has been any harm inflicted on a group. A problem here is that not only does an apparently good explanation of why a person has a certain emotional response turn out to be an error, but that it becomes unclear what does count as a good reason for that person's reaction. A general concern for others may induce anger or despair when we witness egregious harms inflicted on strangers. However, group membership explains and rationalises why our responsiveness can be characterised by a partiality for particular others. If we rid ourselves of this, then the Jew's response to the treatment of other distant Jews is just a matter of his subjective emotional state.

Moral individualism seems to threaten the distinction between the experiencing of well-grounded harms and random, mad and pathological harms. The phenomenology may be indistinguishable, but there does seem to be a difference between the hurt I endure on being unjustly dismissed from my job, and the hurt my mentally disturbed döppelganger suffers just because, in a grip of paranoid delusion, he believes that everyone is trying to harm him. The distinction between the well-grounded suffering of harms and that which is just mistaken, mad or pathological is significant, if not always precise or easy to make. In particular, the kinds of harm which we can be held responsible for inflicting may not include many that are just the result of an individual's personal tastes, dispositions or compulsions.[24] This does not deny the suffering of those who experience pain or anguish when there is no objective reason to do so, but that their suffering is linked to an objective source which can figure in our moral reasoning. If on the other hand moral individualism holds that it is membership-related harms in particular (rather than harms in general) that lack an objective grounding, then it must explain why the distinction breaks down just for this class of harm. As a distinctly moral thesis it must show that it does not rest on the assumption of ontological individualism. The onus seems to be with moral individualism to demonstrate why the natural explanation of an individual's emotional response and claim to have been harmed is in fact an error.

Moving from the weakness of moral individualism's handling of harms a person endures just as a member, I shall turn to assess briefly how it copes with duties which individuals and corporations (particularly the state) are commonly held to owe to groups. I have in mind duties to respect aspects of a group's culture, which are accepted as central to the group's characteristic identity and practices. Consider,

---

24 If I know a person is scared of men wearing glasses and I can (reasonably) avoid wearing my glasses in his presence, then it looks as if I can be criticised for failing to do so. However, if a stranger with the same glasses-aversion falls into the depths of anguish and misery because she sees me walking along the street, I am surely blameless.

for example, claims that Muslim schoolgirls be permitted to wear headscarves in state schools, that Sikh boys be allowed to wear turbans at school and Sikh motorcyclists be exempted from the legal requirement that crash helmets be worn. An obvious individualist analysis is that individuals have needs (and perhaps also rights) with respect to personal and cultural development and that these are to be respected, provided the necessary permissions and exemptions satisfy a constraint of harmlessness to others. Under this understanding, even if claims are couched as claims by or on behalf of a group, it is the needs (or rights) of individuals which ground the moral response.

The problem with this approach is twofold. First, it just ignores once again the collective nature of the harm that a refusal to respect certain practices can generate. It may not just be a question of whether most Muslim schoolgirls are able in practice to wear a headscarf. Rather, it can be important that the group claim be acknowledged as such. Moreover, if the response is framed in terms of individuals and their needs, then this may amount to the denial that the group is something worthy of moral consideration. This is precisely the individualist's point, but the denial itself may generate just the kind of harm the individualist must show is irrelevant in our moral reasoning.

The second problem is one of consistency. If Muslim schoolgirls are permitted to attire themselves (or not) in a certain fashion because it is a question of individual needs, then the individualist must grant everyone what they require in order to satisfy harmlessly the need for individual and cultural development or expression. To define genuine cases of need in terms of group membership (for example being a Sikh, Indian, Jew) seems to either re-introduce the notion that it is the group, as well as the individual, which has value and moral significance or it is just an arbitrary and pragmatic means of restricting 'legitimate' claims.

A moral individualist could just deny that the kind of claims mentioned above are legitimate. Needs based on religious or cultural identity are to be respected and permitted within the sphere of the family and of (voluntary) institutions and groups, but they have no claim on our forbearance or contribution in the public sphere. No group or individual is wronged when state school clothing has to conform to a strictly secular model. The task for the individualist is to elucidate why the claims are not legitimate. One line of thought is that there are indeed group needs, which manifest themselves as the kind of claims mentioned. However, notwithstanding that there are such needs, there are countervailing reasons which undermine them as reasons to act in a certain way in a particular case. There would thus be a sense in which Muslims are harmed by a secular dress code at state schools, but that harm has figured in the deliberations leading to the policy. This is not an avenue of reasoning open to the moral individualist, because it specifically accepts that there is a group need and that the group as such figures in moral reasoning.

The alternative approach open to individualism is to regard cultural and religious needs as matters of taste or choice. To be sure, the individualist can recognise these are tastes and choices of great significance to the individual. Nonetheless, to be refused something of this nature is no ground for moral complaint, and so no-one is treated unjustly or wronged by the denial of the demands. I believe this is a coherent position, but doubt that culturally generated needs are best explained as a matter of individual taste or choices. Again, the importance of certain forms of clothing or religious observance is not obviously explained in terms of taste. It is certainly not an explanation that those who value them actually offer.[25]

I have assumed that the moral individualist accepts that the capacity to suffer harms grounds something's moral status. Granted this assumption I have argued that there is little incentive to deny a group moral status, because some harms can only be endured collectively. Moreover, amongst the harms members of a group can endure as members are those one member suffers when confronted by the plight of another member, namely those suffered in virtue of membership. An understanding of the individual's suffering requires us to recognise the group harm. It is, though, open to the moral individualist to deny that harm is at all relevant in determining moral status. She may agree that there are irreducibly collective harms and that an individual does suffer sometimes as a member. However, moral status may be grounded in rational agency alone, and groups are not moral agents. My point here has not been to show that all versions of moral individualism fail. Rather, it is to indicate a basis on which a group can have moral status and to gesture towards the commitments a successful moral individualism must display. Although here I shall eschew further consideration of how, or whether, such a version can be articulated.

VI   The Welfarist Objection

A group has moral status when it is the source or location of irreducibly social goods and harms. Yet an objection to the possession by groups of moral status is that the irreducibly social practices and goods are only valuable in so far as they contribute to the realisation of a more basic or foundational state or good. The enjoyment of utility, being autonomous or a flourishing person may be regarded as intrinsically valuable, and understood as states or ways of being which individuals can cultivate. Our reasons for action and our judgements ought then to be calibrated according only to the extent that the individuals in our evaluative scope enjoy the relevant state. If moral reasons are analysable in terms of the state or well-being of individuals, then the assignment of moral status to a group can be cast once again in an instrumental light.

---

25 In 2004 legislation became effective in France which banned the wearing of conspicuous religious objects in schools. Such objects include large crucifixes and the Islamic headscarf. By far the greatest attention in both support and opposition to the legislation focused on the banning of the headscarf. I speculate that this was in part because of the relative size of the Moslem population in France (approximately 10 per cent v. 2.5 per cent Jewish population), the on-going conflicts in the Middle East and concern over the (related but separable) phenomena of 'fundamentalism' and terrorism, and the debate concerning the status of the women in Islam. The legislation raises the question of whether the importance of the public display of faith to group members was given proper or adequate regard in the decision to assert a commitment to a particular vision of secularism.

The irreducibly social goods are themselves only to be understood as instrumental in the attainment of some basic value or good. Morally significant states are only those which are discretely enjoyable by the individual.

The descent from moral view of the group can be put in terms of welfarism - the claim that morality is fundamentally a matter of the well-being of individuals.[26] Individual well-being, conceived as a life worth living, has been understood in a variety of ways. In particular debate has centred on the grounds or conditions in virtue of which certain activities or states are constituents of a worthwhile life. For present purposes it suffices to note what has become a standard three-way division. Well-being is variously seen as a matter of (a) *satisfaction* – enjoying or being happy in what one gets; or (b) *fulfilment* – getting what one prefers, desires or selects; or (c) *objective or independent goods* – being a certain way and/or engaging in certain activities which enhance the value of a life. That a life is going well or not is not a matter of satisfaction or fulfilment, but of how a life figures in relation to certain objective goods. We should note also that fulfilment is not (necessarily) a matter of an individual knowing or believing that his preferences, desires or choices have been realised, but of their actually being so.

Moral individualism cannot successfully appeal to welfarism. First, moral concern for the well-being of an individual can entail that one be concerned for the group (the individual and his peers) when the well-being of a member of a group presupposes and is conditional upon the others enjoying just the same (range of) good(s). Furthermore, welfarism seems committed to two views it must defend if it is to amount to an endorsement of moral individualism. It must explain that a group cannot be intrinsically valuable, since something with intrinsic value has a clear claim to moral status. I am not committed to the view that groups can be intrinsically valuable, but the burden of proof is with the individualist. However, even if one doubts that a group can be intrinsically valuable, the welfarist must also demonstrate that a group cannot be extrinsically and non-instrumentally valuable. This weaker position is sufficient to undermine welfarist individualism as a group, thus understood, would be valued for its own sake and so be a suitable candidate for moral status

As a form of moral individualism welfarism can recognise the role of irreducibly social goods and of groups themselves as constituents or contributing elements to the well-being of individuals. The welfarist can accept that some goods are irreducibly social in respect of the necessary and sufficient conditions for their production and enjoyment. However, the moral significance of, say, the personal accomplishments, cultural memberships and personal relations embedded in complex social relations and common understanding, is to be (reductively) located solely in their role as

---

26 See for example Moore and Crisp (1996). I draw on their characterisation of welfarism in the following paragraphs.

constituents of individual well-being: 'whether or not these relations are irreducibly social, their value is entirely decomposable into their contribution to the welfare of individuals'.[27] Irreducibly social goods acquire the role of cultural pre-conditions for the enjoyment of individual well-being. This does not mean that such goods are merely instrumentally valuable, but among those things which are pre-conditions for happiness, recalling Aristotle's distinction between the pure instrumentality of wealth and the role of good looks as a condition for happiness.[28] A thesis about the nature of social goods is detached from one about their moral significance by making their value dependent upon the states of individuals. The value of groups and the practices through which they are constituted is decomposed in terms of the satisfaction, fulfilment or objective good of individuals.

Now, we can ask whether individualism follows from the welfarist thesis that individual well-being is the only good or value which has basic moral significance. One can agree with welfarism that morally significant states or relations are (trivially) states of individuals or relations in which individuals figure, for it is individual persons who experience the relevant states, stand in the relations and whose lives go better or worse. The question remains, though, of what the appropriate response to the individual consists in. If well-being is a matter of satisfaction or fulfilment, then individualism may seem hard to resist, because our moral concern is ultimately directed towards the satisfaction of psychological states or the realisation of wants or preferences, which are identified in relation to a particular individual. However, when the satisfaction or fulfilment is irreducibly social in the sense that the enjoyment or attainment or realisation of a good or choice can only be realised by individuals together – as a group – it would appear that there is a vanishingly small gap between concern for the individual and the group. If the individual's enjoyment of a good presupposes that others will also enjoy it, and the realisation of each person's enjoyment is conditional on others also doing so, then welfarist respect for the individual finds expression in recognition of the moral status of the group. Concern for the welfare of any member of that group entails that one is concerned for them all-together as the group.

Arguably a life goes well when it is characterised by certain objective features regardless of whether these are things an individual enjoys or wants. Moore and Crisp observe that amongst the constituents of well-being we may find pleasure, accomplishment, autonomy and friendship.[29] The assignment of the role of cultural pre-conditions to certain group-constituting practices and values seems to presuppose the point at hand: whether there is an irreducibly social component in the objectively grounded well-being of the individual. A life worth living may for some consist, in part at least, in being a member of a particular group and engaging with others in a certain range of practices. Moreover, an element in a worthwhile life may consist in the recognition of the group(s) to which a person belongs. If it is granted that

---

27 Moore and Crisp (1996) p. 611.

28 This distinction is noted by Moore and Crisp (p. 609).

29 Ibid., p. 600.

membership and participation in the life of a group can enhance the well-being of any individual in whose life they occur',[30] then the individualist understanding of welfarism can be resisted. It is the lives of the members considered as the group which can go better or worse depending on how things stand with the group. That is, on how they engage together and on how the group is regarded by others. Again, it appears that a concern for the well-being of the individual can sometimes entail that individuals are considered together as the group that they form.

The individualist understanding of welfarism can be resisted without rejecting the view that individuals are the loci of welfare and that welfare is morally significant. The point is that concern motivated by regard for the well-being of the individual is sometimes aptly directed at the group. It may be the case that it is as a group that the well-being of individual lives is enhanced through the generation of and access to certain kinds of irreducibly social goods. This is not a claim about the nature of our actual lives, nor is it to be taken as a claim about the actual determinants of well-being. Rather, it seems that groups cannot be ruled out as constitutive elements in the well-being of their members, so that respect for the individual can consist in recognising her as one together with her peers. It is exactly the denial of such a relationship between individual and group that welfarism must demonstrate.

Welfarism as a form of moral individualism is committed to two further claims about groups, which it must defend successfully if it is to rule out the possession of moral status by groups:

C1   Groups cannot be intrinsically valuable

C2   Groups cannot have a non-instrumental role in practical reasoning

Welfarism is committed to C1 on the grounds that something with intrinsic value has a *prima facie* claim to moral status.[31] Welfarism raises the issue of where intrinsic value must be located – within individuals. With C2 the assumption is that groups can only have an instrumental or pre-conditioning role in our deliberations, because if they figured as ends in their own right, then they could again possess moral status. A contrast is commonly drawn between intrinsic and instrumental values, indicating that if the welfarist can show that C1 is the case, then it will follow that groups have only an instrumental value.

An opponent of welfarist individualism can argue that a culture, for example, may be intrinsically valuable because the practices constituting it can be valued in themselves, by both participants internal to them and by outsiders. Taylor has claimed

---

30 Ibid.

31 This does not entail the stronger claim that (recognition of) such a value must be intrinsically motivating. Rather one could say that when value is recognised, or value terms warrantedly deployed, it is, other things being equal and the relevant motivational conditions prevailing, appropriate to regard the valuable object or state of affairs as worthy of moral consideration.

that a culture can be valuable in just this way, through linking the irreducible social nature of the good with its intrinsic value. Thus he observes that,

> a culture is related to the acts and experiences it makes possible in no such (external) way ... It is essentially *linked* to what we have identified as good. Consequently it is hard to see how we could deny it the title of good, not just in some weakened, instrumental sense, like the dam, but as intrinsically good.[32]

Here Taylor contrasts intrinsic with instrumental value. However, that contrast may be a mistaken one. Christine Korsgaard notes that the intrinsic-instrumental contrast conflates two separate distinctions: the intrinsic-extrinsic distinction in the theory of value, and the non-instrumental (being valued for its own sake) – instrumental distinction in the relation of value to practical deliberation.[33] Within an axiological account intrinsic value is identified by Korsgaard as *unconditional* value and extrinsic as *conditional* value. As it turns out on Korsgaard's account the only intrinsic value is the unconditional goodwill. All other goods are extrinsic. Distinct from axiology is the deliberative account, which explains how values are related to the practical deliberations of agents. The instrumental–non-instrumental contrast is located in this account, and its concern is not with the metaphysical nature of value but with how values figure in the practical reasoning of an agent. Leaving the details of Korsgaard's reconstruction of a Kantian position to one side, the distinction she offers suggests a strategy whereby C1 and/or C2 may be blocked.

If a group is to be intrinsically valuable, then its value inheres in the interrelational structure of the group, in the practices, relations and institutions which form it. It is our practices, beliefs and goals which can be both valuable in themselves and in which the group and our membership consists. Their value or disvalue is within their own natures. Group-constituting practices are inherently relational, but their value and that of the group do not depend on any relations extrinsic to the practices and group. The practices and group are not valuable because they stand in relation to some particular individuals, but the value of the practices is in its very nature relational.[34] If a group can be intrinsically valuable, then our practical reasoning permits the assignment to it of moral status (of course, we can imagine social arrangements in which no group is valuable: perhaps life in an extreme and hostile state of nature, or one in a dystopian collectivisation of individuals whose existence is reduced to an automaton-like routine).

One may be unconvinced that there can be relational intrinsic values, or that a group can be intrinsically valuable. However, all that is required to block

---

32 Taylor (1997) p. 137.

33 See 'Two Distinctions in Goodness' in Korsgaard (1996).

34 I draw here on discussion with Dr Alan Thomas on his views concerning the idea of relational intrinsic value.

moral individualism is the possibility that a group can be extrinsically and non-instrumentally valuable, a position in line with Korsgaard's analysis. Extrinsicality does not preclude something being valued for its own sake. A group can be valuable because it stands in a certain relationship with individuals, and figure in our practical reasoning in a non-instrumental fashion. A choir, tribe or culture may be valuable not because it serves any instrumental purpose, but because engaging in the practices constitutive of it and standing in a relationship of membership to it are goods in themselves. The value of a practice can inhere in its being engaged in together by *us*. This is not to say that individuals do not enjoy being in the choir or engaging in the religious rites of the tribe, but that the practices are pursued for their own sake. In particular, group-constituting practices can presuppose and generate the good of membership: the good inherent in forming with others this group, which is valued for itself. A group which is an end in itself in our practical reasoning has a clear claim for moral status, and this denial of C2 is sufficient to undermine welfarist individualism.

VII   The Membership *Simpliciter* Objection

A different kind of objection to the moral status of groups is that membership is of importance in the lives of individuals, but that what is important is just membership *per se*: membership of any group will suffice. To sustain groups individuals may need to engage in the collective fiction that a person's particular attachments have a special importance. Nonetheless, there could just be a fact of the matter that we are the kind of creature for whom simply being a member is what counts as the most important dimension of our lives. If this were the case, a concern for well-being or harms would rank membership *simpliciter* as having particular moral significance. Moreover, if being a member of any group is what is of value, then how can one motivate respect for any particular group? After all, what harm could be done by bringing each person into membership of a single group?

The burden of proof is with the objector, for it is far from obvious that its view of our nature is supportable. Yet, I may, in fact, recognise that my valuing membership of group A could be substituted by my valuing membership of a group B. Analogous claims may be made about loving another or appreciating a work of art. The affective array and configuration of beliefs involved in the actual valuing could have been achieved through a different relationship or experience. Yet my actual attachments enjoy a special place in the considerations of myself and others, because I am engaged with them such that they partly determine and form my ends and my character. It is my actual self, not one of a set of counterfactual selves, who can enjoy values and endure pains. This furnishes my actual memberships with a special place in my judgements and in the considerations of others.[35]

---

35 Of course, when I plan or ponder decisions I am in a sense thinking about my counterfactual or possible selves. When others reason what they should do, judgements are

In concluding this chapter it is important to stress that recognition of a group as morally considerable does not diminish the position of individuals, but represents a greater sensitivity to the roles and positions in which individual lives unfold. Other things being equal, the needs and integrity of the individual, as framed by, for example, a basic negative right of non-molestation, may undermine group considerations. The point may be put in terms of the inviolability of the individual being an essential element in a person's status as a morally considerable entity, and the possession of rights an intrinsic good.[36] Equally, this does not provide grounds for excluding groups from the domain of morally considerable entities. It can be granted that individual rights (or, to free the matter from rights talk, the intrinsic value of non-interference) set constraints on how we assess and act towards a group.

Finally let us return to the marginal farming community dependent for its existence on economic support from the state. In being denied that support the villagers face the *de facto* coercive potential of the state, and they are harmed through the denial of further resources. No-one is killed or tortured, and options for ways of life worth living remain open. Nonetheless, in seeking reasons for the government's action the farmers may be dismayed to hear an explanation framed only in terms of the justice of the distribution to citizens and the rights of individuals. That they have suffered as a group seems to warrant that the group figures in the explanation if they are to be respected as individuals by the state. If one accepts that a harm may be suffered collectively, then the legitimacy of the state's justification for its action may depend on the recognition that its actions touch both individuals and the groups they constitute.

---

frequently made on the basis of what might happen to me if they do this or that. The morally salient feature is that the harm or good, gain or loss is suffered by my actual future self.

36 This is argued by Nagel (1995). Non-interference is not conditional upon, or ratcheted to, the realisation of some other good such as well-being or freedom. The actual absence of coercion or interference is a good which is distinct from those forms of coercion being impermissible. Now, curtailments of freedoms and coercive interference may count as threats to our inviolability depending on whether they restrict us in the public or private sphere. Nagel is then taking our intrinsic worth to ground rights.

Chapter 7

The Possibility of a Group Right

I   Introduction

Groups are sometimes held to possess rights.[1] A striking feature of contemporary politics and of political philosophy has been the increasing attention paid to the significance of the claim that certain kinds of groups possess a right of self-determination. In particular, groups such as nations or peoples, cultural, religious and ethnic groups have been identified as claimants of a right to determine for themselves the nature of their collective life. Over the last twenty years or so there has developed an extensive and wide ranging debate and literature concerning the basis, nature and justification of such claims. Central to this discussion is the relationship between the state and minority groups, such groups being exemplified by (non-immigrant) national minorities such as the Catalans or indigenous peoples of the New World; isolationist (ethnically based) religious groups such as the Amish; and migrant cultural or national groups such as the Bengali community in UK. The politics of recognition and the claim that there are group-differentiated rights is grounded in the thought that in virtue of some salient ways in which such groups differ from the mainstream or dominant cultural group(s), they possess rights to certain exemptions, resources and entitlements. The strongest form such claims to rights takes is the right to a degree of autonomy either within the state or through the attainment of statehood itself.[2]

---

1   Group rights are sometimes described as third generation rights, for example by Waldron (1993) p. 330. First generation rights are the individual liberty (negative) rights of the seventeenth and eighteenth centuries, and second generation rights individual welfare (positive) rights promoted during the twentieth century. This division is useful as an indication of their historical relations. However, group rights are typically expressed as bundles of negative and positive rights. A people's right to self-determination may entail rights against coercion and interference, and also rights to the contribution of others in the form of, for example, the distribution of resources.

2   Perhaps, the right to self-determination is the right most frequently associated with groups. The first article of the *International Covenant on Civil and Political Rights (1966)* states that '(A)ll peoples have the right to self-determination. By virtue of that right they freely determine their political status and freely pursue their economic, social and cultural development'. Recognising that the signatories to the Covenant are states, and so not identical with the peoples being afforded the right, it goes on to require that: '(T)he States parties to the present Covenant, including those having responsibility for the administration of

In this chapter I shall abstract from the detail of much of the discussion on the possible grounds, nature and content of group rights. I examine the general question of whether a group as such can be the bearer of a right, and in particular the external protection right to be left uncoerced in its practices and pursuit of its commitments. The notion of an external protection right is of a right, or package of rights, to 'limit the economic or political power exercised by the larger society over the group, to ensure that resources and institutions on which the minority depends are not vulnerable to majority decisions'.[3] Such rights are commonly contrasted with internal protection or restriction rights, which endow a group with the right to 'limit the liberty of its own individual members in the name of group solidarity or cultural purity'.[4] Such rights appear then to impose serious obstacles on the exercise of individual rights of exit, conscience and choice. For they entail constraints on an individual's freedom to leave the group, renounce commitments and outlooks, or to refuse to engage in traditional or established practices.

The question of whether a group as a group can possess a right follows from the realist thesis that groups exist and from the further claim that they possess moral status. Yet, the truth of both of these views does not entail that a group can have a right. The question is an important one because there may be several senses in which one can deploy the notion of a group right. There is, first, the strong or *sui generis* concept of a group right which attributes the right to the group itself. There is also a weaker or expressive or instrumental basis for group rights. Here, a group possesses a right as a means of realising or expressing the individual and severally held rights of its members. It may turn out that the most effective means of protecting individual liberties, or allowing individuals to realise their individual rights to cultural self-development,[5] is to assign rights to groups. Now, without prejudging whether these are mutually exclusive, it does seem necessary to establish whether the stronger

---

Non-Self-Governing and Trust Territories, shall promote the realisation of the right of self-determination, and shall respect that right in conformity with the provisions of the Charter of the United Nations'.

Self-determination was clearly conceived as a right held by peoples with a claim for statehood or, more modestly, autonomy within a state. The right may be expressed as the demand that a people be able to govern itself through the establishment of a state controlling its own territory. Within states claims are made for greater regional autonomy and capacity to live in accordance with a group's characteristic values and practices. For instance, in Canada the Quebecois, claim the right to 'live in French'. It is perhaps, though, misleading to talk of self-determination as *a* right, because it seems better described as a bundle or package of negative and positive rights, respect for which secures at least the minimal grounds for social, cultural and political development. Our self-determination requires of others that they make certain forbearances and contributions with respect to us.

3   Kymlicka (1995) p. 7.
4   Ibid.
5   For the view that individuals possess just this right see for example Gould (1996) p. 76.

version of a group right is a plausible and coherent one in order to be clear about the kind of claim that is subject to so much discussion and controversy.

At this stage it is important to note that the full-blown notion of a group as such possessing a right need not entail a challenge to or undermine the priority or fundamental status of the basic or human rights possessed by individual persons. Leaving to one side the fuller specification of such human rights the present point is that such rights protect the conditions for or capacity of an individual to have the possibility of (something like) a worthwhile or valuable life. The issue of group rights occurs at the level of 'citizenship rights'. These are rights to ensure the equality of individuals as citizens through equality of access to, for example, health care and education, the right to vote, and the right to a trial by jury.[6] Moreover, citizens have rights to certain entitlements, exemptions, resources or claims in virtue of which any individual citizen has the opportunity to determine and pursue a life its author judges to be of value - a life shaped by particular practices, values and goals. As Miller observes, while such rights underpinning an equality in our pursuit of what may be regarded as a worthwhile life may vary between societies, they are fundamental within a particular political community: 'they are not immutable, but they do serve as trumps'.[7] Group rights are claims about what is required to impart or derive value in a life, not claims about the bare possibility of leading some kind of life at all. To hold that a group as such can possess a right is then to maintain that groups and individuals are both claimants of rights to exemptions, resources, and to political and legal recognition.

Now, if we take rights seriously as moral claims, as moral resources imposing duties on others, then their possession by entities other than individual persons raises the possibility that the interests and needs of an individual agent may be legitimately subordinated in the appropriate circumstances to those of the group. That prospect seems to challenge the very role of rights as securing equality among individuals and as threatening a liberal commitment to moral individualism. This is of course a question about the nature of liberalism and the significance for its articulation of the recognition of the moral significance of groups, and particularly of group rights. In the present work I shall simply, at the end of this chapter, suggest the kind of challenge liberal theory faces rather than offer any substantive analysis of it.

II   The 'Right' Theory of Rights

Building on the harm based account of the moral status of groups, I shall suggest that a group can possess a right to non-interference as a protection against the loss of irreducibly social goods or needs, when such a loss is destructive of what is actually of value in the lives of its members.[8] In such cases the actual value in an

---

6   Compare Miller (2002).

7   Ibid., p. 182.

8   From such needs and consideration of what is of value in the lives of members it might also follow that a group would have a rights-claim to resources and contributions on the part

individual's life inheres in her collective engagement with others, who are tied to her in this dependence on the irreducibly social production of goods through their forms of practices. As noted, there is a class of basic or human rights which individuals possess as protections against violation. I shall not, then, talk about group rights as protections against the egregious assault on groups in the form of wholesale slaughter, genocide or the forced movement of populations. Granted basic individual rights, the role of a group right against such attacks is otiose in that an individual right against molestation is sufficient as a claim over others. Whether any right is sufficient as a means of effective protection is another matter.

It is worth observing, though, that the harm an individual endures when attacked as a member of a group may have a special quality. A consequence of this is that an appeal to the individual right against interference may protect the individual group member if it is respected, but the right will perhaps not reflect or be attuned to the full range of harm to which he is exposed. If I am attacked because I am a member of a certain group, then on the face of it I endure two harms. The personal harm of being attacked and the harm a member experiences when the group is picked upon. I doubt, though, that such harms are simply additive. The harm endured by the victim is more than the sum of the personal and group harms. In being attacked as a member a person has become merely a part of something which is feared, hated or held in contempt, and which is the true object of the assault. In this sense, then, respect for non-violation of the individual and of the group become inseparable. An individual is not merely part of a group, but at the same time her memberships may be essential to who she is.

We can imagine that a particular group is isolated by, or from, others for a special kind of treatment. Its practices, traditions, and language are proscribed. It becomes prohibitively difficult for its members to engage in the relations and interchanges from which the group is formed. The Poles have periodically endured such conditions under Russian, Prussian and German rule; Jews during the Middle Ages would sometimes find themselves with the choice of exile or forced absorption into the majority community. In the late fifteenth and then in the early seventeenth century, a freshly united Spain coerced its Jewish and Moorish populations into assimilation or banishment through the imposition of linguistic, religious and cultural requirements and bans. More recently, we have heard of widespread popular discrimination against Roma communities in post Cold War Eastern Europe. One might also think of Japan which does not officially recognise the presence of a long established Korean minority, the discrimination against the descendants of the lowest feudal caste, nor assign legal recognition of the distinct identities of its Ainu or Okinawan minorities. Likewise the colonial and imperial activities of both the 'Great' European and Asian states suppressed the cultures and identities of subject nations. A threat common to the oppressed groups is that the interrelations, practices and identity in which the group consists are rendered practically impermissible: the cost of engaging in them increases and the opportunities to do so become ever more

---

of others in order to protect the irreducibly social goods.

restricted. The possession by a group of certain rights offers a protection against this kind of treatment, although no guarantee that it will not succumb to such a fate.

On at least one view of rights, groups, as they have been analysed in this book, cannot possess rights because a group is not an agent, and agency is a necessary condition for the possession of rights. Arguments to this effect have been made by, for example, Scruton[9] and Wellman.[10] Reference to group rights is just a way of talking. Note, this does not entail that the reference to the group is merely a way of talking, but that the assignment of a right(s) is. If groups are not agents, then an alternative theory of rights must provide the framework for any claim that groups are indeed apt to bear rights. Any sensible theory of rights takes sane adult humans as paradigm cases of rights holders, and so a constraint on a theory of rights is that it must explain why a sane adult human being has rights.[11]

Rights are sometimes grounded in the needs of an entity, and the harms it may suffer or risk. Joseph Raz has elaborated this notion by saying that something has a right to some forbearance or contribution on the part of others if, other things being equal, an aspect of its well-being is sufficient reason to hold other person(s)

---

9   'Groups Do Not Have Rights', *The Times*: 21 December 1995.

10 Wellman (1996) takes Hohfeld's (1919) taxonomy of legal rights as claims, powers, liberties and immunities as the starting point in his explanation of rights in general. Wellman explains that the function of a right is to distribute control when a moral dispute arises. He argues that a right must contain either a liberty or a power, and therefore only an agent capable of holding a liberty or power can possess a right. A moral liberty consists in the absence of a contrary moral duty, and a moral power is 'the ability to effect some moral consequence by some specific act performed with the rationally imputed intention of effecting some such consequence' (ibid. p. 109). The kind of agency required to hold a power must be one in which the agent can be held capable of bearing a contrary duty, for without being able to sustain the ascription of a duty there could be no liberty. This is of course taking 'liberty' in a sense which goes beyond the simple absence of constraint. Indeed, the suggestion is that to have a moral liberty one must be capable of being morally responsible. That is, one is responsive or sensitive to those values in relation to which moral reasons are directed. To be a rights holder is, according to Wellman, to be the kind of agent capable of recognising moral reasons, which are to be understood as reasons directed towards the promotion of values important in the structuring and maintenance of the social lives of individuals.

11 Except, of course a theory denying that there are rights. There is also space for a theory of rights recognising only groups as rights-holders. Such moral holism is not necessarily objectionable, but it does appear deeply counter-intuitive. I eschew further discussion, but note that a morality sensitive to the needs and harms faced by individuals is likely to be concerned with both the individual considered alone and together with her peers. The practical question of who is harmed or in need can be answered in the singular or the plural. Therefore, to the extent that rights are linked to need and harm and the capacity to suffer it seems difficult to exclude individuals unless all need and harm arises at an irreducibly collective level. A further consideration for those advocating group rights is that a theory of rights, which embraces groups as well as individual persons, may widen the domain of rights-holders to other kinds of entities as well.

to be under a duty.[12] Of course, one must specify how certain needs impose duties on others in order to determine what those duties are and whether in particular circumstances they ought to be honoured. Leaving aside the question of specification for the moment, the key point is that a right is a claim on others that draws its authority from its relation to the actual needs and harms of its holder. Allowing that a responsiveness to the needs and harms of others is a key feature of our practical and evaluative reasoning, the articulation of claims as rights gives expression to a class of particularly pressing or significant needs.

In Chapter 6 I explained how the irreducibly social goods and needs of a group underwrite its moral status. Drawing on the role of such goods and needs, it can be argued that they have such significance for the group that they ground its rights. The (dis)value of a practice or the production of some state of affairs, or attitude consists in its being *ours*. My enjoyment or suffering of it is realised through participation as a member together with others and presupposes its value or harm to us.

A group harm is one that can be suffered by members of a group only in virtue of their membership. It is a harm or loss, the pain of which is presupposed in the valuing by the members of the practices of the group. The harm can arise, even though the opportunities and resources available to each individual may have increased. It is a residual harm shared or participated in by the members of the group after all the harms and benefits which accrue to each one (severally) from some event or state of affairs are taken into consideration. The group harm remains because inherent to membership of the group is a particular good which can only be produced and enjoyed through the interrelations in which the group consists. Such a good may just be the value the members attach to belonging to the group through participation in its group constituting practices. There is no guarantee that the harm could be avoided or compensated by substituting participation in one group with the opportunity to become a member of others, or through the provision of other goods, such as material resources. The harm is specific to the actual engagement together of the members. The collective and uncoerced determination of the practices, goals, values and institutions that form a group may be valuable in themselves for the members. These practices and traditions could themselves be the source of what the members count as valuable in their lives, or as contributing an essential component in a worthwhile life.

If a group is proscribed or if its claims to certain resources or legal status, necessary for its essential forms of interrelations, are unacknowledged, then its members' capacity to be the on-going authors of their identity is undermined, as are the practices established, developed and endorsed in their collective life. Alternatives may be available for each individual or for them collectively, but the harm each suffers as a member together with the others derives from the loss of the particular practices or from the demise of the group itself. This is a group harm in only being capable of being suffered by individuals who stand together in relations of membership, and it can only arise when the group itself or its practices are subject

---

12 See for example Raz (1984).

to threat. Assuming that such harms ground the group right to be left uncoerced in the collective pursuit and articulation of goals and practices, then the right is also collective in its being claimable only by, or on behalf of, the group as a whole.

It may be objected that group rights cannot be grounded in group harms, because we can never differentiate a group harm from ones which are suffered atomistically or singularly by group members. Any harm is suffered by the individual person, and the phenomenology of a singular or group harm may be indistinguishable from the first or third person perspective. Whether the suffering of these individuals is a result of a group harm or not may not be determinable just by looking at the subjective nature or experience of the harm suffered, and it is thus not possible to ground a claim for a group right on it. Such an objection takes the identification of a harm to be purely a matter of how it figures with the individual who endures it. The argument for a group right does not rest on how the harm is for the individual, but on how that harm – whatever its phenomenological aspects – arises such that a particular group – its members collectively - suffer a harm with a common source. For the harm to be a group harm it is not necessary that it share any essential internal phenomenological feature, but that it have the external feature of arising as a harm for these people because of how they are interrelated as members of the group, and of how the group stands in relation to the world. Rescinding the recent assumption of the previous paragraph that there is a group right to be left uncoerced, the question is whether the need, loss or harm a group can suffer with respect to irreducibly social goods is one that is suitable as a ground for that kind of group right.

III   The 'Right' Kind of Harm

One form of argument for group rights appeals to what is taken as the obvious fact that some collective goods are important for the group. From the role and value of certain practices the right to be able to engage in those practices is inferred. I suggest below that the inference is far from obvious. It is insufficient to point to the importance of a group's practices or goals to the group, because their role and significance in the lives of the group's members needs to be elucidated.

Jeremy Waldron has argued that communal or social goods do not just serve the needs of individuals (in respect of, say, each person's well-being or flourishing) but give rise to needs or harms that the group itself can suffer.[13] Membership through the goods and needs entailed by being a member leads to exposure to potential harms intrinsic to that membership, and as such it us together – the group – that stands in need of protection. If certain goods of sufficient importance, those that are irreducibly collective, attach only to groups, then the group is due the protection afforded by rights, and the group's rights are not held in virtue of the claims and needs of individuals considered severally. According to Waldron, this accords with

---

13 See Waldron (1993, pp. 330–69) 'Can Communal Goods Be Human Rights?'

our pre-theoretical way of thinking about these matters since we already 'talk about the rights of groups and the rights of communities'.[14] Indeed,

> particular groups may often stand to some larger entity in a similar relation to that in which individual men and women stand to the state ... The issues, in other words, may have the same sort of shape, and we may think it perfectly appropriate to state those issues using the same sorts of concepts.[15]

This kind of argument for group rights depends upon the inference from the production of group goods to a group right. Waldron identifies the production and enjoyment of certain goods as essentially linked to a group, and concludes that the group has a right to that good. The move is to infer the possession of rights by groups from the existence of such goods on the grounds that it is only groups that can enjoy such goods. In its strongest form the inference depends upon the claim that a certain good, G, can only be possessed by a social group; and that its possession by some particular group, S, is partly constitutive of its being S. In virtue of its constitutive role for S, G is valued and needed; hence S has a right to G.

This approach is susceptible to the criticism that there is no clear reason to accept the validity of the inference. It needs to be shown that the good is important or special in the right sort of way. It is just not sufficient to point to fraternity (or solidarity, cultural participation, etc.) being the kind of good that is dependent upon and constitutive of a group. It must be the kind of good which is of special significance to the members considered jointly. From the claim that something is a good of a group, we cannot just infer that the group has a right to it.[16] We must explain why the good has the kind of significance to the group that underwrites the group's possession of (appropriate) rights. The question thus remains of what determines the sufficiency of an aspect of something's well-being as a ground for a right.

Looking to a harm-based account of individual rights, it is clear that many goods may contribute to a person's well-being. It is implausible to say that she therefore has a right to all of those goods, or a ground for the rights to allow her to enjoy or pursue them, without an account of what well-being or flourishing consists in, and so of the harm that one suffers when deprived of its constituents. Perfectionist or teleological approaches suggest that there is a way or range of ways of being – 'life

---

14 Ibid., p. 361.

15 Ibid., p. 363. In addition to the support garnered from the fact that we do talk of group rights and the parallel structure of the claim for group rights with that for human ones, Waldron notes communal goods may be especially important by being 'partially constitutive of individual autonomy' (p. 367). His aim is not to argue for a thesis in which the particular ground(s) for such communal rights are elaborated, for he accepts that in general there is a plurality of grounds which could ground a claim to the possession of rights. This is not posed as a problem, but as an indication that '(W)e might as well embrace this pluralism, and take advantage of the opportunity it offers to extend the language of rights to claims made on behalf of other (not single individual agents) human entities as well' (ibid.).

16 A point I have heard made by James Griffin.

options' – that are objectively better or more valuable than other ways. The list of valuable ways of conducting one's life may be open-ended, so that there is no single model of virtue or flourishing in respect of which all evaluations are calibrated.[17] Relatedly the constituents and shape of a worthwhile life and the capacity to form judgements concerning them may depend upon context and community. Our lives go objectively better by following some courses rather than others; we realise ourselves by being one way (or some ways) or of a certain character rather than others. In this respect rights can be regarded as functioning to preserve or promote valuable life options.

Our citizenship rights aim to establish a form of equality among us in the pursuit of valuable lives. Among those ways of being are lives in which value is derived from the relations and practices of membership. While it is individuals who have the status of citizens, for some citizens it is the life they share as members of a group that has special or particular significance. Here I take something to be of value not merely in virtue of its being enjoyed, liked or incidentally contributing to the well-being of the person. It is valuable if it is what makes *this* life worthwhile. A particular set of practices or way of being may figure as being of ultimate importance in a person's life. The loss of these things is significant or profound. They are not merely missed or subject to sentimental reminiscence, but the loss of these practices, expressive of certain values, goals and beliefs, empties a particular life of those elements which infused it with value for its holder.

The stress on the sources of a valuable life as grounds for rights may raise the objection that wicked pleasures can be significant in just the right way, unless one provides an account of what an objectively worthwhile life consists in. However, we do not require a specification of the range of good lives to rule out rights to wicked pleasures. A right to, say, torture others requires not only that a person be left uncoerced to pursue her notion of the good, but that others be required to make a contribution to her. In this case others would have to have a duty to offer themselves to the torturer. Such a duty will strike many as absurd, because it clashes directly with the basic negative right to be left unharmed. There is, however, something odd in ruling out rights to wicked ways of being just on the grounds that such rights cannot be held harmlessly. Even if animals do not have rights, it is *prima facie* wrong to inflict pain on them without good reason. Rights do not exhaust moral dialogue or the considerations salient in our practical deliberations and judgements. Wicked practices and pleasures may be fundamental to a (depraved) individual's sense of a valuable or flourishing life, but they do not ground rights because they are wicked: they are ruled out by standards and constraints independent of rights.[18]

The kind of need grounding a *sui generis* group right, is one that cannot be satisfied by respecting the several needs or rights of its members, and the need must

---

17 On a liberal conception of a valuable life one will pursue it in conditions of autonomy. Compare the liberal perfectionsism of Raz (1988).

18 The further task of articulating and justifying those standards is not one to which I shall attend.

be such that a failure to satisfy or respect it would significantly harm the members taken together. The right of the group must be a response to an actual need that maintains and contributes to the value or well-being of that group, or to a harm that threatens it. Simply being a good that is enjoyed and produced collectively does not ground a group right to that good. It must be a necessary element in what is valuable in the life of the group; that is, in the collective engagement of its members together in a network of practices. The sense of fraternity one enjoys as a member of small nation may be welcome, but it is not necessarily constitutive of the good of being part of that group. The value of membership inheres in the practices and traditions which mark us out as this group, and the conduct of which is regarded as valuable in itself.

Again it should be noted that it is the life of each individual which is worthwhile or valuable for her. It might therefore seem sufficient to regard each individual as possessing the right to pursue her notion of the good, subject to a constraint of harmlessness. Although it may be maintained that some lives acquire value through individuals standing in group-constituting interrelations, this does not entail that the group has any rights. However, in response to such a criticism one must stress that the point is that the members considered together – as the group – possess the right(s) because the harm can only be suffered collectively and the protection can only be afforded to them as a body.

A group can suffer a loss or harm through the intentional interference or intervention (or the knowing neglect or failure to act) by others in its practices and patterns of life. The inability to live as it (*we* or *they*) sees fit is a loss sufficient to ground a right against interference in our self-determination. In particular, when it is precisely that capacity to determine the shape of our collective life for ourselves which is essential to the value of membership of the group. The relevant harm inheres in the members of the group being prevented from engaging in, developing and expressing their endorsement of practices, goals and values which make up their actual life together as that group. The loss of this form of life harms them jointly. The harm can only be suffered as the loss of something of value by each person as a member together with the others. The loss of the practice is harmful because its value is produced by and presupposed in the relations and deeds in which it consists. It is sufficient to ground a right when the loss of the way of living is destructive of (a significant element of) what is valuable or worthwhile in the lives of the members. In such cases a concern for the individual prompts us into recognising that they together possess a moral claim on others in the form of a right against intervention in their practices.

Consider a cultural or religious minority within a state dominated by a single cultural group.[19] The state may prohibit the public observance of all religious and traditional practices in order to ensure it has a fully secular public character. This

---

19 The history of their relationship with the state may be significant in evaluating claims.

ban means the minority is no longer able to engage in practices which it values and which are essential to its identity as such.[20]

Banning the public observance of our religion may generate a collective harm. It may render the group constituting practices increasingly difficult, so that the group, as we have understood it, may change in its character. Perhaps from a thriving large-scale group with a distinct but non-hostile place within civil society, it becomes over a number of years a small, extremely tightly knit sect dedicated to the overthrow of the state. This contrasts with the mere withering away of a group, or the changing of its character in the face of an unsympathetic, but non-coercive world. In a pluralist society with a diverse range of options a group may not sustain itself into the future, for example, just because its members drift away or it is unable to attract new ones. Those who continue to form the group as it 'has been' may endure a profound harm as a valued way of life ebbs away. No matter what they do, it may just not be possible to sustain that form of life without the shared commitment of others to it.

A group has no more right to everlasting survival (immortality) than an individual. Death may be an individual misfortune, but we have no right against it in itself, but against those who would expedite it by imposing their will upon us. To be killed because of the coercive intervention of others is to be wronged; to die an inevitable and inescapable hazard. For a group, its foreseeable demise is not enough to ground a right unless that demise results from the intention to wilfully drive it from existence. It should be stressed that the need *I* and *we* have to be part of a thriving congregation or culture does not impose duties on others to stay or join with us. Or at any rate there is need for detailed argument to show that there is such a duty on the part of others.[21] It is one thing to claim that we have a right to be left uncoerced, and quite another to say that others have a duty to engage with us to sustain the practices we consider valuable. Likewise, a person's character may change as her life disappoints and expectations are recast as bitter acceptances. Some lives just do not go well, but it is far from obvious that a person has a right to succeed or to flourish. Instead, we do have rights with respect to encroachments and deprivations that aim to undermine our needs and wants. So with a group, a world in which it, say, struggles to realise its ends is not necessarily one in which it has suffered any harm that could support a rights-claim.

---

20 This is not an ontological claim. A group deprived of the capacity to engage in its most valued practices, those practices in which its members' understanding of themselves as forming the group is articulated, will not necessarily cease to exist. A group, which we can trace through time, and individuate in causal and explanatory terms, may survive the proscription of practices. Indeed, it may even flourish in an 'underground' existence. In facing a hostile state or majority its character – its ' personal' traits – are likely to undergo some development. The moral point is that being of this character is what is actually valuable to its members now. An element of what is important about maintaining the practices and values of the group may often be the importance attached to the group surviving in this form into the future. Put differently, the preservation of this valuable way of life for future members can be a goal and part of why the group is valuable today for its members.

21 See for example Green (1998) for discussion on rights of exit.

In this imaginary case, while unable to practise their faith in public, the individuals of the minority group are fully enfranchised and enjoy the same rights before the law as the majority. Moreover, we can hold that through a redistributive taxation system, and an effective equal opportunities policy, the range of options available to the individuals in that group expands beyond that which would have been possible if the group were to enjoy some greater degree of separation so that it could continue with its public ceremonies. At the same time, then, as suffering a restriction with regard to one kind of activity (just like everyone else), choice for the individuals in the minority group seems to have been enhanced by their possession of equal rights and by the enhanced the range of (valuable) options. The loss for the minority group is in the need to switch to private rather than public religious observance. Yet, if the public observance of certain practices is essential to members' conceptions of what membership entails, to the group having its characteristic identity, it is arguable that much of the value in the lives of those members may have been destroyed. Moreover, it is not just that the group has been unable to sustain itself through an inability to retain members or to maintain practices essential to its historic identity, but the loss has arisen through the imposition of the will of others: in this case by the action of the state. Those practices have not withered because a new generation has been attracted by alternative ways of living, thereby altering the nature or character of the group. The rituals in which the identity of the group and the goals and values of membership are defined and realised have in effect been proscribed.

The good to each individual of having a range of worthwhile options may be simply incommensurable with the good inherent in the practices of the group. It is not a matter of it being true that A (having the range of options) is better/more valuable than B (public observance of certain practices), nor of A and B being of equal value. There is rather a failure of comparability. The loss of certain practices cannot be offset by gains elsewhere, because it is in the nature of that which is lost that there can be no offsetting gains. It might be held that for a harm or loss to be sufficient to ground a right it must not only represent a loss of what is valuable in the lives of the group members, but be irreplaceable. This requirement appears a strong one, but if rights are to be grounded in their role as protections against harm, then the replacement of one (bundle of) good(s) with another one of equal worth can hardly be said to constitute a harm. The impossibility of being able to measure this good I enjoy now against that good which is to replace it suggests that, at least on this occasion, my current good is irreplaceable.

A group can fall victim to such harm only if its practices are significant in the right way. In a pluralist society, marked by a diversity of groups, there is the possibility of underdetermination with regard to which groups are valuable in a right-grounding fashion. National, religious or cultural groups may stand out as prime candidates, but what of other groups? It seems to be a weakness for the view that groups can have rights that *being* a group does not suffice for it to have rights. Being a group does not entail that the group in question has the interrelational structure, which gives rise to the production of irreducibly social goods and needs. Yet, analogously it can be held that not all adult human beings possess rights, because they lack the characteristic capacity to endure harm in the right way. Such creatures might remain objects of moral concern, but they would have dropped from the scope of rights. Whether the analogy is robust or not, it is probably not too helpful. With persons we can make the working assumption that they all have at least a basic right against coercive interference and the right to enjoy equal status as a citizen capable of determining for themselves a worthwhile kind of life. Such an assumption seems less firmly held about groups, particularly if we are confident that many groups will not be valuable in the appropriate way. I am not making the judgement that we should be confident of this possibility. However, the uncertainty of what we should think about groups in general with respect to their claim to actually possess rights contrasts with the certainty we have about the claims of most persons. Perhaps, in practice, the best we can do is to recognise that certain kinds of groups are characteristically sources of value, while leaving open the possibility that in principle any given group could turn out be valuable in a right-grounding fashion.

IV   Group Rights: Recognition and Limits?

Let us assume that a group can have a right to non-interference and self-determination. Possession of a right may be the most powerful kind of moral and political claim available, but – with the exception of the canonical negatively specified human rights against molestation and harm – the claims that issue from them may be legitimately denied. The claims for exemptions and resources on the part of one set of rights holders may clash with the claims of others or with other values which are considered of great importance within the political community. In acting upon the claims of a group or denying those claims the liberal state must justify its actions to all of its citizens, lest it fail to display the transparency essential to the legitimacy of the state's coercive capacity. A fundamental element in any such explanation and justification is that the need of the group be recognised and acknowledged. The group as such and its needs and values are to figure in the deliberations and judgement concerning how claims, exemptions, privileges and resources are to be distributed. The justice with which groups are treated is not to be determined simply by whether claims are met, but by whether the decision about the claim takes seriously the needs and values which motivate the claims.

The way in which a group can figure as such in our deliberations can be illustrated by considering three actual cases. In the first a group seeks an exemption in order to maintain its isolation from mainstream society. In the second a practice central to the group's conception of itself is deemed illegal. In the third a group appeal for protection is denied.[22]

---

22 Note that I am not attempting to analyse the actual reasons offered by the courts for their decisions. Rather, I am suggesting that in order to best explain and justify the decisions that were in fact made we ought to see the group as such as figuring in the deliberative process. It does also seem rather plausible that the cases do suggest that even if group rights are not articulated as such in law, the recognition that there is a group need, and a claim in the form of

In the United States the Amish community enjoys exemptions from certain aspects of federal child abuse legislation in order that Amish children may be withdrawn at a younger age from high school.[23] Strictly speaking it is individuals who enjoy this exemption, and they are taken to be voluntary members of the Amish congregation. In practice the legislation is directed at the group with the purpose of preserving an essential element in the Amish way of life. That life is the engagement together in a range of practices expressive of a particular religious and worldview, and which involves the deliberate and conscious embrace of marginality. The state is not promoting or favouring the Amish life, but is acting to respect the significance of the group in the lives of its members. On the harm based approach to rights suggested here, it looks as if there is a claim on the part of the Amish, and the response of the state is justified as the recognition of a group need and the harm that could follow from its denial. Whether the harm is sufficient in the circumstances to justify respecting the right that the group be free from intervention cannot be settled in advance of a consideration of the details of the context. In the case of the Amish their size and truly marginal position in American society, and a reputation for 'virtuous' living may all count in favour of not intervening.

In the United States somewhat greater controversy has accompanied cases in which infants have been harmed or died because their parents refused to permit medical examination or intervention on the grounds that it is prohibited by the terms of their religious faith. The right of parents to act in this way is supported by religious exemption laws, which allow, under certain circumstances, parents to act in just this way without falling foul of other legislation, and in particular laws against child abuse. While a range of religious groups have been involved in instances of medical refusal I shall take as representative a case involving Christian Science.

The Church of Christ The Scientist prohibits 'non-mechanical' medical intervention. Very roughly, Christian Science holds that the world of 'Mind' rather than matter constitutes what is real. A commitment to this view entails the rejection of medical intervention in favour of prayer.[24] The only permissible medical attention is that involving purely mechanical procedures such as the delivery of children, the setting of bones and dental work. In recent years some Christian Scientist parents have found themselves in litigation with medical authorities in the United States over parental refusal to consent to treatment for their children. In some cases refusal has followed a diagnosis, which had yielded a poor prognosis. Here, the difficult

---

a group right being in effect asserted, may explain the legislative and juridical attitude of the state in certain contexts.

23 Historically, this arrangement can be regarded as a compromise between the Amish and Federal authorities. Until the twentieth century the Amish had been permitted to educate their children entirely at home. Compromise took the form of requiring the Amish to send their children to school, but with a lower legal leaving age. The Supreme Court ruling putting this into effect aimed at restricting the coercive control over minors, while respecting the centrality of certain practices to the Amish way of life.

24 I believe there is a debate within Christian Science over the permissibility of diagnosis, although its official doctrine is broadly opposed to it.

decision is whether to allow a child to die, thereby avoiding the likelihood of pointless suffering. It is by no means clear that religious conviction is an inappropriate basis for forming a decision. More controversial, and germane to the issue of group rights, are cases in which the refusal to obtain even a diagnosis has resulted directly in the otherwise avoidable death of a child. For example, in 1986 the response of his parents to two year old Robyn Twitchell's vomiting and stomach pain was to gather with some fellow practitioners to pray. Four days later the child died. An autopsy revealed that death followed complications arising from a bowel blockage, a problem that could have been dealt with simply and effectively had the child been taken to hospital.[25]

Living out a commitment to the world of Mind and the power of prayer is absolutely essential to Christian Scientists. It is in collectively engaging in practices bearing witness to such a commitment that the group's character is expressed, and from which its members' lives draw much of their value. That commitment, though, carries a cost in terms of the potential danger to infants, who cannot possibly be held to have made anything like a voluntary commitment to the church. To put matters in these terms is to suppose that prayer is not a more effective means than medical intervention. One opposing view would be that when a child dies, following the refusal to obtain medical attention, the problem is internal to Christian Science; it may be that people were not praying 'hard' enough. However, the right to live in accordance with this belief system and its practices is circumscribed by the involuntary danger into which infant members of the group can be plunged. Even if fatalities result from failings in the praying, consideration for children unable to make any choice about their membership looks a plausible basis for intervention in the practices of Christian Science.

Nonetheless, there does remain the harm that the group suffers as a result of the restriction in being able to live in accordance with one its central tenets. Indeed, from the perspective of Christian Science, the harm the child can suffer is exactly what is at issue. Now, I happen to believe there are strong arguments to doubt the coherence of a commitment to the World of Mind. However, liberalism cannot rule out a way of being, an entire set of practices, if they are otherwise harmless, and it faces the difficulty of showing Christian Scientists that their attitude towards medical intervention does indeed count as (potentially) harmful for infants and young children. On the latter point there may just be no agreement. Should religious exemptions not be allowed in such circumstances, the liberal state can maintain that it has acted non-arbitrarily and in a measured fashion if it is able to demonstrate that the importance and value of the practices of Christian Science have been considered. The state has intervened in the life of the group, but it has recognised that the group has goods and needs, which as far as possible the state seeks to respect.

---

25 This case is discussed in May (1996). The parents were initially found guilty of involuntary manslaughter. In 1993 this verdict was overturned on appeal. It would appear that the kind of compromise established between the Amish and the federal Authorities is yet to be fully worked out.

Sometimes, then, group needs and claims clash with other important needs and values within a particular social or political context. A different kind of example is provided by the incident in which the village of Skokie was targeted in 1977 by American Nazis for a march because it was inhabited largely by concentration camp survivors. The local authority issued ordinances banning the march, but it was permitted to go ahead on appeal by the Supreme Court on the grounds that the ordinances infringed the First Amendment provisions on free speech.[26] Now, the Nazi action was clearly directed at causing distress to the village as a community, to harm them together as a group. Furthermore, the march could be seen as an attempt to insult or intimidate the Jewish community as a whole. The case has been analysed in terms of the growing importance of the notion of state neutrality and the rise of the 'unencumbered self' in American political culture and thought.[27] The thrust of their argument is that in not punishing defamation against groups the Supreme Court was shifting to a view that the only relevant harms were those suffered directly by an individual, whether that be by way of physical assault or injury to her reputation. The law was losing sight of the significance of the context or group in which the individual was situated and drew value.

Putting to one side the proper interpretation of judicial attitudes, the Skokie case would also be consistent with the view that the court decided that not just any group harm grounds a rights claim. In light of the present analysis of group rights it is uncertain that the Skokie villagers, or the wider Jewish community, had a legitimate rights claim based on harm against those who would march. First, the harm suffered must be considered within the context in which it arises. Other factors, such freedom of speech issues could undercut any appeal based on the harm that would actually arise. Second, there is surely a sense in which such a powerful instrument as a right can only be legitimately invoked when the need or danger is pressing. The Nazi march would be hurtful and cruel in many respects. It would not, though, endanger the Jewish community or the life its members had built. The state sanction under which the Nazis were marching was not one that could plausibly be read as a warning from the state to this minority. The Skokie villagers and Jewish community as a whole could look after themselves well enough without an appeal to the right that they be protected from insult.[28] This is not to say that the group did not have a right to defend itself, but that the legitimacy of a claim is calibrated by reference to the actual harm or risk with which the group is faced.

The appeal to a group right as a protection against the collective harms following the denial of, say, religious practices or autonomy is justified by the inadequacy

---

26 With the legal support of the ACLU the Nazi group led by Frank Collin succeeded in having the ordinances and an injunction against the march judged to be unconstitutional. Having achieved this, Collin offered to cancel the Stokie march if the Nazis could hold a rally in Marquette Park, Chicago. The Supreme Court refused to block the larger rally in Chicago which finally took place on 9 July 1978. A helpful synopsis of the events is to be found at the Illinois Periodical On-line Project – http://www.lib.niu.edu/ipo/ii781111.html.

27 Sandel (1996).

28 Compare Sadurski (1990).

of individual rights to secure the necessary protections. The appeal to group rights is directly linked to the plural voice which expresses the need for an irreducibly social good. It is not *I*, but *we* who have the right to live in this way, because its value is in our engagement together in the practices that make up this group and pattern of life. Freedom of individual religious conscience, or the freedom to live in accordance with one's own values and goals, do not give the individual the claims on others that they respect the right of a community to live in a particular fashion. Rather, individual rights protect the individual from the coercion of others in the development and pursuit of her own ideals and goals, if any. To respect individuals in this way may not be sufficient to secure the liberties (and resources) necessary for the group in which their lives take shape and acquire much of what is valuable.

V   The Liberal State and Group Rights

I shall conclude the chapter by sketching the challenge that the acknowledgement of group rights poses to liberal theory. If groups are recognised as being normatively significant in a way that endows them with rights, then liberal theory must be able to explain three issues. First, it ought to render pellucid how the recognition of group rights is consistent with the moral individualism to which liberal theory is committed, or explain away the apparent commitment. Second, liberal theory needs to make clear why certain kinds of groups are suitable candidates for rights while others are not. Third, in specifying the content of group rights liberal theory must ensure that it can either respect the difference between external protection and internal restriction rights, or explain why the latter may be in some cases acceptable to the liberal. In addressing these issues the liberal must also be clear whether group rights are to be understood as *sui generis* or instrumental, and to ensure that the responses to each part of the challenge are consistent with one another.

Putting matters in a rather general way, the liberal state is one that regards its citizens as free, equal, self-determining individuals, and the state is committed to moral individualism – the moral primacy of individual persons. The freedom and equality of individuals is expressed through the possession of common rights and the institutional procedures of the state. The liberal state is tolerant of cultural and national diversity among its citizens and non-citizen migrant populations. Cultural membership and participation in the practices of membership is something for the individual to determine for herself.

This is a general way of putting matters since liberal theory is not a single doctrine, but a range or family of views. A liberal could hold that there is just one really valuable way of life – being a liberal. With this ethical version of liberal theory toleration of other forms of life goes hand in hand with an effort on the part of the state to get all of its citizens to be good (enough) liberals. Or, one could characterise liberalism in perfectionsist terms through its commitment to autonomy. There is an open ended range of valuable lives, which are those pursued autonomously. The main role of the state is to secure for its citizens conditions of autonomy. The state ought to promote the practices, institutions and values which underpin the capacity to be autonomous and to rule out or discourage those forms of life which are not valuable. Distinct from either an 'ethical' or 'perfectionsist' liberalism are two further ways in which contemporary liberalism has been expressed. One is the 'political' turn associated with *inter alia* Rawls and Larmore[29] and the other is the 'liberal culturalism' of, for example, Kymlicka, Tamir and Miller.[30] Through both turns liberalism highlights the moral and explanatory significance of groups – for example, nations, religious and cultural communities – and individual membership thereof. At the same time the theories remain distinctively liberal in their defence or presupposition of canonical liberal values and institutional structures.

Liberal theory (in general) has been characterised in part by a commitment to moral individualism – the moral primacy of individual persons. A central concern of liberalism is the justification of the coercive power of the state as it is deployed against the individual. This is emphasised in, for example, the turn towards 'political liberalism' and its focus upon the principles to regulate the basic political and social institutions. The interests of the individual are enshrined in her rights, which define the limits of the state and map her path through the procedural structures in which the coercive power of the state is expressed. This turn in liberalism is 'political' because it seeks to eschew any commitment to a particular conception of the good or life-plan. Its neutrality does not spring from a void nor does it purport to establish a moral vacuum. There is a moral base to the liberal neutral state.[31] It presupposes a commitment to rational dialogue, in which there is an acceptance that differing, and potentially irreconcilable, views may be reasonable, and to a shared view of individuals as equally worthy of respect. The deployment of rights therefore springs from a prior view about the normative structure of a society. To argue that a group (or individual) has a right to something irreconcilable with a liberal conception of the regulation of a society is to take on the role of a Sisyphus, in which the required gradient is supplied by the moral content underwriting the appeal to rights in the first place.

The basic case for liberal theory to accord groups rights is that a commonality or community of shared individual citizenship rights is insufficiently sensitive to the needs, values, commitments and constraints that can arise as a result of one's membership of a cultural group. In particular, when that group is a minority group within a wider, dominant national community – the kind of community which finds expression in the idea of a nation state. Being a citizen expresses an identity, membership of a political community. However, cultural or national identities may

---

29 In particular Larmore (1987); Rawls (1996).

30 See, for example, Kymlicka (1995), Tamir (1993), Miller (1995).

31 Neutrality is here understood as the state's commitment not to promote any particular conception of the good or forms of life though its institutional procedures, laws and so on. The neutrality is at least constrained by a commitemnt to some basic liberal principles and it is a neutrality with respect to aim, rather than an active management of the kinds of lives and communities that do exist.

serve to undermine access to real equality of status as a citizen. For example, my religious commitments and the fact that my first language is not the official state language may serve to disadvantage me in terms of educational and employment opportunities notwithstanding my full possession of rights. Furthermore, the formal equality of citizenship may be insufficient to secure the resources, protections or exemptions needed to sustain the good of one's cultural or national identity. Indeed, the claims of national identity may stretch to the rejection of the very idea of citizenship of *this* state and at least to the demand that *we* ought to enjoy control over substantial areas of our life – we ought to be autonomous.

The liberal might then feel entitled to ask whether membership is *really* a private matter or a public kind of good? Does membership – as the foregoing sections have suggested – ground a claim as, say, a need or is it all just a matter of choice? The first part of the challenge to liberal theory arises if one thinks there can be group rights. For now groups appear alongside individuals in the domain of rights holders, and that is a *prima facie* denial of moral individualism. Against this one might hold that moral individualism is expressed through our basic or human rights. On this view it may become a minimalist claim in that it protects just the bare possibility of a kind of life. Furthermore, there emerges the question of whether the worth, effectiveness or value of such human rights can be undermined or enhanced by the kind and content of citizenship rights individuals enjoy. One attempt to dissolve the appearance of a problem for liberal theory may be to argue that group rights are only instrumental in giving effect to individual rights and other desirable ends or values. Now, though, a further question arises. Does this instrumental attitude to groups provide liberal theory with a stable basis to discriminate between groups? For, it seems possible that different kinds of group – clubs or associations – may promote those ends to just the same degree while not being recognised as possessing equal standing or significance.

The third element in the challenge to the liberal concerns the relationship between the external protection right of a group to security and self-determination and the internal restriction rights a group might exercise over its members. A liberal (culturalist) defence of group rights sees such rights as a means to ensure equality of members of minority groups as citizens capable of exercising choice over the course of their lives. To put matters roughly, the claim is that group rights are consistent with liberalism when they secure the freedom of individuals within a group and promote equality between groups.[32] The liberal is highly suspicious of internal restrictions, for they seem to undermine the freedom of individuals. However, in granting the external protection of (some degree of) political autonomy to a group, the liberal state may be in effect opening the way for the creation of internal restriction rights. Furthermore, a group may claim that it needs internal restriction rights in order to survive as a group. If the state takes the value of a group and membership seriously, then surely the very existence of the group is the most pressing of grounds for its claims to be met.

---

32 See Kymlicka (1995) esp. Chap. 3.

It is intuitively plausible that a right is only grounded in the suffering of a harm if the practice or good being denied or impaired satisfies a constraint of harmlessness. The clarity of this Millian principle contrasts with the difficulty in specifying what harm amounts to. Working with the basic notion that the enjoyment of a right by one party be consistent with its enjoyment by any other, an immediate limitation on the claims of a group is apparent. One group can not legitimately have a right that excludes others from also possessing it. Moreover, at first glance, it appears absurd to permit a group to require members to participate in practices which the liberal must judge as manifestly wrong.

The self-immolation of widows in the practice of suttee,[33] clitoridectomy (the surgical removal of the clitoris, which is a feature of some of the so called circumcision practices associated with, for example, certain traditional Sudanese and other East African female rites of passage ceremonies), and child marriage in some rural communities in the United States have been criticised as essentially coercive. The 'participants-victims' are never in a position to make a voluntary choice or endorsement of the practice. It is maintained that they are therefore simply the victims of physical abuse, which undermines the call for protection of a group need. Yet, the account of group rights I have adumbrated looks as if it must take into consideration the actual harm that the members of such groups will suffer if such practices are effectively proscribed. Leaving unattended difficult and controversial issues concerning the dynamics of harm and the operative notion of voluntary or informed consent, it seems clear that establishing whether a particular practice is abusive may prove difficult to determine. In particular it is likely to require a careful investigation of how the victims regard their own position.

Furthermore, judgement concerning a particular practice may need to be sensitive to the ways and extent to which the practice itself is subject to critical scrutiny and revision within the culture in which it is practised. However, let us grant that clitoridectomy or child-marriage in the Appalachians do represent abuses of individuals. One could say that there is just a straight clash of individual rights with the claim for a group right to continue the practice, and that the individual right against molestation will trump the group right. No right can have as its ground or purpose the imposition of a coercive harm on another rights bearer, and this is a feature of the liberal context in which rights are embedded.[34]

The right of a group to determine its own course does not entail that it has a right to engage in internally coercive practices that go beyond standards, expectations or commitments woven into the liberal framework of rights. Of course, there remains much more to be said on the relationship between and the distinctiveness of rights of protection and restriction. In particular, a pressing issue for liberals may not be whether groups have a right to non-interference, but of what the weight and extent are of claims made with respect to such a right. The distinction between external and internal rights is a neat one. However, once we grant the normative significance of

---

33 Outlawed by the Indian colonial authorities in 1829.
34 I leave aside questions of the right to be punished.

group needs it may not be an easy distinction to maintain when we must specify the content of a rights claim.

The claims that *we* have as a group to engage in our form of collective life may not threaten your right to some kind of life, but it could decisively undermine what is of value in your life through, for example, the distribution of resources or the impact of permissions and entitlements afforded to the group. If one takes seriously the notion that group harms ground group rights, then there arises the possibility that the protection of the group from harm may curtail the ability of certain individuals to pursue what they consider to be a valuable life. It is intuitively compelling from a liberal perspective that a group has no right to demand that individuals who do not wish to remain as members do so, nor that a group be permitted to coerce them into participating in practices vital to the group. Yet, at the same time, it is not obvious that a group has *no* right to demand certain sacrifices from its members (especially those who are willingly members), as when, for example, the group is placed under severe threat.

A fully fledged theory of group rights must address in detail the conceptual underpinning of the relationship between individual and group, but this is not the purpose of the present chapter which has been to adumbrate the plausibility of admitting groups into the domain of rights holders. The foregoing arguments suggest that the actual significance of irreducibly social needs and goods do provide a basis for developing a theory of group rights. An endorsement of a harm based ground for group rights means dealing with the underdetermination of which groups are valuable in the right way and of explaining the relationship between group and individual rights. An acceptance of group rights is not one that need be made by the ontological holist, nor by one who recognises the status of groups as sources of obligations and duties. Holism furnishes us with an understanding of groups through which we can see how irreducible social harms and needs are generated, and through which we grasp how the group can influence and shape the lives of its members. The assignment of rights to groups, though, must ultimately be settled by moral and political theory. Moving from moral status and rights, the next chapter asks if groups can sustain moral evaluation or judgement.

Chapter 8

The Moral Evaluation of Groups

I   Introduction

Having considered whether groups can possess moral status and rights, it is natural to ask if groups can also be the objects of moral evaluation and judgement. It is natural because moral status, possession of rights and aptness for moral judgement come together in our paradigm of a fully-fledged moral agent – the sane adult human being. In being capable of sustaining judgements a moral agent is presupposed to be able to deliberate and act in certain ways, and is considered the legitimate target for certain forms of action. In particular, persons are judged in terms of responsibility, praised or blamed, rewarded or punished. Both our attitudes and actions towards groups ought then to be informed by whether they are appropriate objects of moral judgements.

Possession of moral status and rights does not entail the capacity or aptness to be judged.[1] While a concern for the harm something can endure may underwrite its moral status and even endow it with rights, something more seems to be needed than the potential to be exposed to harm in order to render an entity apt for moral judgement. Ultimately, the elucidation of this 'something more' requires a theory of the necessary and sufficient conditions determining aptness for judgement; or, alternatively, perhaps an analysis of the family of properties around which our judgmental practices converge. The specification of such an account is a matter of deep and long-standing controversy within moral theory. At one level it seems pretty clear that moral accountability hangs on the extent to which a person is regarded as free or autonomous. However, questions as to the nature of the control an autonomous subject must have over his/her actions, cognitive and affective states, and even dispositions and appetites, quickly dim the light briefly cast by that obvious intuition.

In looking at whether groups are morally evaluable one could analyse groups in light of one's preferred theory of moral accountability, or the theory one takes to be most amenable to viewing groups as morally evaluable. Difficulties with this approach to the present topic appear on two fronts. On the first, the problem is just in the selection of a basis for evaluation and moral accountability. A discussion of the relevant issues threatens to take us too far afield from the central concerns of

---

1   Or, more precisely, on some theories of status and rights it does not.

the present work, although a full consideration of the evaluability of groups would need to engage with the relevant debate in moral theory. It is also far from clear what the most compelling account of moral accountability is. To hold that a capacity to endure harm is a basis for moral status and rights is contestable, but it is not question-begging once we have elucidated the nature of the harm. To say, for example, that moral accountability depends upon the subject's autonomy immediately raises the question of how to specify autonomy. Over what is the subject autonomous? Her actions, intentions (if these are not taken to be actions), desires, dispositions? Of course, cogent positions stake out the territory of the debate in moral theory, but stipulating a particular account here may just amount to a kind of handwaving.

The problem of specifying a theory of moral accountability is joined on a second front by one that arises from what seems to me to be a natural way of thinking about the moral evaluation of groups and the question of whether a group can be morally responsible. I have again described a view as 'natural', and this is really no more than a way of signalling views which have a certain intuitive force.[2] I begin from the belief that whatever a theory of moral evaluation and responsibility specifies, it will pick out certain conditions or properties which are features of persons – or rather moral agents understood as a restriction on the kind term person; and groups are in no obvious sense persons or agents. There may be deep and intractable disputes about what makes a person morally accountable, but there is the sense that it is a property(s) of persons. This is not to say they are exclusively possessed by persons, but we begin from a consideration of persons. Now, since I doubt that groups are properly understood as persons and believe our conceptions of moral responsibility are framed as consideration of persons, the following views arise when thinking about our judgements of groups.

First, much of our talk about group responsibility may just confuse the causal and explanatory role of a group with the judgements we make of its members individually, and in particular judgements relating to their personal commitment to and endorsement of the group's values, goals and practices. The anger and frenzy of the rampaging mob may result in some innocent persons being crushed. We may criticise individuals (perhaps all of them) for being part of the mob – each should have known better - but to hold the mob morally responsible is not entailed by the fact that the mob *qua* body was causally responsible for the injuries.

---

2   I doubt that a philosophical position is any the worse for starting from intuition. It is worth noting David Lewis's reflections in the Introduction to Lewis (1983) p. x:

Our 'intuitions' are simply opinions; our philosophical theories are the same. Some are commonsensical, some are sophisticated; some are particular, some general; some more firmly held, some less. But they are all opinions, and a reasonable goal for a philosopher is to bring them into equilibrium. Our common task is to find out what equilibria there are that can withstand examination, but it remains for each of us to come to rest at one or another of them. If we lose our moorings in everyday common sense, our fault is not that we ignore part of the evidence. Rather, the trouble is that we settle for a very inadequate equilibrium.

I opt to pass over the task of further elucidating the notion of our everyday common sense.

Second when we do assess a group as a group in evaluative terms it often seems to have more the shape of an aesthetic judgement. That is, we tend to see it as instantiating or expressing a certain value. Thus we may hold that Aztec culture was bad or ugly, but not hold the Aztec people morally responsible for the deaths it inflicted through sacrifice. Moreover, our judgement is not necessarily directed at the badness of the state of affairs brought about by the group when that state is assessed in terms of suffering or pain. In the case of Aztec culture, it is plausible that being sacrificed was either an honour or met with acceptance – perhaps an ordinary hazard within the terms of pre-Columbian Meso-American culture. The historic detail does not matter here. The point is that a group can strike us as good or bad in itself. On the calculus of utility the world may be a better place if contemporary neo-Nazis set up an isolated state of their own in the wilds of Idaho. Moreover, in doing so they threaten no other person's rights, and probably have a right to harmlessly engage in their voluntarily undertaken life together.[3] Nonetheless, it would be reasonable to judge that this group is bad because of its very nature, the goals and practices expressed through and underwriting its practices. It might be morally inappropriate to take action against it, but quite in order to decry it as bad and, perhaps, ugly.

Third, I believe we do sometimes evaluate groups morally. We assess a group in terms of goodness, right and virtue, and these judgements provide reasons for action.[4] However, it seems possible that there are degrees of moral judgement. A full-blown moral agent like an unimpaired human adult is judged to one standard, and entities which approach possession of her qualities, but fall short in some way, are judged to another. This is perhaps illustrated in our dealings with children as they mature and with persons who are in some way partially impaired in their cognitive faculties. The language of judgements, appraisal and responsibility does not appear fine grained enough to distinguish degrees of capacity to be judged. The man, the child and the group can all be said to have done wrong or to be bad. It does seem to me, though, that we recognise that different standards and expectations may apply to each class of judged.

This is not to say that we should think of groups as being evaluable or held accountable in *some sense*. Larry May, for example, has argued that we ought to assign moral responsibility to groups because this enables group-based harms to be addressed. Consider, for instance, the harms caused by a rampaging or rioting mob. Although May recognises that groups lack the intentional capacities necessary for moral agency, the identification of members with each other and shared goals and intentions produces the solidarity and cohesiveness of a single body. May claims it is:

> best to conceive of the responsibility of mobs in collective terms because the very intent
> to act [here it is clear that the intent is that of each of its members] comes from the sense

---

3   Detail can be added to the story to ensure that children are protected from being brought up in that environment; perhaps the community is voluntarily sterilised under conditions of informed consent.

4   If not necessarily the motivation to so act, but that is another debate.

of solidarity which the members feel toward each other, perhaps as a result of recognising a common enemy.[5]

He goes on to maintain that because individual members of a group may not intend to bring about a certain outcome, they cannot be held personally morally responsible, but that since a group's actions were determined by the relations between its members, and in particular their sharing in certain 'pre-reflective' intentions, there is a sense in which the group can be held morally responsible. Thus:

> the members of mobs have the two chief characteristics which are necessary for the ascription of moral responsibility: participation and intention. But since the intention is not a reflective state for most members, the members of mobs should not be held individually responsible for the harms caused by them. Rather, collective responsibility is, in a sense, the appropriate category to apply to mobs.[6]

The motivation to hold the group responsible *in a sense* appears to be that it allows a moral ascription to be made to an entity when there is really no basis for doing so, except the instrumental one of addressing a class of harms (group-based ones) better than could otherwise be achieved. Or, more charitably it is a way of expressing the sense in which action issued from commonalities or shared features among individuals. Again, it is to be doubted that an ascription of moral responsibility to those individuals collectively is appropriate. A difficulty for May's view is that the individual mob members are not in the right state to be held personally responsible, and the mob (a fiction within May's analysis) as such lacks the capacity to possess intentional states.

This attribution of moral responsibility *in a sense* is quite distinct from the suggestion that accountability may come in degrees linked to the capacity an entity has to sustain the relevant kind of judgements. In particular, there may be a certain point up to which one expects something (say a child) to be able to reflect on its actions and motivations in a way that grounds moral judgements about it. It is thus not in a sense that we hold children morally responsible, but up to a point. The interesting issue with groups is not whether we can find good reasons to treat them as if they were morally accountable (i.e. responsible in a sense), but whether they are the kind of thing whose nature elicits from us moral judgements within the bounds drawn by their capacities.

Rather than attempt to show that groups are fully-fledged moral agents like the typical human person, I shall consider if there is a minimal condition associated with moral agency – a hallmark of being considered apt to be judged – which groups can satisfy. In doing so it may then be appropriate to regard a group as being

---

5   May (1987) p. 80. My insertion.

6   May (1987) p. 83. The notion of pre-reflective intention is developed by May from Sartre. Very roughly, individuals do not have an intention to riot or act together as a mob, but they are 'configured' or disposed to do so by the solidarity characterising the relations in which they stand.

capable of bearing some degree of moral judgement. Again appealing to intuition I shall suggest that to be judged in moral terms a group must have, at a minimum, a capacity for collective reflection and deliberation. It is in this capacity that we can locate the ability of a group to exercise some degree of control over its actions. If one is convinced that a group can possess the appropriate capacity for reflection and deliberation, then at least an overhasty denial that groups can be judged is blocked.

II Moral Evaluation

Although I have used moral judgement and evaluation interchangeably, the different terms reflect separable dimensions of our moral assessments (a term I hope to be neutral for present purposes). Roughly speaking, we make moral evaluations or form judgements about another's actions, intentions, beliefs, desires, values, goals, feelings and character. Such assessments are expressed in terms of whether or not the object of a judgement is right, good or virtuous. Our assessments would seem then to fall into two categories. We judge a person's conduct before the moral law, holding her responsible for infringements in the absence of a suitable excuse. We judge a person to have acted rightly or wrongly. Or, we evaluate persons on the basis of what we could broadly call their character and motivations. We evaluate a person as good or bad, virtuous or vicious. Now, the relationship between these faces of assessment and of whether they reflect a dichotomy in moral stances is deep and interesting, but not one I shall address. Of concern to both a law based and character driven approach to moral assessment is the voluntariness or control a person can have over her actions and motivations. To put matters in a crude and oversimplified way, there is a matrix of positions on the metaphysical issue of the degree of control we can exercise over our actions and of the limits control imposes on our moral accountability for those actions. To this set of relations can be added the question of whether, or to what degree, a person is required to have control over his/her motivations, which in turn raises the question of how to characterise our motivations – desires, beliefs, intentions, dispositions, appetites and so on.

When we make moral judgements it appears that we presuppose the person being judged to be capable of: (a) forming and acting on intentions; (b) reflecting on goals, values and actions and adjusting them in light of the reflective process and new information; and, perhaps, (c) we also expect that the object of judgement be capable of the appropriate emotional response to her actions – in particular to experience shame, guilt and remorse. The first condition captures the thesis that moral evaluations are made of entities which act on the basis of their intentions and which are thus connected in a responsibility grounding fashion to their deeds and outcomes.[7] A familiar explanation of why the group – the members collectively – can

---

7   We can imagine someone who acts without forming intentions – an instance of such an action might be a mother forcing her way through a crowded room just on seeing her child

be held responsible is because the members share an intention to act together (as a group) in the relevant way, the likely outcome was common knowledge among them and they did act together in the relevant fashion.[8] Individuals can be held collectively or jointly responsible because they are appropriately linked to the relevant outcome by their sharing or participating in the intention(s) and deeds that led to its production.

In the small group examples which tend to feature in the discussion of shared intentions there is plausibility to the notion that we can share intentions in a way that binds us together as a group and in virtue of which we together as the group are morally accountable. However, particularly in large, complex groups in which many of the relations between more or less distant individuals are mediated by practices and institutions it appears unlikely that all the members will share intentions about goals and actions in a way that connects them directly to the production of the events and states for which the group is causally responsible. A challenge is, then, to explain if there is a ground for speaking in terms of group responsibility when the shared intention to produce the relevant event or state is absent.[9] Realism must explain – or explain away the appearance of – the nature of our talk about the responsibility of groups. For on the realist view this is not a mere shorthand form of talk about individuals, but reference to the group itself.

III   Collective Evaluation

From a school class held in detention to a people subjected to international sanctions (typically through punitive actions taken against a state), there appears little reticence in our readiness to make judgements of, attribute moral predicates to, and take action directed at groups. In evaluating groups as, for example, being praise or blameworthy, good or bad, worthy of admiration or to be reviled, we go beyond regarding them as moral patients to whom we owe certain duties or as the holders of rights. It looks as if groups are being held capable of acting in ways that elicit moral judgements or evaluations of the actor. If a group as a group can be judged in moral terms then the first, and perhaps both, of the following kind of claims should come out as being true or non-trivially false.[10]

---

in danger of being crushed. To the extent that such a person can deliberate on the values and attitudes which frame their stance towards and understanding of the world she is not obviously rule out as an appropriate object of judgement.

8   A number of different and plausible accounts of shared intention have been developed in recent years. See e.g. Bratman (1992), Gilbert (1997), Searle (1995), Tuomela and Miller (1988), and Tuomela (1995).

9   Or to show against appearances that there is suitably robust sense in which the members do collectively participate or share in the salient intentions or attitudes, which can support the attribution of moral judgement.

10   At any rate judgements about groups will be as truth apt as those of individuals, and as prone to problems of indeterminacy and underdetermination.

G1   The German People bears moral responsibility for the development of the Nazi state.
G2   The German People ought to feel shame and remorse if G1 is true.

We should note immediately that the beliefs and emotions through which the shame and remorse of the people find their expression are beliefs and emotions of individual members. This is not to say that group shame, or other emotions of self-assessment, are therefore necessarily analysable in terms of individual shame or whatever. There is a distinction between the 'I' thought an individual has with respect to her own shame and the 'we' thought about the shame of her group. A person may steal from another and (especially if caught) sincerely express her sense of shame. She recognises the blame that attaches to her action and accepts that she is the appropriate object of judgement. The belief that 'I am ashamed' and the emotion of shame arise from her assessment of and response to her own actions, the judgement of her by others and perhaps her contribution to some state of affairs. In this case to the fact that she deliberately stole something.

Contrasting with this sense of personal shame grounded in personal blameworthiness is the notion of group or collective shame. Here the individual has a 'we' thought. The judgement is that the group is to blame, with the consequence that as members we participate in the shame of the group. This is not shame that attaches to an individual's particular actions. Nor is it a sum of shame in which each member has some individualisable or quantifiable share.[11] The shame we have in respect of the group and its actions or character is distinct from our particular personal contributions, and is grounded in the fact that we are members. Importantly, a 'we' thought presupposes that others share it. Even if in fact they do not, they ought to if an individual is warranted in possessing it. Therefore, even if my emotional response were phenomenologically indistinguishable from that I experience with personal shame, the beliefs I have about my own blameworthiness and the appropriate actions of myself and others will be markedly different from those I have when I am *personally* ashamed. If an aspect of blaming a group is that it exhibits an appropriate emotional response then its members should possess (or be criticised for not possessing) the appropriate 'we' thoughts. If G2 is true, then the appropriate expression of shame on the part of individual Germans takes form '*we* are ashamed'.

It is worth stressing that the present point is with the evaluation of a group as such. That is, a judgement is made of it *qua* body, its members being judged together as a single and unified whole. The point is to be stressed because it appears perfectly coherent (in a sense) to say that I believe Germans to be wicked or admirable or whatever. I make a judgement about individuals who are German, and when I say 'The German People is characterised by wickedness' I express my evaluation of the individual Germans. Now, I may explain this judgement of individuals in terms of their membership of a group; perhaps, they cannot help but be wicked given the structure and nature of their group. Nonetheless, my judgement

11 Gilbert (1997) also makes this point.

is about individual persons and it is grounded in a property that these certain individuals happen to share. It is a judgement that can be changed in a way that a judgement about the group as such cannot. I may come across a 'good' German, thereby revising my belief to holding that most, but not all, Germans are wicked. In contrast to this a judgement about the group is not revisable in such a way in light of evidence that particular members may have contrary, or even contradictory properties from those that ground our judgement of the group. If there is a distinct judgement to be made of the group, then the judgement must be of *its* actions, goals and values. The point at hand is whether we have any basis for thinking that a group *qua* group can be judged morally, or if in fact our judgements of groups are just an aggregation of judgements about its members as individuals.

If there is to be a basis for holding a group to be morally evaluable, then it is grounded in its interrelational structure. In making a judgement about a group we are expressing a view about its individual members considered together, a judgement which is irreducible to the aggregation of the several assessment of each of the individuals.

IV   Deliberative Capacity

Groups lack the cognitive and affective structures and capacities of persons. Through the relations which constitute it, a group may have a capacity to process or handle information that is greater than the sum of its individuals' capacities, or different in its nature and properties. A group lacks, though, the mind of a self-conscious agent, and in virtue of which such an agent is considered capable of bearing moral evaluations. Yet, if a group has the practices that allow its members to reflect and deliberate upon the group's character, goals and practices, and to bring about changes in those goals and ways of being, then it is plausible to regard the members as collectively or jointly accountable for the nature and actions of the group. That is, the group as such has a reflective capacity within the relations through which it is constituted. It is important here to stress that the mere potential to have such reflective practices is too general a ground on which to hold a group accountable. Any group could in principle develop the appropriate practices. Furthermore, it looks too demanding to hold that every member must participate directly in the practices and institutions enabling collective reflection. Rather, the practices and institutions of reflection must be available to the group – its members taken together – as it engages in the potentially (and typically) complex array of practices in which it consists. Also the practices or structures in which the reflective capacity inheres must be able to exert an influence within the group in their own right. It is not enough that there is a capacity. The practices and institutions through which that capacity is realised must have an influence within the life of the group, and as such possess an explanatory role in an understanding or description of the group.

It is a task for the social sciences to furnish details of the forms these relations actually take, or indeed the extent to which we can say of a particular group that any such capacity is present. There is no *a priori* reason to suppose that groups must be morally evaluable in virtue of the shape of their interrelational structure. However, there is reason to think that, where the appropriate mechanisms for deliberation are available, the processes of reviewing and revising aspects of a group's values and practices are ones that can only be undertaken by the members together – by the group.

While I emphasise here the role of deliberative capacity in assessing the capacity of groups to sustain moral judgements, a fully worked out account of group or collective moral responsibility may be multi-criterial; or, at any rate offer a much richer notion of collective or group deliberation. For example, in showing how 'it makes sense to hold collective groups … responsible for the effects of what they do in such a way that individual members of those collectives can properly be held liable for the ensuing costs', David Miller suggest two models of collective responsibility.[12] On the 'like-minded' model members share aims and outlooks, and recognise their like-mindedness.[13] The group acts in certain ways and produces the states it does because its members share certain attitudes or contribute to their currency through membership. On the 'co-operative practice model' members are collectively responsible because they share fairly in the benefits produced from their participation in group constituting practices.[14] In confronting the judgements we actually have to make of groups we shall in practice need to recognise a range of considerations including the degree to which there is a capacity for deliberation, a shared set of attitudes and the distribution of benefits among its membership. That noted, the capacity to reflect and deliberate upon how we are and what we do seems absolutely central to any attempt to assign something like full-blown responsibility to a group.

The practices of a group, and the values or goals in which they are framed, arise from and are sustained by the on-going engagement of the individual members and the effects of the group as a whole on each of them. To talk of group practices, goals or attitudes is to pick them out because they are irreducibly social in their form of production and maintenance. An individual, for example, may harbour a racist attitude. A group can be said to value and endorse such an attitude through the way in which its members interrelate. Of course, the attitudes of individuals support and feed into the forms of relations in which they stand, but a group is not racist only if all (or most) of its members actually share such a view. Rather, a group is racist (or whatever) if the values, goals and practices through which it is structured entail

---

12 Miller (2004) p. 248. This paper focuses on the question of national responsibility. The discussion does not presuppose a commitment to the ontological holism defended in this book.

13 Ibid., p. 251

14 For example, by being workers in a collectively owned and democratically organised factory – see Miller (2004) p. 253.

the endorsement of such an attitude – whether or not individual members actually consciously endorse it. It may be that few members of a group would consider themselves to be racist, but that the practices of the group encourage a view of the world and the pursuit of goals, which do ultimately entail the presumption of the inferiority of groups distinguishable on grounds of, say, physical features. That which is valued, perhaps above other goals, by a group may only be realisable in ways that are harmful to other individuals or groups. Our claim to a particular territory, or to privileges over others, may be embedded in the ways in which we interrelate and the practices through which we lead our lives as members of the group.[15]

One way in which a group can change its values and practices is if each of its members determines to revise his attitudes in such a way that the patterns of interrelations alter so that the former values and practices can no longer be sustained. Here, we can think of a community in which each (or most) of the members is transformed by religious conversion when faced by, for example, an exceptional individual preacher. In this kind of case the group may change because of changes in the nature of its parts, and the way in which they (can) subsequently interact. A group can also review and revise its values and practices as part of the way in which its members interrelate, so that the process of review is not analysable in terms of the isolated actions of particular individuals. Rather, consideration of the nature of the values and practices is an aspect of those practices, an activity typically mediated by norms defining particular practices, the establishment of institutions or forums as public spheres, and through tradition. If a group fails to revise its wicked goals or practices given the availability of mechanisms for doing so, then it can be held morally evaluable in light of its values and actions.

An immediate objection is that the capacity for collective revision is necessary, but not sufficient for such an evaluation. It may be that given the range of values and attitudes available to the group, it could only consistently articulate and endorse what we consider wicked ends.[16] The objection is well made. Ultimately, it seems a question for ethnographic study to determine whether a group can be said to lack the cultural and conceptual resources to be able to recognise that its values and practices are at least open to moral criticism (or praise), and that such criticism may be framed in terms which are not immediately answerable by appeal to the values currently endorsed by the group.

Leaving open the matter of whether the historical and sociological evidence suggests that the German People does share some of the moral blame for the emergence of the Third Reich, there is a conceptual framework in which to place the question and

---

15 One might wonder whether a group composed of racists, but which is not racist as a group is possible. In its actions and relations the practices and relations constitutive of the group do not issue in racist acts, foster such an outlook and so on. While empirically unlikely perhaps because of the manifest tensions between the attitudes and commitments of its members and the relations and practices which constrain their realisation through the group, it does not involve any conceptual absurdity.

16 The same point can be made with respect to good or worthy ends. If the group could not have done otherwise, then should we praise the group? I think not, but as Baier (1990) has pointed out our treatment of unintended or inevitable good is not symmetrical with that of similarly caused harm.

to guide what counts as evidence. We can ask whether the group was characterised by the practices, institutions, intellectual and conceptual context and traditions in which the membership could review and attempt to revise its goals, values and the practices themselves. The process of review and revision may take place at a number of levels and within a variety of forums and through a range of practices.[17] The reflective capacity of a group need not be a function of any single sub-unit or practices or institution, but inhere in the interplay between different aspects and elements of the group. A culture amenable to critical review and the maintenance of institutions in which debate, review and revision can take place, is not one in which every member participates directly in these debates, but it is one in which the practice is sustained by the forms of interrelations in which the group consists. The valuing, for example, of freedom of speech does not entail its universal exercise by the membership of a group, but is part of the typically complex array of relations and attitudes through which members are held together. Of course, the ability of a people to bear witness to its values and practices can be constrained by their suppression at the hands of a determined state. Just as individuals can be coerced, so a group as a whole can be forced into certain forms of practice because its capacity to assess or change them is impaired.

The practices and attitudes of a group are produced collectively, and it is the members as a unit which is the object of moral evaluation. It is the individuals considered as a whole – as the group – which can review and revise. If we are satisfied that a group has this reflective capacity, then, notwithstanding how else it differs from a person, it is appropriate to look at the group in judgmental terms. We may not hold it morally responsible in just the same way as a person, but we can say that to some degree the group is morally accountable.

Two challenges to the practice of holding groups responsible ought to be noted. First, there is the question of whether the capacity to be held responsible entails the ability to display the appropriate moral emotions. If so, the issue arises of whether a group can indeed express such emotions. The second challenge considers the permissibility of acting upon the judgement formed about the group. This objection holds that in taking the group as the target of action individuals who are personally innocent of any morally salient contribution to the relevant group produced outcome may unduly suffer or be rewarded simply by virtue of their membership.

V   Experiencing the Emotion

One may doubt that a group can feel in the way it would need to in order to respect the demand of G2 – that the people feel shame and be remorseful. Even if we can identify an analogue of a person's capacity to determine and deliberate about her goals, values and actions in a group's mechanisms for collective reflection, there is no immediately obvious analogue for the capacity to experience and express emotion. If one is convinced that emotions of self-assessment like guilt, pride and shame are only properly felt with

---

17 This may certainly be the case with large and complex groups, such as a nation or people.

respect to what a person has done herself,[18] then it is difficult to see how a group itself could have the appropriate emotional response.

I suspect there is no single account of group emotions. Indeed, there seems to be distinct senses in which the notion of a group emotion appears applicable. Individuals may come to share emotions through reflection about their group and the nature of membership of the group. Or through their standing together as group members, which both fosters and is supported by the effects of sympathetic imagination or the occurrence of a kind of emotional contagion.[19]

Perhaps the way in which a group can properly be said to express the appropriate moral emotion may be through its members coming to experience that emotion just in virtue of being a member. All the members together – as a group – ought to stand affectively to the world in a certain way for the common reason that such an emotional response is demanded by the nature of the deeds of the group. Now, to motivate the plausibility of this sense of a group emotion the conviction that guilt, pride and shame are strictly first personal is to be resisted. Recalling the distinction adumbrated earlier between 'I' and 'we' thoughts, there may be cases in which an individual ought to experience a certain emotional reaction upon reflection of the nature or action of her group. The emotion is experienced as one that *we* share, or that my fellow members ought at any rate to share with me if they properly understand what it is to be a member and are capable of having such feelings. A person may have made no direct contribution to some good or evil deed, but her association as a member is a sufficient connection to take pride in or feel shame at the group. Sometimes it may be that membership entails that a person is disposed to respond emotionally to the deeds of the group, regardless of one's own direct contribution. To be a true member entails that one just does respond in certain ways in particular contexts. To take pride in *our* achievements and feel shame at *our* failures may just be part of what it is to be a member. In this case, a member is not led to an emotional response by reflection, but is already attuned emotionally to the group's actions. Now, it can be objected that such an emotion is not warranted just because of the lack of direct contribution. I cannot settle this matter here, but my aim is to point out candidate situations in which the notion of group emotion looks employable.

However, it is only in an extended sense that one would talk of the group *being* in a state of anxiety or *feeling* excitement or grief, for the experience of the emotion remains within each of the members. There is no group mind or consciousness in which the excitement or grief can be felt by the group as a subject of that experience.[20] Note, that this is not to say that certain emotional episodes (and perhaps some emotions?) do not

---

18 For example Taylor (1985) argues that guilt itself cannot be vicarious; feelings of guilt cannot arise from the omissions of others (p. 91). The phrase 'emotions of self-assessment' is the subtitle of Taylor's *Pride, Shame and Guilt*. Gilbert (1997) argues that such emotions can be felt by individuals in virtue of their participation in the joint commitment of plural subjects.

19 See brief discussion in Chapter 4.

20 At any rate there would need to be a compelling argument for a commitment to the notion of a group literally possessing a mind of such a nature.

depend upon individuals being in a group, but that it is difficult to motivate an intuitive sense in which a group as such experiences emotion like a person.

While acknowledging that the felt experience of the emotion is 'within the skin' of each of the members, and that for each it is uniquely her experience in the access she has to it,[21] there is an irreducibly social dimension to the experiencing of certain emotions. Let us say that G1 is true, and that therefore by G2 the German People ought to feel ashamed and remorseful. The requirement is directed at the members as a whole – all-together. Each member ought to feel the emotion appropriate in light of the actions and attitudes of her group. The shame and remorse is not prompted by an individual person's deeds, values or character, but by the group's. If I ought to possess these feelings of assessment, then all of us ought to. My emotions of assessment are not provoked by or directed at me alone, but by and at myself and my fellows together. Moreover, the group's deeds or character are the appropriate source of my emotional response only if all the members ought to feel this way in light of them. The very same deeds could provoke the same emotion in me and some others, say of pride or shame, because of each of our direct involvement in their production. The group-based emotion is prompted not by the extent to which I am directly or significantly involved in the relevant events or states of affairs, but by my membership. If I do not have the appropriate emotional response to the actions of the group, then this could be a failing on my part. Or, if the members generally lack the appropriate affective response, then it may be that the group is to be blamed for the way in which it has structured or influenced its members. We judge a people to have responded appropriately to its actions when its members share a sense of guilt or pride or whatever in virtue of the deeds or attitude of the group.[22] Of course, this is not to say that our judgements of groups are always impeccable. A group may have values and a structure such that its members share and express insincere feelings about the group's deeds. It may look as if the group attitude has changed, but this is merely a veneer.

Although an individual may have an emotional response to, or in virtue of, his group's actions or character, one might still ask whether members *ought* to feel anything with respect to the group. That is, membership of a group can explain 'we' thoughts and feelings of collective shame without showing that there exists appropriate grounds for holding the group morally responsible. I ought to feel ashamed or guilty for *my* misdeeds, but ought I experience shame or guilt for what the group has done? The judgement that members ought to feel a certain way with respect to the acts of their group can be grounded in a group's capacity for collective determination and revision.

---

21 I take it that each individual has unique and direct access to a token of a common or shared kind of experience.

22 What percentage of the group must share in the appropriate feeling if we are to judge that the group has responded (or not) as morality would demand? The obvious answer is most of the group should do so, as unanimity seems practically unlikely and not necessary given considerations of the on-going maintenance of the group. It may be, though, that rather fewer than most of the members need to share the emotion. Perhaps it is sufficient for the group to respond in the right way for only a few members to feel, say, guilt or pride provided most of the others do not have a contrary emotion with respect to the same deed or attitude.

Its members are together thereby suitably connected to the group's actions and attitudes to be held morally accountable. With moral accountability comes the requirement that one has responded fully (or as fully as one can) to the situation at hand when one's beliefs, actions and feelings are appropriately attuned to its moral demands. While experiencing an emotion may always affect the subject of that experience, the source of the same emotion can be different. I may be ashamed of myself, my brother and my group. The basis for feeling the emotion, and being judged as having to possess it, is that I am suitably connected with its source or the object at which it is directed.

VI   A Moral Objection

It can be granted that a group can be structured so that its members can collectively determine and reflect upon its goals, deeds and character. Yet, one may still object to the evaluation of a group in moral terms, even if it is only to a certain degree. The structure of the group, the pattern of its constitutive relations, can explain why individual members have certain values and pursue their ends in particular ways. It may also help to explain why individuals experience pride, shame, guilt and remorse as responses to the actions of their groups. Yet, the kind of analysis suggested in the previous section for why it might be plausible to assess groups in moral terms may strike some as illustrating only the ways in which a group can influence and affect its members. The group would be limited to this kind of role because the foregoing analysis cannot explain why an apparently important moral principle disappears from sight. The principle is that individuals can only be held accountable for attitudes, intentions and actions that they have freely determined and carried out.

The evaluation of a group appears to entail judgements being formed about individuals whether or not they had any free or direct role in the relevant event or states of affairs, or were indeed victims of their group. One can respond to this worry by pointing out that group or collective evaluation does not entail any personal judgement of particular members. It is carried out on a joint only basis, rather than a joint and several one. There is a difference between making a judgement of the group and a judgement of individuals considered singularly.

A problem remains, though. The distinction between group and individual evaluation aims to respect the principle that personal accountability be determined by a person's own choices, attitudes and actions. A significant part of morality is taking action towards those who have been judged. Centrally we punish and reward. Given the restriction on personal accountability it appears difficult to see how a group evaluation could issue in action, if that action entails directing action at (some of) the individual members. Theories of moral accountability and the grounds for morally justified action are clearly connected. That a person is properly held responsible for a an action features significantly in what counts as morally justifiable way of dealing with them – in determining the nature of the action to be appropriately directed against them. Holding a group responsible seems to leave underdetermined how we should treat any particular individual. It is possible to utter statements of praise or blame at the group, but as soon as we act in way that empowers or constrains, help or harms, particular individuals, it appears an individual may be (in effect) held personally accountable for actions or attitudes over which she had no control. Determining that the group is to blame cannot of itself lead to any action which impacts on the lives of its individual members, because each deserves to be treated in accordance with her own attitudes and actions. An understanding of the group can inform our judgement of the individual members, but, according to this line of argument, our judgement of the group cannot of itself decisively inform our action with respect to the members. Collective evaluation would seem not to be action-guiding in the way we expect of moral judgements.

This is a difficulty in knowing how to treat a group in a way that affects individuals fairly as members while somehow remaining sensitive to their individual, singularly specifiable, contributions, omissions and attitudes. Imagine the liberal minded minority in a racist, aggressive and oppressive people. Let us say that the people is held responsible for its systematic discrimination against a small group. Perhaps, the racist people is forced to give up certain of its practices and to engage in a process of public reflection and debate.[23] This may change the group in such a way that much of what all its members took as valuable in their collective life together is diminished along with its morally unacceptable practices. It may turn out that the group cannot endure or survive without grave loss in the sense of continuity and worth that even the liberal members valued. Perhaps given the original nature of the group this is a reasonable burden for all, including the liberals, to bear. For as members all participated in the constitution and character of the group. However, that it is reasonable for all to suffer does not appear to follow just from the fact that the remedies directed against the group address the morally objectionable aspects of its nature.

Although there is this constraint on moving from the judgement that a group is, for example, wicked to taking action against it, the evaluation of groups does have a role in our practical reasoning and our understanding of groups. First, acknowledgement that a group is morally accountable is one of the ways in which individual persons can develop their own moral character. In recognising that my group has endorsed a morally despicable practice I can come to (re)assess my own role and values. Furthermore, recognition that we *qua* group are morally accountable can encourage the review and assessment of the practices and values of the group itself. In doing so the way in which the group exerts a causal impact on the world, and the way in which it influences the character and actions of its members may undergo development.

It can also be the case that individuals are personally culpable because they fail to participate within the mechanisms or forums available to review and revise the

---

23 Of course everything needs to be said about how this would be undertaken.

values and practices of the group. Indeed, individuals may seek to personally endorse those practices either by direct participation or approval of those who do: had they been in the same situation they would have acted in just that fashion. There are of course limits on what an individual person can be expected to do, and the options she has will be partly be determined by the group. Nonetheless, in recognising that there is a judgement to be directed at the group, we come to see a context in which individuals can also be evaluated: that is, individuals can be assessed in terms of their participation within a group. Indeed, this is may be a common form of individual evaluation. Returning to the German People it seems that loyal but squeamish Nazis are personally blameworthy for mass exterminations in a way that scared, coerced liberal train drivers on the death camp line are not, even though the latter would have been directly involved in transporting victims to their extermination.

Sometimes it may be clear that a group's actions are indeed actively endorsed by its members, and that there is very close fit between group and personal values and goals. In such a case the group and the members reflect and support the values of each other, and in observing one we witness what is morally salient about the other. It is probable that certain groups are constituted precisely because members share certain attitudes and goals, and the on-going maintenance of the group inheres in their personal endorsement of its goals and their collective engagement in the pursuit of those goals. Here we can think of groups dedicated to extreme and active political or religious goals, and in which there is little scope for personal agnosticism – either as a way of maintaining membership or as a means of sustaining the group in its particular form. Of course, in advance of social scientific investigation we cannot tell how many groups are like this.[24]

With persons the question can be raised of whether a significant change in their nature or character through time relieves them today of responsibility for past actions. So too with groups: to what degree is a group today morally responsible for the events and states for which it has been causally responsible? Consider demands that 'White America' today is responsible for the relative disadvantage of 'Black America',[25] particularly through its exploitation of slavery. Likewise the peoples of colonial nations are held morally accountable for the treatment of their former colonies, and the on-going difficulties encountered by their peoples as a result of the colonial legacy. Conceding that a group was to blame for its past actions, it can be argued that through the mechanisms of collective reflection and revision the old goals and attitudes can be adjusted – and indeed are today radically different from the past attitudes and goals which framed the pursuit of morally unacceptable, wicked and

---

24 It is noteworthy that when action is taken against a group as such, in the form of, say, economic sanctions, it is not (never?) justified on the grounds that the people deserve it, or that consideration of the individuals suggests each is sufficiently blameworthy, but on pragmatic or 'realist' grounds.

25 The scare quotes are meant to indicate this is shorthand for a range of candidate groups: white Americans; the Rich; the Southerners and so on. Nothing in the present point hangs on the detail of the claims.

bad practices (Perhaps, for example, one might conclude that the German People in the first part of the twentieth century was morally responsible for the emergence of the Nazi state while recognising that the character of the group has undergone radical shifts in the second half of the century). Nonetheless, it can be insisted that obligations were created as a result of the past actions, and that therefore the 'reformed' group today must discharge these obligations. This claim might be plausibly constrained by recognition that to fully discharge some obligations may be ruinous for the party bearing liability, and that ruination would be unjust. In effect a claim for compensation does penalise individuals today, who are morally innocent of contribution towards or endorsement of the practices and attitudes in virtue of which the obligations are said to have arisen.[26]

If the group today has reformed its goals and attitudes, then to hold it morally accountable for its past actions we must discount the significance of its change of character. One might try to argue that it is not the same group because it has changed so much. This seems implausible if the group today stands in relations of causal continuity and narrative role so that we individuate just the one (developing or evolving) group through time in our explanations and descriptions. It is controversial whether an individual person whose character or personality changes profoundly is to be held morally accountable now for her past deeds.[27] Against the view that a individual profoundly changed in character escapes responsibility for past deeds, though, are considerations that a person is responsible for her actions throughout the course of her life, and that justice demands that she receive her due. We should perhaps not be optimistic that any clear answer should be available with respect to groups. The revision of practices and goals, and perhaps the acknowledgement by the group that it had acted badly in the past, may be the most that can be demanded today of the group as such. If a group fails to reform morally, then we are brought back to the question of how to treat it in a way that respects the principle of individual

---

26 Here the question is whether a group has obligations in respect of its past misdeeds, and there are typically calls that the obligation be discharged in the form of an acknowledgement of the wrongdoing and a redistribution of resources. Demands for the same kind of redistribution of resources, and perhaps also where necessary the establishment of constitutional safeguards against repetition, could also be grounded on rather different grounds. For example, the advantages enjoyed today by one group relative to another may not have been properly or fairly paid for. The claim would not be a past wrong needs to be acknowledged so much as an outstanding debt honoured. More radically, a call for redistribution may arise because there is no moral justification for such inequality between groups regardless of how it has arisen.

27 Perhaps this is most pressing in cases involving the death penalty. Sensitive to arguments concerning the significance of the change in personality on the justice of carrying out the sentence advocates of capital punishment sometimes stress the importance of timely execution to ensure that the guilty person(ality) is put to death. See, for example, Van Den Haag (1985) who also appeals to the notion that the personhood be analysed in terms of person-stages.

accountability. There is no quick answer, or practical algorithms resulting from an analysis of groups and their moral accountability. Nonetheless in recognising that groups can be evaluated to some degree in moral terms our practical reasoning acquires both a depth and scope that is responsive to the potential complexity of the social domain we inhabit.

Chapter 9

Concluding Remarks

By explaining that our best understanding of social groups is as composite material particulars, I hope to have furnished an ontological underpinning to the widely felt sense that groups are significant in the unfolding of our lives in the personal, communal and political spheres. There is a quite literal sense in which we are absorbed into and bump against groups. In caring for the individual and displaying recognition for her needs and claims, we must sometimes acknowledge that she is tied together with her peers as a group.

Of course an ontological underpinning is just that, and much work remains to be done on all aspects of the social world. For example, in developing a semantic analysis of first person plural statements it seems likely that 'we' is sometimes referring to the group in just the same way as 'it'. When the band of rebels is about to be executed by the forces of the regime oppressing the minority people to which they belong, the band's leader may declare that 'we will never go away'. Read as a claim about the people this is may indeed prove to be the case; read as a reference to the rebel band it is a triumph of optimism. This is just a simple example, suggesting that a realist social ontology may help to capture formally more of the expressive richness of natural language.

Other areas in which the ontological analysis here may contribute are in studies of how groups facilitate the cognitive and cultural functioning of individuals,[1] and of how groups as such possess a processing power or cognitive-like capacity distinct from their individual members.[2] The mindedness of groups and corporations is certainly an area that can stand much more work. In political theory and science, and in the practical task of policy formulation, interesting light may be cast by an understanding of groups and corporations as entities with a responsive capacity in their own right. In economics and psychology the recognition of groups as real, material entities with causal powers may inform theory formation, the ever expanding deployment of game theoretical approaches and methods, and the construction of experiments. A particularly pressing need is to deepen our understanding of the bases for and the mechanisms of the appropriate attribution of moral responsibility and legal liability to groups. Questions of political obligation may, for example, be informed by a sense that membership can act as very real constraint on the demands that can realistically be made of individuals. On the heels of recent anthropological investigation, the conception of a group can be extended and tested by considering the nature of the kind of interrelations taking place (and made possible) by the recent growth in the capacity and sophistication of telecommunications and information

---

1   Compare Kusch (1999), although I take issue with his constructivist approach.
2   As discussed in Hutchins (1995).

technology.[3] We should consider whether increasing technological capacity and options means we are engaging in more of the same kind of practices, or whether genuinely new kinds of interchanges and social objects are emerging.

A conception of a social group as a composite material particular means we need not accord social groups a special metaphysical place any more than we need to confine them to the metaphorical slums. The recognition that groups are material particulars supports a broadly naturalist approach to the social sciences. Now, this is not to say that holism is necessary for such an approach, merely that it forms an element in one defence of a naturalist view. In the context of the present work I shall not expand on this issue, but I shall conclude by adumbrating why I understand holism to help underpin naturalism.

A naturalist approach is one that takes there to be a substantive sense in which there are continuities between the natural and social sciences. That continuity may no longer be sought in the form of a common methodology drawn from the practices of the hard sciences, or in a shared commitment to the discovery and elucidation of laws as the hallmark of a scientific domain of enquiry. Given the doubts and controversy concerning the nature and status of natural scientific claims and methodology, a naturalist approach to the social sciences no longer means attempting to ape the so called proper methods of the hard sciences. Naturalism is perhaps better conceived as a two way street. Different domains of enquiry seek to delineate and elucidate the salient features of a mind-independent world from their particular perspectives, and in doing so they may cast light upon or inform other domains of enquiry. Scientific practice is constrained and shaped by both the nature of the world and by the interests and perspective of a particular field or branch of study. In recognising that groups are objects in the world, the natural and social sciences find that at a high order of taxonomic classification they are studying the same kinds of thing – material particulars.[4] Moreover a proper task of the social sciences emerges as the engagement with that investigation into the nature and structure of our world.

Interpretivist and critical perspectives in the social sciences are essential in understanding the nature of our interactions, the significance of reflection and reflexivity in the patterns of interrelations and the degree and kind of control self-conscious rational agents can exert over their own actions and destiny. Nonetheless, groups are formed and we have reason to take them as possessing their own powers and properties, which in turn help shape the nature of our world. It is a world to be understood and divided not merely in accordance with our interests, understanding and critical perspective, but in a way that is constrained by the nature and powers of the objects that inhabit it. Among those objects are individual persons and social groups.

---

3   See for example Hakken (1999).

4   The individualist could also make this claim, the proper object of social scientific study being individual persons. However, she must first explain away reference to groups.

Bibliography

Aristotle (1983), *The Politics* (revised edition), trans. T. Sinclair, London: Penguin.

Baier, A. (1990), *Moral Prejudices*, Cambridge, MA: Harvard University Press.

Benn, S. (1988), *A Theory of Freedom*, Cambridge: Cambridge University Press.

Beckermann, A., Flohr, H. and Kim, J. (eds) (1992), *Emergence or Reduction: Essays on the Prospects for Nonreductive Physicalism*, Berlin: de Gruyter & Co.

Brandt, R. (1965), 'The Concepts of Obligation and Duty', *Mind*, 73, pp. 374–93.

Bratman, M. (1992), 'Shared Cooperative Activity', *Philosophical Review*, 101(2), pp. 327–41.

Buchanan, D. and Huczynski, A. (1985), *Organizational Behaviour: An Introductory Text*, London: Prentice Hall.

Burge, T. (1979), 'Individualism and the Mental', *Midwest Studies in Philosophy*, 4, pp. 73–121.

Burke, M. (1997), 'Coinciding Objects: Reply to Lowe and Denkel', *Analysis*, 57(1), pp. 11–18.

Campbell, J. (1986), *Essays in Anglo-Saxon History*, London: Hambledon Press.

Carter, A. (1990), 'On Individualism, Collectivism and Interrelationism', *Heythrop Journal*, XXXI, pp. 23–38.

Cartwright, N. (1983), *How The Laws of Physics Lie*, Oxford: Oxford University Press.

Cartwright, N. (1994), 'Fundamentalism vs. The Patchwork of Laws', *Proceedings of The Aristotelian Society*, IVC, pp. 279–92.

Chalmers, D. (1996), *The Conscious Mind*, New York: Oxford University Press.

Churchland, P.M. (1981), 'Eliminative Materialism and the Propositional Attitudes', *Journal of Philosophy*, 78, pp. 67–90.

Clanchy, M. (1983), *England and Europe 1066 – 1272*, Glasgow: Fontana.

Cooley, C. (1964), 'Primary Groups' in L. Coser, and B. Rosenberg, *Sociological Theory*, London: Macmillan (reprinted from Cooley (1909) *Social Organisations*, London: Scribner's).

Copp, D. (1984), 'What Collectives Are: Agency, Individualism and Legal Theory', *Dialogue*, XXIII, pp. 249–69.

Cruse, A. (1979), 'On The Transitivity of the Part-Whole Relationship', *Journal of Linguistics*, 15, pp. 29–38.

Currie, G. (1984), 'Individualism and Global Supervenience', *British Journal for the Philosophy of Science*, 35, pp. 345–58.

Dan-Cohen, M. (1986), *Rights, Persons and Organizations*, Berkeley: University of California Press.

Davidson, D. (1970), 'Events as Particulars', *Nous*, 4, pp. 25–32.

Davidson, D. (1971), 'Agency' in R. Binkley, R. Bronaugh and A. Marras (eds), *Agent, Action and Reason*, Tornonto: University of Toronto Press.

Davidson, D. (1980), *Essays on Actions and Events*, Oxford: Oxford University Press (1980).

Davidson, D. (1987), 'Knowing One's Own Mind', *Proceedings and Addresses of the American Philosophical Association*, 60(3), pp. 441–58.

Dennett, D. (1991), *Consciousness Explained*, Boston: Little Brown.

Dupré, J. (1993), *The Disorder of Things*, Cambridge, MA: Harvard University Press.

Durkheim, E. (1982/1895), *The Rules of Sociological Method* (trans W. Halls), London: Macmillan.

Durkheim, E. (1982/1908), 'The Method of Sociology', *Les Documents du Progrès*, 2, pp. 131–2 repr. as an appendix in Durkheim (1982/1895).

Elster, J. (1999), *Alchemies of the Mind*, Cambridge: Cambridge University Press.

Fodor, J. (1974), 'Special Sciences (Or The Disunity of Science As A Working Hypothesis)', *Synthese*, 28, pp. 97–115.

French, P. (1979), 'The Corporation As a Moral Person', *American Philosophical Quarterly*, 16(3), pp. 207–15.

French, P. (1983), 'Kinds and Persons', *Philosophy and Phenomenological Research*, XLIX(2), pp. 241–54.

French, P. (1984), *Collective and Corporate Responsibility*, New York: Columbia University Press.

French, P. (1992), *Responsibility Matters*, Lawrence: University Press of Kansas.

Fukayama, F. (1995), *Trust: The Social Values and the Creation of Prosperity*, New York: Simon and Schuster.

Gellner, E. (1956), 'Explanations in History', *Proceedings of the Aristotelian Society*, 30, pp. 157–76.

Ghiselin, M. (1987), 'Species Concepts, Individuality and Objectivity', *Biology and Philosophy*, 39, pp. 225–42.

Gibbard, A. (1975), 'Contingent Identity', *Journal of Philosophical Logic*, 4, pp. 187–221.

Giddens, A. (1997), *Sociology* (Third Edition), Cambridge: Polity Press.

Gilbert, M. (1987), 'Modeling Collective Belief', *Synthese*, 73, pp. 185–204.

Gilbert, M. (1989), *On Social Facts*, Princeton: Princeton University Press.

Gilbert, M. (1990), 'Walking Together', *Midwest Studies in Philosophy*, 15, pp. 1–14.

Gilbert, M. (1993), 'Group Membership and Political Obligation', *The Monist*, 76, pp. 119–31.

Gilbert, M. (1996), *Living Together*, Lanham: Rowman & Littlefield.

Gilbert, M. (1997), 'What Is It For Us To Intend?', in *The Philosophy and Logic of Social Action*, J. Holmstrom-Hintikka, and R. Tuomela (eds), Dordrecht: Kluwer Academic.

Gilbert, M. (1999), 'Obligation and Joint Commitment', *Utilitas*, 11(2), pp. 143–63.

Gilbert, M. (2000), *Sociality and Responsibility*, Lanham: Rowman & Littlefield.

Goldie, P. (1999), 'How We Think of Others' Emotions', *Mind and Language*, 14(4), pp. 394–423.

Goldie, P. (2000), *The Emotions: A Philosophical Exploration*, Oxford: Clarendon Press.

Gould, C. (1996), 'Group Rights and Social Ontology', *The Philosophical Forum*, XXVIII, pp. 73–86.

Green, L. (1998), 'Rights of Exit', *Legal Theory*, 4, pp. 165–85.

Griffiths, P. (1997), *What Emotions Really Are*, London: University of Chicago Press.

Hakken, D. (1999), *Cyborgs@Cyberspace? An Ethnographer Looks to the Future*, London: Routledge.

Hare, R. (1952), *The Language of Morals*, Oxford: Oxford University Press.

Hellman, G. and Thompson, F. (1975), 'Physicalism: Ontology, Determination, and Reduction', *Journal of Philosophy*, 72, pp. 551–64.

Hohfeld, W. (1964/1919), *Fundamental Legal Conceptions*, London and New Haven: Greenwood Press.

Hossack, K. (2000), 'Plurals and Complexes', *British Journal for the Philosophy of Science*, 51(3), pp. 411–43.

Hull, D. (1978), 'A Matter of Individuality', *Philosophy of Science*, 45, pp. 335–60.

Hume, D. (1978/1739), *A Treatise of Human Nature* (2nd Edition) (ed. P.H. Nidditch), Oxford: Oxford University Press.

Hutchins, E. (1995), *Cognition in the Wild*, Cambridge, MA: MIT Press.

Jackson, F. (1998), *From Metaphysics to Ethics: A Defence of Conceptual Analysis*, Oxford: Oxford University Press.

Jackson, F. and Pettit, P. (1990), 'Program Explanation: A General Perspective', *Analysis*, 50(2), pp. 107–17.

James, S. (1984), *The Content of Social Explanation*, Cambridge: Cambridge University Press.

Kemeny, J. and Oppenheim, P. (1956), 'On Reduction', *Philosophical Studies*, 7, pp. 6–19.

Kilpi, J. (1998), *The Ethics of Bankruptcy*, London: Routledge.

Kim, J. (1989), 'The Myth of Non-reductive Materialism', *Proceedings and Addresses of The American Philosophical Association*, 63, pp. 31–47.

Kim, J. (1990), 'Supervenience as a Philosophical Concept', *Metaphilosophy*, 21, pp. 1–27.

Kim, M. (1992), 'Downward Causation and Emergence' in A. Beckermann, H. Flohr and J. Kim (eds), *Emergence or Reduction: Essays on the prospects of Nonreductive Physicalism*, Berlin: de Gruyter & Co.

Kitcher, P. (1979), 'Natural Kinds and Unnatural Persons', *Philosophy*, 54, pp. 541–7.

Korsgaard, C (1996), *Creating The Kingdom of Ends*, Cambridge: Cambridge University Press.

Kripke, S. (1972/1980), *Naming and Necessity*, Oxford: Oxford University Press.

Kuhn, T. (1977), 'The Essential Tension: Tradition and Innovation in the Scientific Record' in T. Kuhn (ed.), *The Essential Tension: Selected Studies in Scientific Tradition and Change*, London: University of Chicago Press.

Kusch, D. (1999), *Psychological Knowledge*, London: Routledge.

Kymlicka, W. (1995), *Multicultural Citizenship*, Oxford: Clarendon Press.

Larmore, C. (1987), *Patterns of Moral Complexity*, Cambridge: Cambridge University Press.

Leibniz, G. (1934/1714), *Monadology* in *Philosophical Writings*, London: Everyman.

Lebra, T. (1989), 'Adoption Among the Hereditary Elite of Japan: Status Preservation Through Mobility', *Ethnology*, 28, pp. 185–218.

Lefebvre, G. (1949), *The Coming of The French Revolution* (trans. R Palmer), Princeton: Princeton University Press.

Levey, S. (1997), 'Coincidence and principles of composition', *Analysis*, 57(1) pp. 1–10.

Lewis, D. (1969), *Convention: A Philosophical Study*, Cambridge, MA: Harvard University Press.

Lewis, D. (1973), *Counterfactuals*, Oxford: Blackwell.

Lewis, D. (1976), 'Survival and Identity' in A. Rorty (ed.), *The Identities of Persons*, University of California Press.

Lewis, D. (1983), *Philosophical Papers* (Volume 1), New York: Oxford University Press.

Lewis, D. (1986), *On the Plurality of Worlds*, Oxford: Blackwell.

Locke, J. (1975/1690), *An Essay Concerning Human Understanding* (ed. P.H. Nidditch), Oxford.

McMahon, C. (1994), *Authority and Democracy*, Princeton: Princeton University Press.

Mandelbaum, M. (1955), 'Societal Facts', *The British Journal of Sociology*, 6, pp. 305–17.

Mandelbaum, M. (1957), 'Societal Laws', *The British Journal for the Philosophy of Science*, 8, pp. 211–24.

May, L. (1987), *The Morality of Groups*, Notre Dame: University of Notre Dame.

May, L. (1996), *The Socially Responsive Self*, Chicago: The University of Chicago Press.

Mellor, D. (1982), 'The Reduction of Society', *Philosophy*, 57, pp. 51–75.

Miller, D. (1995), *On Nationality*, Oxford: Clarendon Press.

Miller, D. (2002), 'Group Rights, Human Rights and Citizenship', *European Journal of Philosophy*, 10, pp. 178–95.

Miller, D. (2004), 'Holding Nations Responsible', *Ethics*, 114, pp. 240–68.

Miller, R. (1978), 'Methodological Individualism and Social Explanation', *Philosophy of Science*, 45, pp. 387–414.

Moore, A. and Crisp, R. (1996), 'Welfarism in Moral Theory', *Australasian Journal of Philosophy*, 74 (4), pp. 598–613.

Moore, G. (1922), 'The Concept of Value' in G. Moore (ed.), *Philosophical Studies*, London: Routledge and Kegan Paul.

Nagel, T. (1995), 'Personal Rights and Public Space', *Philosophy and Public Affairs*, 24, pp. 83–107.

O'Neill, J. (ed.) (1973), *Modes of Individualism and Collectivism*, London: Heineman.

Oppenheim, P. and Putnam, H. (1958), 'The Unity of Science as a Working Hypothesis', in H. Feigl, M. Scriven and G. Maxwell (eds), *Minnesota Studies in The Philosophy of Science*, vol. II, Minneapolis, University of Minnesota Press.

Papineau, D. (2002), *Understanding Consciousness*, Oxford: Oxford University Press.

Perry, J. (1979), 'The Problem of The Essential Indexical', *Nôus*, 13, pp. 3–21.

Pettit, P. (1996), *The Common Mind (With Postscript)*, New York: Oxford University Press.

Putnam, H. (1973), 'Meaning and Reference', *The Journal of Philosophy*, 70, pp. 699–711.

Quine, W. (1960), *Word and Object*, Cambridge, MA: MIT Press.

Quine, W. (1980), 'On What There Is', reprinted in W. Quine (ed.), *From a Logical Point of View*, Cambridge: Harvard University Press.

Quinton, A. (1975), 'Social Objects', *Proceedings of The Aristotelian Society*, 75, pp. 1–27.

Rawls, J. (1996), *Political Liberalism* (2nd Edition), New York: Columbia University Press.

Rousseau, J. (1968/1762), *The Social Contract* (trans. M. Cranston), London: Penguin.

Raz, J. (1984), 'Rights', *Mind*, 93, pp. 194–214.

Raz, J. (1988), *The Morality of Freedom*, Oxford: Clarendon Press.

Ruben, D-H. (1985), *The Metaphysics of The Social World*, London: Routledge & Kegan Paul.

Sadurski, W. (1990), *Moral Pluralism and Legal Neutrality*, Dordrecht: Kluwer.

Sandel, M. (1996), *Democracy's Discontent America in Search of a Public Philosophy*, Cambridge, MA: Harvard University Press.

Schatzki, T. (1988), 'The Nature of Social Reality', *Philosophy and Phenomenological Research*, XLIX (2), pp. 239–60.

Schatzki, T. (1996), *Social Practices*, Cambridge: Cambridge University Press.

Scheler, M. (1954/1913), *The Nature of Sympathy* (trans. P. Heath), London: Routledge.

Scruton, R. (1989), 'Corporate Persons', *Proceedings of The Aristotelian Society*, Supp. Volume 63, pp. 239–66.

Scruton, R. (1994), *Modern Philosophy: An Introduction and Survey*, London: Sinclair-Stevenson.

Searle, J. (1995), *The Construction of Social Reality*, London: Penguin Books.

Simons, P. (1987), *Parts: A Study in Ontology*, Oxford: Clarendon Press.

Simmel, G. (1971/1908), 'How is Society Possible?', in D. Levine (ed.), *Georg Simmel: On Individuality and Social Forms*, Chicago: University of Chicago Press.

Sober, E. (1993), *Philosophy of Biology*, Oxford: Oxford University Press.

Sanford, D. (1970), 'Locke Leibniz, and Wiggins On Being in the Same Place at the Same Time', *The Philosophical Review*, LXXIX, pp. 75–82.

Stern, J. (1984), *Hitler: The Führer and the People*, London: Fontana.

Strawson, P. (1959), *Individuals: An Essay in Descriptive Metaphysics*, London: Routledge.

Swindler, J.K. (1996), 'Social Intentions: Aggregate, Collective and General', *Philosophy of the Social Sciences*, 26, pp. 61–76.

Tamir, Y. (1993), *Liberal Nationalism*, Princeton: Princeton University Press.

Taylor, B. (1993), 'On Natural Properties in Metaphysics', *Mind*, 102, pp. 81–100.

Taylor, C. (1997), *Philosophical Arguments*, Cambridge, MA: Harvard University Press.

Taylor, G. (1985), *Pride, Shame and Guilt: The Emotions of Self-Assessment*, Oxford: Clarendon.

Thompson, J. (1983), 'Parthood and Identity Across Time', *The Journal of Philosophy*, LXXX, pp. 201–20.

Tidman, P. (1993), 'The Epistemology of Evil Possibilities', *Faith and Philosophy*, 10, pp. 181–97.

Tuomela, R. (1995), *The Importance of Us*, Stanford: Stanford University Press.

Tuomela, R. and Miller, K. (1988), 'We Intentions', *Philosophical Studies*, 53, pp. 367–89.

Van Den Haag, E. (1985), 'Refuting Reiman and Nathanson', *Philosophy & Public Affairs*, 14, pp. 165–76.

van Frassen, B. (1980), *The Scientific Image*, Oxford: Clarendon Press.

Waldron, J. (1993), *Liberal Rights*, Cambridge: Cambridge University Press.

Warren, M. (1997), *Moral Status*, Oxford: Clarendon Press.

Watkins, J. (1952), 'Ideal Types and Historical Explanation', *The British Journal for the Philosophy of Science*, 3, pp. 22–43.

Watkins, J. (1955), 'Methodological Individualism: A Reply', *Philosophy of Science*, 22, pp. 58–62.

Watkins, J. (1957), 'Historical Explanation in the Social Sciences', *The British Journal for the Philosophy of Science*, 8, pp. 104–17.

Weber, M. (1978/1922), *Economy and Society*, Berkeley: University of California Press.

Wellman, C. (1996), *Real Rights*, Oxford: Oxford University Press.

Werhane, P. (1985), *Persons, Rights and Corporations*, Engelwood Cliffs: Prentice Hall.

Wiggins, D. (1968), 'On Being in the Same Place at the Same Time', *The Philosophical Review*, LXXVII, pp. 90–95.

Wiggins, D. (1980), *Sameness and Substance*, Oxford: Oxford University Press.

Worsley, P. (ed.) (1977), *Introducing Sociology*, London: Penguin Books.

Zimmerman, D. (1996), 'Could Extended Objects be Made out of Simple Parts? An Argument for Atomless Gunk', *Philosophy and Phenomenological Research*, 56, pp. 1–29.

Index

accountability, corporations 134–5
Alexander, Samuel 27
Amish 105, 175
   group rights 188
The Angry Silence 83
animal groups 129–30
Aristotle 100
   on happiness 169
   on the state 97
atomism, and ontological individualism
   23–4

Boethius 149
Bradley, F.H. 6, 133
bridge principles, reductionism 25–6
'bully', etymology 84
bullying, by groups 83–4

Campbell, J. 81
Carter, Alan, on interrelationism 44–5
conceivability, and possibility 117–18
constructivism, groups 43
Cooley, Charles H., on primary groups 58–9
Copp, David 21
   groups, mereological analysis 47–51
corporations
   accountability 134–5
   computerised 142
   continuity 139–40
   definitions 136–7
   groups, distinction 6, 131–3, 138–42,
      146–7
   intentionalism 145
   legal personality 137, 142
   longevity 133–4
   mindedness 146–7
   moral agency 132, 134, 136, 143–4,
      147–50
   nature of 131–2
   ontological status 136–42
   partnerships, distinction 137n. 15
   personhood, attribution 142–7, 149

punishability 149
as rule-based entities 135–6, 137–8
significance 133–6
as unifying force 133
'Coventry, sending to' 82–3
Crisp, R. 169
cultural norms, groups 105

Dan-Cohen, Meir 142
Davidson, D. 145
deliberative capacity, groups 204–10
diachronic identity, groups 119–23 *see also*
      synchronic identity
Durkheim, Emile 70, 97–8

eliminativism 14
   meaning 16
Elster, J. 89
entities
   moral status, case for 154
   non-material 8
essences 124–5
   and taxonomic ordering 125–6
   see also kind
events, role of groups 77
exile
   function of 81–2
   as punishment 82
explanation
   and holism 76
   nature of 75
   role, groups 5, 77–8, 98

family
   definition 30
   varieties of 30–32
fictionalism, and interrelational
      individualism 42
Fodor, J. 29–30
Frederick II 1
Frege, Gottlob 16–17
French, Peter 143, 144, 145, 146